S0-BNW-433

No Traveler Returns

The Story of Hitler's Greatest Crime

No Traveler Returns

By HENRY SHOSKES

Edited,
With a Prologue and an Epilogue
By CURT RIESS

1945

DOUBLEDAY, DORAN AND COMPANY, INC.
Garden City, New York

PRINTED IN THE UNITED STATES
AT
THE COUNTRY LIFE PRESS, GARDEN CITY, N. Y.

FIRST EDITION

CONTENTS

PART THREE: THE FIGHT

Prologue

It was one morning in the middle of August 1944, when a medium-sized, stockily built man, with an intelligent face and lively eyes hidden behind glasses, came to my office and introduced himself as Dr. Henry Shoskes.

I remember the day very well. It was still extremely hot in New York, and everybody who could get away was out of town. The newspapers had been carrying exciting and encouraging headlines. The Nazi rout in France had begun; Paris was being encircled by American troops. It seemed only a question of days till it would fall to us. General Montgomery had spoken of a "definite, complete, decisive Nazi defeat" and had promised his troops that the end of war was in sight. Rumania was about to break with Hitler, and the Russians were driving into Rumania. Throughout all the occupied countries the people were revolting against the Nazi regime. In Warsaw the revolt had taken the form of organized military resistance on the first of August. Little had yet leaked out about the war of the Polish underground army against the Germans. But even from those meager reports it was clear that it was a fight for life and death. That very morning a Warsaw broadcast had stated that underground troops had captured Warsaw's main telephone exchange after a seven-hour battle and were resisting a tank-supported German counterattack. The Germans had cut off the water supply and the Poles were digging wells everywhere in Warsaw. . . .

Dr. Henry Shoskes introduced himself as a Polish refugee. It seemed that before the outbreak of the war he had been the general manager of the Central Cooperative Bank in Warsaw, which controlled 650 cooperatives comprising a membership of 280,000. He had paid many visits to the United States, North Africa, and the Middle East, on behalf of various government agencies, and had also traveled, for business or other reasons, to Germany, France, Soviet Russia, et cetera. He had written numerous articles on these travels and other experiences. Finally, he had played an outstanding role in the Jewish communities of Poland.

Dr. Shoskes opened a rather impressively fat brief case. "I have here material on the uprising in Warsaw," he said, looking straight at me through his thick glasses. "Authentic material. It's a tremendous story. I have been told that you are interested in any piece of evidence connected with the fight against Hitler. I thought of doing a book based on this material. Perhaps you can advise or aid me."

I was astonished. "How is it that you have so much material when even the best-informed news agencies and papers carry only a few lines? It seems that only trickles of information leak out of Warsaw, while the fight is still in full swing."

Dr. Shoskes shook his head. "I'm not speaking about the uprising which is taking place just now. I am speaking of an uprising which took place in 1943. The uprising of the Jews in the Warsaw Ghetto in April and May 1943. Don't you remember?"

I was disappointed. Yes, I remembered that I had read the stories the papers carried about the heroic fight the Jews had put up in the Warsaw Ghetto. Like a vast number of other Americans, I had been quite moved—nay, more, even shocked and perturbed—by that story, and had felt it to be one of the outstanding deeds of heroism of World War II.

But—and this is what I told Dr. Shoskes—there were so many other performances of heroism which had taken place more recently. There were so many other stories which were exciting and moving. Yes, I remembered, and probably so did many other newspaper readers in this country, how shocked the world was at the treatment of the Polish Jews at the hand of the Hitlerites. But so many stories of atrocities had filled the front pages since then. So many things had happened. One could not remember everything. Every day brought a new story, new excitement, new shocks. I did not think that the American public would be very much interested in a thorough and complete account of what had happened in the Warsaw Ghetto two years or even longer ago. I was quite sure that I was not too eager to hear about it.

Dr. Shoskes shook his head. He did not take no for an answer. He began to take reports from his brief case, photostats, notes, handwritten accounts, in Polish and Yiddish. He began to tell stories. All of them dealt with people who had lived in the Warsaw Ghetto: how they had suffered; how they had died from starvation, from numerous diseases artificially accelerated by the Nazis. How the Nazis had begun to exterminate them, first by the hundreds, then by the tens of thousands. How within the relatively short time of two years they had brought down the population of the ghetto of Warsaw from something like five hundred thousand to less than forty thousand people.

There were stories I had read before, facts I had heard of before, but the vast majority of what I learned now I had never read, not in any paper, magazine, or book. The tale of Dr. Shoskes was not a tale of black and white. Not all the Germans were black villains; not all the Jews were angels. It was a moving tale, though, full of life. The ghetto became to me more than just a word about which I could not imagine very much. The ghetto became a community like many other communities, a city full of people, a world full of people.

For, strangely enough, everything that had happened in the world during the years when the Warsaw Ghetto existed seemed to have happened in this ghetto, too, even though it was cut off from the rest of the world. There were the same discussions and fights in the ghetto as in the rest of the world as to what to do about the Fascists: to appease them or to fight them. There were people who were decided to have nothing whatever to do with the Nazis, and others—though only a few, it is true—who gladly collaborated if they were given a chance. There were stupid people who thought that everything would eventually arrange itself, even though they did nothing about it, and intelligent ones who, unwilling to fool themselves, saw clearly the catastrophe that was to come. There were people who tried to attend to "business as usual" and those who knew that a decision which would be of importance for centuries to come was now in the making.

And then there was the fight of those who were left in the ghetto to perish. A fight which from the very first was completely hopeless. What could a handful of badly armed Jews, many of them women and children, do against the mighty Wehrmacht? But it was a fight, nevertheless, which shook not only Warsaw but the entire world. It was a fight comparable only to the greatest exhibitions of courage in history, such as the celebrated Battle of Thermopylae where three hundred Spartans fought against an overwhelmingly superior Persian army. Indeed it was almost even greater than that fight, for were not the Spartans professional soldiers, equipped and trained for such a fight, while the Jews of Warsaw were amateurs, untrained, and depending mainly on their strength of purpose, their belief in their cause, to carry them through?

Did I tell Dr. Shoskes that I didn't think anybody would be interested in an account of this battle because it had happened more than a year ago? No, for I suddenly realized that I was completely wrong. What, I began to think, are two or even ten years? What, for that matter, are one hundred years in the face of an event of such historical importance? Now I knew, beyond peradventure or doubt, that this story must be told, that for generations to come people would want to hear the story of this fight.

The account which Dr. Shoskes gave me on that day and during many days which followed was based on many sources. He had in his possession a great number of reports from the Polish underground, some of them printed, some of them handwritten. There were also a number of Polish underground papers; then there were the reports of representatives of the Polish government-in-exile, and finally there were the statements of numerous witnesses. Dr. Shoskes himself was one of these witnesses. He had known all those who had played important parts in the tragedy of the Warsaw Ghetto for the greater part of his life; some of them were his intimate friends. He had seen with his own eyes many of the things he told me about. He had spoken to many of the Nazis who were instrumental in the organization and finally in the destruction of the ghetto.

I suggested that he should write the story of the ghetto as he had seen it; as a number of incidents from his own experience. He shook his head: "I don't think that is the right approach. Leave me out of it. The story I have to tell is so much bigger than I am . . . so much bigger than all of us. I just want to tell the story."

He was right. I realized this story was bigger than anyone who could tell it. It was a great story—just as great as those who had written it with their own blood, who had died to make the story. Since they, the ones who had fallen, could not tell it, it had to be told for them.

When Dr. Shoskes began his account I found that there was not merely one story; there were dozens, hundreds of stories. Most of them were gruesome, desperate, atrocious. I wondered if anybody could take so many accounts of assassinations, cruelties, starvation. Then I slowly began to realize that there were not really so many accounts, that there was just one account, one story, a running story, strange, singular, which had never happened before anywhere in the world and which, therefore, had never been told. Only very few incidents which are part of this one great story have yet come to our attention through newspaper accounts. Since these accounts dealt with what in the language of journalism is called sensations, the readers had been given the impression that the whole story of the ghetto of Warsaw consisted of nothing but such sensations—murders, atrocities, inhuman acts. Now I began to understand that these seemingly unrelated "sensations" represented but a few visible parts of one great entity, of a story which so far had been submerged and had now been dug up by Dr. Shoskes.

It was a new story and still an old one. It was the old great human tragedy of guilt and punishment, of the pursuit of happiness and the final frustration of lost illusions and of men growing beyond their own stature to do deeds which survive themselves.

When Dr. Shoskes started I had been unwilling to listen, but before he ended I knew that it was my duty to listen and that it would be the duty of all of us to listen to this story. Later generations may read the account of the Warsaw Ghetto as history, and they may rejoice in the greatness to which people can grow when their dignity is challenged and the very ideals for which they live are threatened, though these people were little people with no aspirations to greatness, people who just wanted to get along, with no intention of putting up a great fight.

But this is not enough for us who have been alive while the tragedy of the ghetto of Warsaw took place—though, being a few thousand miles away, we were almost unconscious of its taking place. We have a deeper connection with it because we are alive. We are not permitted to forget about it, because in a way we were instrumental in bringing it about. The whole civilized world which permitted Fascism to grow and to attack innocent and helpless people is guilty of the deeds which Fascism committed. It is no excuse to say now that we didn't know what the Fascists would do, because we chose not to know, we chose to look the other way, we chose to isolate ourselves. Like Cain, we felt that we were not our brother's keeper, and it was thus that the unspeakable happened in our time.

In the eyes of posterity we will never be absolved from our guilt for the crimes committed in our time. But we can at least atone by ceasing to fool ourselves; by taking cognizance of what has happened; by not looking the other way; by not isolating ourselves now; by recognizing what went on in this world of ours while we were contented to mind what we falsely believed to be our own business.

Dr. Shoskes went on talking for days and weeks. Out of the countless reports of witnesses and documents, and from what he remembered from his own experiences, the world of the Warsaw Ghetto began to form itself before our eyes. Men and women now long dead came alive again. They started to think, to feel. They started to speak and to act. We saw them as though we were living with them.

I thought it might be a good idea for Dr. Shoskes to tell the story just as he had told it to me first, with people speaking their own language, thinking their own thoughts, moving in their own rhythm. I know that thus something has been put on paper which in the scientific sense of the word cannot be termed a report or an account. But in a higher sense it is just that. Because nothing, not a word, not a thought, is fictitious. Everything Dr. Shoskes tells through the mouth or through the thoughts of others—even when apparently he could not have been there to listen to these people—is based on documentary proof, on accounts of witnesses, on his intimate knowledge of these people.

Even as Dr. Shoskes continued his account to me, the newspapers carried more and more about the uprising of the Poles of Warsaw which had begun on August 1, 1944. We read about British and American planes flying nine hundred miles to bring supplies to the embattled Poles. We read about German infantry and tank attacks which failed to dislodge the heroes of Warsaw. The older part of the city was under steady barrage from German airplanes. More than 150,000 civilians, many of them women and children, were taken as hostages by the Germans. A twenty-four-hour curfew had been imposed on the entire city, and only old women were allowed to appear on the street from noon to 2 P.M.

And the Germans continued to shell Warsaw with their heavy artillery, destroying all the principal buildings and shooting down anyone who tried to extinguish the fire. The air was full of the roar of the cannon. . . .

"It must be just the way it was in 1939, when the Germans shelled Warsaw for twenty-one days," said Dr. Shoskes. "They hardly stopped for a minute. I can still hear it. I still remember one morning in a little synagogue . . ."

CURT RIESS

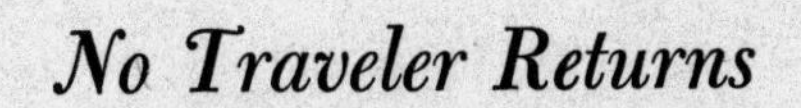
No Traveler Returns

Part One: The Slaves

Chapter I

Enter the Nazis

The synagogue, a small one, attended in normal times mainly by poor people, tradesmen, artisans, and workers, was crowded with worshipers. Above the heavy roar of the cannon one could hear the broken voice of the cantor singing, "On the Day of Atonement it is judged how many shall pass away and how many shall be born; who shall live and who shall die; who shall perish by fire and who shall perish by water; who by the sword and who by wild beasts; who by thirst . . . But penitence, prayer, and charity may avert the severe decree."

Never did these words fit the circumstances in which they were sung so well as on that Day of Atonement, September 23, 1939. For who among the worshipers knew whether this was not his last day on earth?

The Germans had bombed and shelled Warsaw all during the night. There had been hardly a minute when the roar and thunder of the cannon, the whistling sound of falling bombs did not make the Polish people wonder whether it was their turn this time; when the streets did not shake with the concussion of explosions, and the roar of hundreds of houses falling made them feel that at any moment they, too, might be buried, the living along with the dead.

Only a few days before, during the Jewish New Year, the Germans had shelled and utterly destroyed a great part of the Jewish district of Warsaw, and thousands had been buried under the debris. A German radio reporter had tersely informed his public, "Last night we sent New Year's gifts to the Chosen People."

Chosen people, indeed! thought Professor Mayer Balaban, who was one of those present in the synagogue that morning. This short, stocky man, with the energetic, intelligent face framed by a beautiful long white beard, was famed as a historian of the Polish and the Jewish people. He taught history at the University of Warsaw and occasionally he also functioned as a rabbi in one of the main synagogues of the capital. In spite of his long beard he did not look like a rabbi. His eyes behind thick glasses, wide-awake, good-natured eyes, eyes which saw a great deal, which wanted to know and to make certain, gave more the impression of the scientist. And there was his fine, almost womanly mouth which was so often on the verge of a smile that seemed to say that nothing the eyes saw should be taken too seriously. . . .

Chosen people, indeed, thought Professor Balaban. Ever since the German bombardment had begun, the "chosen people," together with the rest of the population of Warsaw, had huddled in cellars, praying in their different ways to the same common God, praying for the dead and the living alike, for the hundreds of thousands of innocent victims of a people gone mad with dreams of world conquest, and for the millions of victims to be, though those who prayed did not know yet that they themselves were to be the chief ones among those victims.

The old professor turned to a man next to him, much taller than he and much younger, one of his favorite pupils, a well-known historian in his own right, Dr. Emanuel Ringelblum. "Look," Balaban murmured.

Dr. Ringelblum followed the direction of his eyes and noted in the congregation many young and middle-aged men, wealthy and successful businessmen and doctors and lawyers.

Balaban said: "This is, I am sure, the first time in years that many of these people have been inside the synagogue. They have been too busy with their own affairs, too concerned with their worldly interests, to think of religion, of going to the synagogue, of praying. But now they are afraid. And so, like children, they have come here, to seek courage and comfort from the old prayers of their childhood faith. But they have even forgotten the words. They are content simply to repeat the words the old men are saying."

It was true. They were afraid. But as they repeated together the words so long ignored and almost forgotten—"O Father in Heaven, have pity on us and our children. O Father, Our King, do this for the sake of those who were slain in Thy name. Father in Heaven, avenge before our eyes the blood of Thy servants that has been spilled"—their fright lessened and they began to forget where they were and why they were there.

Through the windows they could see the big department stores on the Iron Place burning. Then a building only a few yards away from the synagogue was hit by a rain of bombs. The windows trembled and broke. Clouds of smoke penetrated the synagogue. The rabbi blessed the worshipers. Strangely enough they showed no signs of panic. Slowly they left the synagogue and emerged into the streets filled with mortal dangers. Then they began to run.

Balaban and Ringelblum were among the last ones to leave the synagogue. Balaban's face did not show any fear. "This is no worse than the last war," he murmured. He had been a chaplain in the Austrian Army during World War I. After a while he added, "No, it isn't any worse—not yet."

At the corner he turned around once more. Now the synagogue was on fire. It must have been hit by incendiary bombs a few seconds after they had left. Ringelblum's face was pale with sadness. Professor Balaban patted him gently on the shoulder as though to comfort him.

"Perhaps the fire will carry the prayers and tears of our poor people to Heaven," he said.

Warsaw resisted for twenty-one days. It fell on September 27. On October first, German troops marched into the city.

In those twenty-one days more than thirty thousand people had been killed and more than one hundred thousand wounded. Almost half the buildings had been completely destroyed or severely damaged. Hundreds of thousands of homeless wandered the streets. Corpses were crushed under ruins or lying in houses; there seemed no possibility of burying all of them. There was almost no food left, and no ammunition at all. Otherwise Warsaw would never have given up.

It was shortly after 10 A.M. of October 3, when Professor Balaban arrived at the Jewish Community Building in Grzybowska Street, a large old building where, since the second day of the invasion of Poland by Hitler, the Emergency Committee for the Jewish People had been in constant session. Ever since the siege of Warsaw had begun, the Jews had collaborated closely with the Central Committee for Defense under the heroic mayor of Warsaw, Stephan Starzynski. On that morning the members of the committee and a few of the more prominent Jews met there to discuss what could be done to help the numerous Jewish refugees who had come to Warsaw ahead of the Nazi army. They were sitting around in small groups telling each other all the rumors which were filling Warsaw at an amazing speed.

"This morning the Germans sent soup kitchens into the streets and trucks loaded with loaves of bread," one of them reported. "They urged us to stand in line so we could get fed. They had their newsreel cameras there, too, and they took pictures to show how nicely they were treating us. They told us we should look eager to get the food, and after we'd gotten it we should show how overjoyed and grateful we were."

Balaban smiled for a moment. "I suppose," he said, "they're going to show these movies all over the world to prove how wonderful they are."

The first speaker continued, "As soon as they had finished taking their pictures, they disappeared, taking their soup and their bread along with them. They obviously have no intention of wasting their food on us."

Another one reported, "This morning I saw two German soldiers stopping passers-by and searching their pockets. They took everything they could find."

"You can see this all over town. It seems that the German command has granted the troops freedom to loot. They may not have given a specific command, but the officers obligingly look the other way."

"I can't believe it." The man who spoke was Adam Czerniakow, a tall, powerfully built man with a broad, intelligent face, an outstanding engineer who had held an important position in the Ministry of Commerce and Industry and who was considered one of the leaders of the Jewish community in Warsaw. "I can't believe it," he repeated. "After all, German officers . . . they wouldn't do such things. They have a tradition; they've certain ideas of how to behave, even in wartime."

Balaban looked at him and shrugged. "I'm afraid, my friend, you haven't seen anything yet. As far as the looting of troops is concerned, it's a time-honored tradition of conquerors. It happened in ancient times and in the Middle Ages too."

Czerniakow shook his head. "But we are living in the twentieth century."

"I don't think that the Germans believe that wars have changed much since the Middle Ages," Balaban answered.

Just as he spoke they heard a loud hammering at the doors of the building, then a crash as of breaking timber, and the doors gave way. True, they had not even been locked, but those who entered seemed to feel it necessary to do so by force.

The first to come into the room where the committee was assembled was a man clad in the uniform of an officer of the Gestapo, a tall, fat man with a red face covered with many scars. Later it was learned that he was Captain Batz, chief of the Jewish section of the Gestapo in Warsaw. He held in his hand a whip which he swung through the air as he shouted, "All of you Jews . . . come, get out of here now." He was followed by a few young men in black uniforms who proceeded to push the elderly Jews out of the room and down the stairs.

But before they had reached the courtyard Captain Batz was after them. "Who has the money?" he shouted. "I want the money . . . at once."

There was a moment's silence.

Then Adam Czerniakow took a step forward. "I am the treasurer," he said.

The captain nodded. "Come along." He went upstairs again, followed by Czerniakow. There he took out a gun. "Hand over the money," he barked.

Czerniakow hesitated a moment. Then he went over to the safe and opened it. The German grabbed the entire contents without giving Czerniakow a chance to do anything about it.

"You have just taken 97,000 zlotys [about $20,000]," the treasurer remarked calmly. "Will you give me a receipt?"

Captain Batz looked at him for a moment and then he laughed till his face was even redder than normally. "Sure, you'll get a receipt. Come back for it the day after the world revolution." When Czerniakow turned to go, Batz shouted, "Wait, I'm not through with you yet. I have a lot to straighten out with you Jews. You'd better get together some kind of a representation, a kind of a council." He used the German word *Judenrat.* "I'll give you twenty-four hours to get a Judenrat together. It should have . . . let me see . . . Oh well, twenty-four members, outstanding members of all parties and groups of Jews. To start with, I need a census of the Jewish population of Warsaw. I want to know exactly how many of you Jews I have to deal with."

Czerniakow cleared his throat. "Since you have taken all the money we had, I hardly see how we can finance our activities. After all, to take a census . . ."

Captain Batz began to laugh again, his brutal and senseless laugh. "Never mind that. You'll have a lot of income from the cemeteries. Thousands of Jews are going to have to be buried during the next weeks and months. And then there will be more . . . you'll see. Now, get out!"

Abraham Alter, the rabbi of Gur, the great wonder rabbi of Poland, had found a temporary refuge at 6 Twarda Street in Warsaw. For Gur had fallen into the hands of the Nazis soon after the invasion began; the synagogue of the wonder rabbi was converted into a stable and his Talmudic Academy became a military brothel for the members of the Wehrmacht.

There used to be quite a few "wonder rabbis" in Poland. Some of them, it is true, were crooks and fakers who cynically used the superstitions of their followers to make money. They sold blessings for business enterprises or to childless women who longed to become mothers. But Abraham Alter was not this kind of a wonder rabbi. He kept aloof from everyday life, devoting himself entirely to the study of the Talmud and other religious books and to interpreting the Talmud to his followers, who numbered hundreds of thousands. On every Jewish holiday they flocked to Gur to visit the large synagogue, the Talmudic Academy and the holy quarters of the wonder rabbi for consolation and common prayer. But they saw him only rarely. He was a frail old man, almost eighty years old when the war broke out, and for some time his health had been failing and his voice was too weak to be heard in a large synagogue.

When the Germans advanced it was only with the greatest of difficulty that his followers were able to get him out of Gur and to hide him in Warsaw. Early in October his eldest son was killed by a stray bullet from the gun of a Nazi who was amusing himself by shooting at random in the streets of Warsaw. The dead son could not be buried immediately, for there were so many ahead of him. So the rabbi had his son's body brought to his room, where it now lay on the floor covered with a black sheet and surrounded with burning candles. The entire room was filled with friends and followers of the rabbi who had come to be with him in this hour of distress. They were praying.

Suddenly the door burst open. A detachment of German soldiers entered. They'd come for a special purpose. So many houses were in ruins, so many streets were impassable, that men were needed to clear up the mess. The Germans thought it a good idea to force the Jews to do this, and they had started hunting them down. Any Jew walking the streets was likely to be grabbed and pressed into service. After a day or two of this the Jews did not appear on the streets any more. The Nazis therefore decided that they would have to go after them in their houses. And it was on such an errand that the soldiers appeared now at Rabbi Alter's place of refuge.

They were overjoyed at the picture which presented itself to them. "Look at those beards!" one of them shouted. "White beards, black beards, red beards! Aren't we lucky?" Laughing with fiendish glee, they pulled out knives and scissors, threw themselves on the Jews, and proceeded to cut the beards. They laughed and laughed. Evidently they found this sort of game highly amusing. Some of them, however, disdaining such refined methods, simply tore at the beards till the hair came loose from the bleeding skin.

The Jews, most of them old men, made no attempt to ward the soldiers off. They did not implore them to let up, nor did they cry out. They knew this might be their end. They realized that the Nazis might start to shoot if they so pleased, but they kept quiet and calm.

In the corner, half reclining on his bed, the wonder rabbi lay, watching the scene and murmuring words of a prayer, his gentle yet magnetic eyes full of pity, love, and a kind of surprised worry for his friends, and at the same time full of defiance for the assailants. The only strength the old man had left was in his eyes. A few of the German soldiers came over to where he was lying. They came laughingly, and they were about to seize him too. Then something happened to them. Perhaps they looked into his eyes. They stood still for a moment. They seemed nervous, almost frightened. The laughter died on their lips. Then they turned around and left the room, pushing the friends of the wonder rabbi before them.

They led the men to a block of houses in the neighborhood where some cleaning up had to be done and ordered them to jump into the still-smoldering ruins.

A sergeant stepped forward and demanded that the Jews should dance and sing. "You certainly must know a lot of juicy Jewish melodies," he said.

The old Jews did not understand what they were supposed to do. The sergeant barked his order again; he was losing patience. Some of the soldiers pointed their guns unmistakably at the Jews. One of the victims who understood German whispered a translation of the order to the others. And now they began to move slowly around among the stones and debris in a strange and pitiful *danse macabre,* in time to a melody which one of them sang.

He sang in Hebrew. "By the rivers of Babylon, there we sat, and we also wept when we remembered Zion." His voice, soft and halting at first, grew louder and stronger. "O daughter of Babylon, who art wasted, happy he that repayeth thee thy recompense for what thou hast done to us." And now his voice filled the street, and it seemed as though the poor old Jews dancing to the melody had forgotten where they were and why they were there. "Happy he, that seizeth and dasheth thy babes against the rock."

One of the members of the Judenrat who had witnessed the scene went to see Captain Batz. Since the captain was out, he was shown to his right-hand man, Gruppenfuehrer Mende. Mende looked more intelligent than Batz. He had the face of an intellectual, somewhat reminiscent of Dr. Goebbels.

The Jew described what he had just seen and spoke of the man hunts going on in the streets of Warsaw. He went on to say that the Jewish Council thought this sort of thing shameful. "Furthermore," he added, "the practical results are negligible. Old white-bearded men cannot do this type of manual labor."

Mende remained silent. The other one then proposed that the Jewish community should organize Jewish laborers into battalions. Thus some real work could be done, and the old and infirm could be spared.

Mende smiled ironically. "Well, so you don't like the way we try to make you Jews work? I admit your way may be more effective. Let's try it, anyway." He got up. "Can you organize three thousand workers by tomorrow morning and assemble them for us in the courtyard of the

Jewish community house?" He waited till the other man had opened the door and then called after him, "You understand, of course, that we can't stop our men entirely from hunting in the streets. They must have some fun, you see."

The Jewish Community Building had been given back to the Judenrat so that there was a place from which to operate. When the members learned that they were to assemble three thousand workers by the next morning, they were aghast. How was it possible, they thought, to get that many workers in so short a time in a big city where the telephones were not functioning, where there were no newspapers yet, no radio and no means of transport? It was decided that all employees and members of the Judenrat should repair to the Jewish section, where they would go from house to house asking for volunteers. They were to say that the Jewish Council would supply all volunteer workers with bread and soup. They thought this might be as good an inducement as any, since so many Jews were completely destitute.

The next morning it was raining hard, and it was very cold. But by seven o'clock the courtyard of the Jewish Community Building was crowded with people, many more than could be used. The gates had to be closed. But there were still more, thousands of them, thronging the neighboring streets, trying to get in, shouting, crying, "We want work! We want bread!"

Gruppenfuehrer Mende and his men showed up only after the Jews had waited for more than three hours in the rain. They paved their way through the masses with whips. Mende seemed surprised that so many had come to work, but he made no comment.

From that day on, every morning at six, the prescribed number of Jews assembled in the courtyard to be led away by Mende's men, and every night at seven they were brought back. Then, on October 26, the governor general for the Occupied Polish Territories, Hans Frank, issued a decree which said: "Compulsory labor for the Jews shall be introduced, effective immediately. The Jews shall be formed into forced labor groups for this purpose."

There was no compensation for this work, of course. Many of the Jews were beaten up with rubber clubs after they had finished their twelve-hour stretch. Evidently the Germans considered this the right sort of compensation. And, anyhow, they had to have their fun.

Chapter II

Shadows of the Ghetto

Captain Batz had come to the office of Adam Czerniakow, the newly elected president of the Jewish Council, to discuss something of the "utmost importance," so he said. It was November 2, a Thursday.

The Gestapo chief smiled briefly. "You are aware, of course, that our Warsaw garrison has a great many young men in it. They are normal, healthy fellows, active and virile. But they have no chance here to lead a normal sex life. And they are suffering from the lack of it. Of course there are the prostitutes. But—well—it seems that there have been a large number of infections. We had to stop that sort of thing. But something has to be done for the men. The Gestapo has therefore decided that the Judenrat must set up a brothel."

"Surely you are joking!" Czerniakow did not look at the captain.

"You will soon learn that the Gestapo never jokes." Batz glared at Czerniakow a moment and then continued. "Let us see. . . . Come to my office at Gestapo headquarters day after tomorrow at five in the afternoon. Room thirty-seven, kindly note. And bring with you the men to whom you can entrust the job of setting up this brothel."

Czerniakow's forehead grew moist but he refrained from wiping it.

Apparently unmindful of the consternation his words aroused in his listener, Batz continued calmly: "There must be two such places, one for the officers and another for the men. The officers' place should be very comfortable, even elegant, if you know what I mean . . . the best furniture . . . and, of course, the best possible beds." He laughed his idiotic laugh. "Incidentally, these houses should be good paying propositions. You Jews will make a handsome profit."

Czerniakow was almost unable to speak. Several times he started and stopped. What could he tell the man? Should he explain to him that neither he nor any of his colleagues would dream of helping to carry out such an assignment? And would it do any good if he did say so? At length, however, he managed to find words to express his opposition to the revolting proposal. But Batz merely raised his eyebrows in astonishment.

"Really, my good man, you are taking these things much too seriously. You are a man of the world, aren't you? After all, we are being rather generous. We are willing to let you make some money. And we are even willing to forget about the Nuremberg Laws—you know, sexual intercourse with non-Aryan women. Just get a few good-looking Jewish girls. War is war, and to hell with all the race laws for the present."

"I cannot make any reply to this disgusting suggestion. And I must decline to come to your office day after tomorrow."

"Oh no, you won't." The captain reached for the calendar on the desk, turned over two leaves, and wrote down, "Case X."

"That will remind you," he said, and turned to go. "When you come, just mention that you want to talk to me about Case X. You see, there is a young girl working as my secretary. I don't want to offend her."

Czerniakow did not report to Gestapo headquarters on the appointed day. He remained at his desk in the Jewish Community Building, working on his reports and glancing from time to time at his desk calendar, where the words "Case X" stared threateningly up at him. He wondered whether they would arrest him. He was almost certain they would.

At half-past five a car stopped in front of the building. A minute later the door of Czerniakow's office was flung open and Batz entered. His face was purple, and he was almost speechless with rage. He brandished a short whip.

Czerniakow got up, ready for anything.

"So you didn't keep our appointment after all!" When Czerniakow still did not speak, the German continued: "Well, you are lucky at that. It seems that we can't find suitable quarters for our brothels. All the buildings which might have suited our purpose have been damaged by our artillery or burned down. Of course we wanted to confiscate a house belonging to a Jew. But we couldn't even find one belonging to a Christian which suited our purposes. Well, we'll take the matter up later. And in the not-too-distant future, I can promise you that."

With these words he was gone.

He came back again the following Tuesday, late at night. Early that afternoon Czerniakow had received an order to assemble the members of the Judenrat. Only twenty-two of the twenty-four could come. One had been arrested and taken to a German concentration camp the day before, and another one had disappeared as he was trying to make his getaway across the frontier.

The twenty-two men waited in the assembly room of the Community Building. The electric lights were still not functioning, and the only light in the room was furnished by a few small candles. Among those present were some of the most prominent Jews: a senator, a congressman, a leading industrialist, the leader of the orthodox Jews, Professor Balaban, and Arthur Zygielbojm, an alderman of the city of Warsaw and an important leader in the workers' union movement. None of them were seated, for they were unwilling to be forced to rise when the Germans entered. No one uttered a word.

Shortly before midnight they heard a few automobiles slowly making their way through the streets that were still littered with all kind of wreckage. A few German officers climbed out of the cars and entered the assembly room. Batz barked a command, an orderly brought flashlights, and one of the Germans proceeded to read aloud something from a paper which he had taken from his pocket. The Jews were to find twenty-four men to act as their deputy councilmen. This had to be done within the next fifteen minutes.

The members of the Jewish Council remained silent. The same thought was in all their minds: This could mean only that they were going to be arrested and held as hostages.

After a moment the Jews proceeded to a corner of the room to discuss the situation. Only Balaban remained where he was. So it has come, he thought. Well, he had expected it. He looked at the wall, on which the flashlights were throwing grotesque shadows. Yes, he reflected, he had known that it would come. But he had not thought that it would come quite so soon. It seemed, he reflected, that it was a crime to be born a Jew. . . .

In the corner the others were still arguing. Some thought it might be best to refuse to make any move at all. The Germans could not do any more than arrest and kill them, and they would do that anyway. Czerniakow was of a different opinion, however. He thought it was better to try to find some *modus vivendi* with the Germans. After all, if the Nazis started by killing off all the Jewish leaders first, it was a certainty that they would eventually wipe out the entire Jewish population of Warsaw.

But what to do? They were all agreed that they could not get twenty-four men of any standing or responsibility within such a short space of time—if they could get anybody at all to stick his neck out at any time, in the circumstances.

The German officers had settled down to await the next move on the part of the Jewish leaders. One of them took out his watch: "Only thirteen minutes left," he announced. And he meant it, too.

The Jewish representatives made a quick decision. Three of them ran downstairs to the funeral society across the street. There, as they had expected, they found a number of gravediggers, pallbearers, shroud makers, hearse drivers, and professional mourners. They took twenty-four of them along, promising them a few zlotys in return for their help. Of course these men were not precisely representative of the Warsaw community, but then nobody else could have been found in so short a time.

When they returned with their new-found deputies the German officers got up and ordered the Jews to line up in two rows: on one side the members of the council, on the other, facing them, the newly acquired deputy councilors.

Then they heard Batz reading the following decree:

"In order to preserve the German Army and the Aryan population of Poland from any corrupting Jewish influence, a ghetto will be established in Warsaw, within the boundaries designated on the accompanying map. All the Jews residing outside the ghetto must move inside its confines within three days. The ghetto will be fenced off with barbed wire. Guards will be posted between the hours of 7 A.M. and 6 P.M., during which time no Jew will be permitted to leave the ghetto."

The Jews listened in silence. They were too stunned to speak. And they waited for what they thought was certain to come now: their arrest. They knew it was quite impossible to achieve what the decree demanded within the short space of three days. They would be taken along as hostages and would be shot if the deputy councilmen did not achieve the impossible task laid out for them.

Then came the final surprise of the evening. Turning to the twenty-two members of the Judenrat, Batz declared, "It's your responsibility now, gentlemen. As to the deputies you have selected . . . we'll take them along. If you don't act according to the decree, I'm afraid we'll have to shoot them."

The pallbearers and gravediggers and shroud makers began to clamor and weep. They had wanted to make a few zlotys; they did not want to die. But to no avail. The Germans marched them off.

With the flashlights gone, it was almost dark in the large room. Then everybody seemed to talk at the same time. All of them felt that it was impossible to do what the Germans wanted. Somebody estimated that more than 150,000 Jews were living in sections outside the ghetto limits. How could so many people be transferred from their homes within three days? And removed—where to? To the bomb-wrecked, devastated sections of Nalewki and Smocza streets, where only the poorest of the poor lived, where already six to ten persons were crowded together in one small room.

Only Professor Balaban kept silent. He felt the weirdness of this night more than any of the others. Everything seemed so unreal—even those around him, men he had known and esteemed all his life. Here they were now, racking their brains to find some practical solution of the situation. But none of them thought of what seemed to him the real issue: of the enormity of the crime which was about to be committed on the Jews in general, degrading them once more to the status of subhuman beings, confined to restricted areas, allowed to live only behind barbed wire.

Finally he said, "Why don't we face it right now? There is nothing we can do. This problem cannot be solved. And should we solve it?" He shook his head. "I think not. We should not have anything to do with any attempt to drive us back into the ghetto. After all, haven't we fought many hundred years to get out of it?"

Czerniakow could not agree. "We have to do something. We have to act in some way. We cannot just sit there."

Someone had the idea that a delegation should go to Gestapo headquarters in the morning. But the others thought there would be hardly any sense in appealing to Captain Batz. Another one said, "Why not appeal to General von Neumann-Neurode? The decree was read in his name."

"But that is against the law. We were told that all Jews in occupied Poland are placed under the jurisdiction of the Gestapo and that it is forbidden to us to approach any other authority."

Adam Czerniaków, though, thought it might be a good idea to appeal to the general, in spite of this ruling. "It's our only chance, in any event," he said, "even if it's only an outside chance. But I think we might get somewhere. After all, German officers aren't as bad as the Nazis. Perhaps the general will be fair and understand our difficulty."

At ten the next morning a delegation led by Czerniakow arrived at the general's headquarters on Sachson Place, in the building formerly occupied by the Polish Commandantur. After a short wait an adjutant ushered in the general.

Neumann-Neurode turned out to be a tall, gray-haired, distinguished-looking gentleman with a monocle. He shook hands with the Jews, asked them to sit down, then sat down and looked at them expectantly.

Czerniakow outlined the situation, concluding with these words: "There is no doubt that such a mass evacuation, if carried out in so short a time, will have certain dangerous repercussions. Already epidemics are raging in the city. Such a hasty mass move as this could serve to spread them, eventually even endangering the German soldiers."

The general almost dropped his monocle in his surprise. "I assure you I know nothing about an order to evacuate . . . how many did you say? . . . one hundred and fifty thousand people or more. I'm positive that I never signed any such order. Why . . . it's preposterous!"

"Then you agree that such an evacuation is impossible?"

"Of course I agree! Quite impossible! Why, it's preposterous! Preposterous!" The longer he talked the more furious he became. Suddenly he rose, asked his visitors to go out into the adjoining room and wait there, and closed the door behind them.

A few minutes later Captain Batz rushed through the waiting room and into the general's office. Through the closed doors the Jews in the outer room could hear the general's excited voice talking rapidly and shouting the word "preposterous" at regular intervals. Batz they could not hear at all. After a while the door opened again and Batz came out, a chastened look on his face.

Then Neumann-Neurode appeared. "Gentlemen," he said in his suave manner, "an understanding in this whole matter must be reached with the Gestapo. But I think that that can be managed."

The delegation decided that perhaps they had better call on Captain Batz immediately. But in the end they decided that it might be best to send Czerniakow by himself.

Batz was waiting. He had Czerniakow shown in by four heavily armed Gestapo men. He was very angry and moved about constantly, in his hand a little whip which seemed, as if by chance, always about to touch Czerniakow's face. "How did you dirty Jews dare to go over my head?" he shouted.

"General Neumann-Neurode has suggested that we should reach an understanding," the president of the Judenrat said.

"What kind of understanding?" Batz was swinging his cane in the air.

"About the ghetto, the evacuation . . ."

"What about it?"

"Well, it hardly seems possible to move so many people within three days."

"Who said it was possible? It's all a misunderstanding." Batz began to shout. "A misunderstanding, I tell you! Perhaps you wanted to misunderstand me. I never said anything about moving Jews at the present time."

Czerniakow spoke calmly. "I'm sorry that we misunderstood you."

"You better be." The Gestapo chief crossed the room several times. "The general said something about epidemics and that a sudden evacuation might endanger the health of the army. Did you by any chance suggest anything like that to him?"

"I believe we did mention such a possibility."

Batz began to laugh. "That's rich. How tricky you Jews are! One

might almost believe that you are really concerned with the welfare of our army!"

Meanwhile the rumor had spread among the Jews of Warsaw that a ghetto was to be established within three days. They immediately became panicky. No one knew where the limits of the ghetto were to be. No one knew whether they could stay where they were or whether they would be evicted from their homes. Thousands of people milled in front of the Jewish Community Building. It was impossible to get through any street near by. Everybody talked at once. Rumors were spreading like wildfire. Everybody had heard something—usually something different—and with every hour the mood of those who were waiting in front of the Community Building became more desperate. Fashionably dressed ladies rubbed elbows with poor workers; orthodox Jews with long beards stood next to young lawyers and doctors; old women fainted; mothers held their babies high up so they would not get crushed. All of them wanted the Community Council to resist the demands of the Gestapo, no matter what the cost might be. Not even when they finally heard that nothing definite was decided yet, but that in any case the ghetto ordinance was temporarily postponed, did they calm down entirely.

Then Arthur Zygielbojm jumped on an overturned refuse box to talk to the people in the street. He was a rather small and fragile man, and his thin, intelligent face and the way he carried himself showed signs of a youth of hardships and privations. He had been a worker in his youth. He had taught himself how to read and to write, had joined the Social Democratic party, and had become one of the leaders in the struggle of the socialists against the injustices of the Tsarist regime. He had played an important part, first as alderman of the city of Lodz and later of the city of Warsaw and in the workers' union movement. He knew how to address mass gatherings, and this occasion gave him an opportunity to display his powers thus. Addressing himself particularly to the workers in the crowd, he told the people to keep discipline and not to permit themselves to be aroused. "The Nazis will try everything to provoke you, to make you do things which will give them a right to interfere. Don't give them that chance. Keep calm! Go home and wait for further developments!"

Zygielbojm took his life in his hands when he spoke these words. The Gestapo could have arrested him on the spot for inciting the people against the Germans. But the little, energetic man who had worked so singleheartedly all his life for the party was full of courage. And the last days had made him lose all regard for personal danger.

There was no sleep that night for any of the members of the Jewish Council. They knew that since the news of the ghetto had spread among the Jews, many of them were already packing and on the verge of moving. They had to let them know that they could stay where they were. So they ran from street to street to carry the word to them. The night was cold and it was raining hard. In the devastated, mud-soaked sections of Bagna, Panska, and Twarda streets the people were already carrying out their children, their pillows and blankets and bedding. They cried with joy when they heard the good news that they were being allowed, for the time being, at least, to remain in their old, broken-down homes.

The next day Captain Batz ordered Czerniakow back to Gestapo headquarters. A few of the other members walked with him to the door and then waited for him to come out. He did not stay long. Captain Batz, he reported, had been in excellent mood. He had agreed to release the badly scared deputy councilmen. "As to the ghetto project," Czerniakow said, "the captain assured me that it was postponed indefinitely."

It was still raining hard when the Jews made their way from Gestapo headquarters back to the Community Building. There were three miles to walk. They walked like men in a trance; they were happy beyond words.

Professor Balaban was waiting in Czerniakow's office.

"A great disaster has been averted," Czerniakow told him, taking both of his hands.

"I wish I could be as happy as you are," Balaban replied. "But I fear I cannot."

"You were always a pessimist. I told you there is always a way to get along—even with the Germans. You'll see. Everything will come out all right."

"I am not a pessimist. I am just considering facts." The old professor wondered for a fleeting moment whether he would not be happier if he could make himself indulge in wishful thinking as Czerniakow and so many of the others did. The Nazis blame everything that is wrong with the world on the Jews, he thought. They have sworn to annihilate them. What could prevent them from going through with their plan? He had no doubt how it all would end. He did not want to think of it too often, but his trained mind, accustomed as it was to watching and analyzing everything that went on, could not be lulled into a state of false security by the apparently good turn events had taken for the moment. Nor could he refrain from watching and making note of everything that happened, with the detachment of a scientist, no matter how unhappy it made him to see it.

He was to see a great many things in those days. . . .

Crowds of Jewish people filtering slowly through the streets of Warsaw on their way to the Jewish Community Building—a sad procession of aged men, women, and children, tired, dirty, clad in rags, led by an old woman carrying the Torah in her arms.

They came from Sierpc, a town about forty miles from Warsaw. The day before, the German authorities had given the order that all Jews would have to leave the town within a half hour. They were herded into the market place before they were expelled. The Germans then ordered the orchestra of the fire department to play happy tunes because now their town was to be freed from the Jews. The Polish musicians wept as they played, to see the great misery of the Jews with whom they had lived peaceably for so many generations.

The Jews who were thus driven out were followed by a detachment of German cavalry who pursued them for eighteen hours right up to the gates of Warsaw. The refugees had to move quickly. Many of the older ones and the sick, who were unable to travel, had to be left behind. When the old rabbi who marched at the head with the Torah became exhausted, it was his wife who took the Torah from his arms and led the others. Not long afterward the rabbi collapsed, and a few minutes later he was dead. They buried him hastily, driven by the shouts of their German pursuers to "Move on!" There was no time to weep or pray.

The people of Warsaw were soon to become used to the sight of whole communities, entire villages or towns on the march, wandering like lost souls. It seemed as though every German commander had decided to keep the Jews out of "his" city, "his" town, "his" district. But no one had any idea—nor, indeed, did anyone care—where these Jews were to go.

It was during the first days of December that Professor Balaban met Stefan de Ropp, the well-known professor in the School of Economics at Poznán, who had been General Polish Commissioner at the New York World's Fair in 1939. De Ropp, who had made a sensational escape from Poznán after being tipped off as to his imminent arrest, told Balaban that the Germans had deported 1,200,000 men, women, and children from western Poland, the part of the country the Nazis had decided to incorporate into Greater Germany. This forced wholesale migration had taken just about two months. Needless to say, the German officials saw to it that the better-situated Poles were compelled to move first, leaving behind all their property, which thus fell into the hands of the Germans. Needless to say, too, the Germans acted as brutally as they could, making things as difficult as possible for the Poles, in the hope that many of them would freeze or starve before they had reached regions where they still had a right to exist—the so-called Government General.

"Still, they have a place to go to," Dr. Ringelblum said to Balaban. "But where are we Jews to go? They are allowed to live, but we are supposed to disappear from earth."

Balaban nodded. "Yes. That is precisely what we are supposed to do. Disappear from the earth. No place to go to." He smiled sadly. "And to think that I have spent the better part of my life as a historian to prove that we Polish Jews have just as much right to live in Poland as any other Pole, since, after all, we have been here just as long as most of the non-Jewish Poles." Professor Balaban, the author of an authoritative history of the Jews in Poland, had always stood for the thesis that the Jews in Poland were not there as guests, but as citizens, and that they had every right to stay there. "But what is a lifetime of study, of argument, of scientific research?" he commented sadly. "The Germans come with their tanks and their dive bombers and settle the issue once and for all."

They published dozens of decrees of humiliating nature to set the Jews apart from the Poles once and for all: Jews had to wear badges with the Star of David; Jews were not allowed to travel in trains; Jews were not allowed to use busses or taxis; Jews were not allowed to enter parks, theaters, or bathing houses; their property was confiscated; their bank accounts were frozen; their businesses were taken away from them.

All this happened during the first weeks of the occupation of Poland. The Nazis displayed an ever-growing brutality and cynicism in their treatment of the Jews. Nazi soldiers clipping the beards of old Jews was a daily sight in the streets of Warsaw. The only beards which were safe were those of the men who worked in the Community Building. In a moment of good-natured mockery Gruppenfuehrer Mende had decreed that the entire Judenrat and its employees should be provided with documents which not only allowed them to pass through the streets unmolested, but specifically protected their beards. When Balaban received this document he remarked, "I feel that I ought to tear this paper up. Why should we have privileges? But then I have worn my beard so long—I've become a bit fond of it." And he pocketed the Nazi document.

Most of the Poles turned away in disgust when they witnessed German soldiers chase old bearded Jews and cut swastikas into their long beards. Boys in their teens, who in normal circumstances would have been busy in school, thought it an amusing spectacle. They also thought it fun when the old Jews were driven to some kind of menial labor by Gestapo men armed with whips. They cried out with delight, "Look, look! They are like so many stray curs in a dogcatcher's cage!"

But the Nazis soon turned from such lighthearted sport and resorted to cold-blooded murder.

A thief who was about to be arrested by a Polish policeman drew his gun and shot the officer. Such an occurrence as this happens in every large city from time to time. But in this particular case the thief happened to be a Jew. That gave the Germans an opportunity to take charge. Two days later the Gestapo surrounded the building where the shots had been fired and arrested all the Jews who were living there and every Jew who happened to be there at that time, fifty-three in all. On the morning of the third day after the arrest, November 13, these fifty-three men were shot. The mass slaughter was kept a secret for a while, because the Gestapo wanted the Jewish Community to pay a fine of 300,000 zlotys for the assassination of the Polish policeman—an enormous sum which they duly collected. Then the *Krakauer Zeitung*, the official German newspaper in Poland, reported briefly that "because of their reprehensible conduct during the police investigations, fifty-three male Jews from the house at 9 Walewski Street were shot."

Even this first mass murder did not yet create panic. Rather, it aroused complete consternation. Only a very few Jews saw the sign on the wall and decided to flee Warsaw and the country, no matter how great the odds against the success of such an attempt. Almost all of them stayed on, paralyzed by their fear and hoping against hope. They did, it is true, recognize the gravity of the situation. They knew that all of them were in mortal danger. And while they did little or nothing to save themselves, they did do everything in their power to save those among their number whom they regarded as the most worthy. One of these was the wonder rabbi of Gur, Abraham Alter. Countless notes were smuggled out of Poland, all of them cries of help for the venerable rabbi. Hundreds—nay, thousands—of his followers who did nothing to save themselves or their families implored their friends abroad to do something so that the rabbi might be rescued.

The wonder rabbi had thousands of followers in every country, the United States along with the rest. In January 1940 word was finally received here that Abraham Alter was still alive, but, like every other Polish Jew, in constant danger. A special committee was formed to save him and his family. The State Department in Washington and other Allied governments were willing enough to help with visas, but saw no way of getting the rabbi, a Polish citizen, out of occupied Poland, for by that time Jews were no longer permitted to travel in Polish trains.

A complicated and fantastic plan was conceived and carried out. A certain neutral diplomat went to Italy—that country was not yet in the war—and found there an influential person who was, in turn, willing to go to Warsaw on the rescue mission. Once there, he began trying to bribe his way through the Gestapo. Eventually, after having spent a great deal of money thus, he finally reached a Nazi, Colonel Tebens, who it was thought would be able to do something in the matter because of his key position in the Transportation Board of the Government General.

Herr Tebens had been expecting to hear from the Italian, for his intelligence department had already informed him of the reasons for the latter's arrival in Warsaw. Tebens was willing to play ball.

"I don't care for the rabbi one way or the other," he declared cynically. "Certainly I can arrange transportation for him. But it will cost you a good deal of money. And it must be American money."

The Italian wondered why Tebens insisted on American money.

"Our mark is subject to so many changes," the Nazi explained a little sadly.

At length a sum was agreed upon. However, this was only the beginning. It was impossible to effect the rabbi's escape unless certain other officers of the Gestapo collaborated. There was, for instance, the head of the security department, the head of the political division of the Gestapo, the head of the Jewish section of the Gestapo, Captain Batz, and many other officials connected with the running of railroads. And they all wanted to be paid. Every Nazi seemed to have his price. None was above taking money—even Jewish money—provided it was paid in good American dollars.

The deal was finally closed and consummated. The rabbi and a few members of his family were put into a railroad car which was then hermetically sealed. Up to the moment the train crossed the German frontier, the special car was closely guarded by the Gestapo officials who had been bribed. No German officials or soldiers were allowed to enter.

When these officials returned to Warsaw they immediately began to quarrel with each other about how the money was to be divided. Berlin got wind of the affair, and an investigation was started which ended with the removal of a number of those who had been bribed. Captain Batz and Colonel Tebens, however, were able to save their skins—for the time being, at least.

The wonder rabbi and his family finally arrived in Palestine. A few lives—a mere handful—had been saved. But more than three and one half million Jews were still left in mortal danger.

The escape of the wonder rabbi occurred from Warsaw in the middle of April 1940, and only a few days later, during the Jewish Passover holidays, the first pogrom was staged there. Suddenly the streets of Warsaw were full of certain types of the underworld, juvenile hoodlums and other irresponsible elements who before had hardly dared to show themselves in broad daylight. Now they proceeded to beat up, rob, and kill Jews. They knew there would be no consequences, for they had been told so by the Gestapo men who brought them into the streets. In fact, the Germans had made it clear that whoever killed a Jew might be assured of the gratefulness of the Third Reich. About a thousand young ruffians took part in this affair. They broke and looted Jewish shops while German soldiers stood by and took pictures of the scene. A few representatives of the Jewish Community rushed to Gestapo headquarters to complain. They were promised help by Captain Batz. But when they left the Gestapo Building the hoodlums were waiting for them to beat them up. No doubt they had been tipped off.

In order to make it seem as though everything that was done was perfectly straightforward and legal, Captain Batz arranged pictures taken showing a few Germans beating up these hoodlums. These pictures were to furnish documentary proof that the Germans had intervened on the side of law and order and in defense of the attacked Jews. But, unfortunately, the scene in which a Gestapo official paid the hoodlums a few zlotys for permitting themselves to be beaten up for the benefit of the camera was one that was not filmed.

The first pogrom lasted four days. When it was all over, Gruppenfuehrer Mende put in an appearance at the Jewish Community Building. He told Czerniakow and Balaban that he was very sorry that all this had happened, but that it was not the doings of the Germans. After all, if the Polish population felt that way about the Jews . . . After a pause he continued, "I may be able to do something to prevent further outbreaks of this kind. But I must have a written complaint signed by you, and a request to act against the Polish criminals who have attacked the Jews.

Professor Balaban said quickly, "We'll think it over."

After the German had left, Czerniakow remarked, "Perhaps we should take advantage of this opportunity. If we make our protest strong enough, the Germans may get the idea that we don't take everything lying down."

Professor Balaban slowly got up. The little stockily built man seemed to have grown in size. He put his hand flat on Czerniakow's desk. "We are not going to do anything of the sort. We are not going to send any written statement. Don't you understand? All they want is to have something signed by us, some kind of complaint against the Poles so that they can play the Poles and the Jews against each other." He smiled. "It is an old trick. *Divide et impera.* The old Romans knew it very well. Every conquering general in the history of the world has used this trick. We are not going to fall into this trap. We are not going to complain to the Gestapo."

Chapter III

The Gates Are Closed

On October 16, 1940, the German authorities issued a decree that a ghetto was to be established in Warsaw. All Jews had to move into it, and the Poles who lived there had to move out. The dead line was set for October 31.

October 16 also marked the beginning of the Sukkoth holidays. This holiday, which lasts for nine days, is celebrated in memory of the many years the Jews wandered in the desert after their escape from Egypt. In order to keep the laws of Sukkoth, Jews have to move out of their houses and live for eight days in makeshift, roofless huts or cabañas—a reminder of those in which they lived during their wandering in the desert. Of course it was impossible for the Jews in Warsaw to observe the Sukkoth holidays as they used to in the olden days. The Germans refused to grant them permission to build their little huts. Indeed, they had forbidden the Jews to practice any of their religious rites at all. But this did not deter many of the Jews from meeting secretly in private homes and saying the Sukkoth prayers.

The decree of October 16 meant several things. In the first place, the part of Warsaw which was to become the ghetto was by no means inhabited by Jews only. Roughly about eighty thousand "Aryan" Poles were living there. They would have to move out within a fortnight and find a place to stay in some other part of the city. On the other hand, more than 140,000 Warsaw Jews were living in houses and streets situated outside the newly created ghetto. They were supposed to move into the ghetto within the same short space of time.

The district which was to become the ghetto had always been the poorest and most overcrowded one in Warsaw. And it had been made still more overcrowded since the beginning of the war by the influx of more than ten thousand refugee Jews, as well as by the fact that many of the houses had been bombed out of existence or partly ruined. And now 60,000 more—the difference between the 140,000 who were to move in and the 80,000 who had to move out—had somehow to be accommodated.

The confusion in the streets of Warsaw surpassed all description. Some two hundred thousand people were frantically trying to move to new quarters, or at least into the prescribed district. Two hundred thousand people with no means of transport, for there were no horses, no trucks, no cars of any kind, only pushcarts which you had to push yourself. You could not load a pushcart with too many things. What would become of your property which you left behind? The Nazis "confiscated" it. But sometimes they even confiscated the things you had finally been able to take along on your pushcart, if these things happened to catch their fancy. What happened to your apartment outside the ghetto? It was confiscated. What happened to your business outside the ghetto? It, too, was confiscated. What happened to the money due to you outside the ghetto? It was conveniently forgotten about.

The ghetto . . . At first the Jews used the expression ironically, as if it were a good joke on themselves. But the word soon became the center of their lives. There was nothing left for them to think about, to speak about, to interest themselves in, but the ghetto.

They had to consider themselves lucky if they were able to find any room at all in this ghetto. The narrow, winding streets bordered by the old, dilapidated houses were crowded with people carrying or pushing their few belongings before them, looking up at the dark façades in search of a place where they and their families could go. Every doorbell was rung: Is there a vacant room here? Every passer-by was stopped: Can you tell me where I can find a room? Every neighborhood child was bribed with a few zlotys: Do you know of any room?

Children who had lost their parents stood crying in the street. Mothers with haunted looks knocked on every door right up to the attic, determined to find a place where at least their children could sleep. Fathers raced to the Community Building in the hope of getting some address, any address, where a room, or a part of a room, might be available. They filled the cafés, where there was always a chance that they might hear of a still-vacant place.

There was so little time. And the nearer the dead line came the thicker the crowd became, the more desperate the people, the greater the confusion.

In the midst of all this turmoil, concerned as they were with the pressing question of getting a place to live, few of the Jews realized that walls had begun to appear in the ghetto—slowly, almost imperceptibly, and in many places at once. Some of these walls grew up in the middle of a street, dividing it arbitrarily into two parts. Others appeared between two neighboring houses. The Nazis used Jewish masons to do the work, but wherever a wall was there were armed Nazi guards watching the workers closely. In still other places the Nazis built fences of barbed wire or used Jews to construct them for them.

The end of October came and passed, and still nothing happened. Many of the Christian Poles had still not moved out of the ghetto, and many of the Jews had not yet come in. And still the Nazis did nothing about it. Apparently they had realized that the resettlement could not be achieved in so few days as they had given. By the first week of November the confusion had begun to die down. Most of the Jews had now found at least a place to sleep inside the ghetto. Many of them did not stay there except at night. Every morning they went to their businesses, their factories, their places of employment, as they had done all their lives. They thought they would go on doing it for the rest of their lives.

Then, on November 16, 1940, the ghetto was shut off from the rest of Warsaw. There had been no warning. It was a morning like every other morning. Most of the Jews, men and women who worked in stores, factories, or offices outside the ghetto—and almost all of them did—made themselves ready for work. They went on their way and in due time came to the point at which their street crossed the frontier between the ghetto and the rest of Warsaw. But on that morning they could proceed no farther. The Nazis had strung a fence of barbed wire across the street and were patrolling the spot in order to prevent anyone from going from the ghetto into Warsaw proper.

The people who were thus stopped from reaching their places of work tried other streets . . . with the same results. In one night the Germans had cut the ghetto off from the rest of the world.

The news that the ghetto had been closed spread like wildfire. From every house the Jews issued, running over to where the barbed wire had been strung. As they looked at it their faces became gray, their shoulders sagged, their eyes were without hope. Now they were trapped. Now they were left in houses and rooms much too small for their needs, cut off from their resources, from their business, from their places of employment. Now indeed they were left to be forgotten, to rot away, to die.

The city of Greater Warsaw extended over about thirty-four square miles and had roughly twelve thousand houses. The ghetto itself comprised about nine square miles. It was situated in the northern part of the city, which had always been the poorest part of Warsaw. It comprised 1,692 houses in all, most of them one- or two-story buildings.

In this ghetto there were almost no trees at all. The courtyards of the bigger houses were used as markets for the whole block. There was only one park—Krashinsky Park—in that part of the city, but the Germans, when they devised the frontiers of the ghetto, saw to it that it was left outside. There was not a single playground for children. There were a few nice streets, though. There was Leszno Street, a broad avenue with many shops running from east to west and cutting the ghetto into a northern and a southern half. There was also Sienna Street, almost at the southern end, a quiet district without shops, where people with means could reside. And there was Twarda Street, where the well-to-do orthodox Jews lived. But aside from these few streets the rest was almost entirely slums.

The unfinished wall around the ghetto continued to grow. Jewish masons were no longer employed—the Nazis did not trust them since it had been discovered that they had put in bricks so loosely that they could easily break them out later on. Their places were now taken by Poles. The barbed wires disappeared, and soon a whole system of walls surrounded the ghetto, walls eight feet high and covered with broken glass. They were constantly patrolled by German and Polish police. There were eleven gates leading into the ghetto. These, too, were constantly guarded. Only Jews with special permits were allowed to pass through.

There were a few leaks, though, in this barrier that had been thought out with such typical German thoroughness. In the first place, there were some houses that had been destroyed by German shells and bombs, which were situated partly inside and partly outside the ghetto, the cellars of which served as underground tunnels. Then there was the Church of All Saints and the new Court Building in Leszno Street, both of which had entrances from the Warsaw side and the ghetto side. To get into the Court Building you had to be called as a witness or be a party yourself to a lawsuit of some kind. This, of course, could be arranged. It was in these two places, the church and the Court Building, that Jews and members of the Polish underground were to meet later on. But this was very much later.

How were the Poles taking this outrage that had been committed against the dignity of the Jews, who, after all, were Polish citizens, too? Many of the Jewish leaders began to wonder. Arthur Zygielbojm, who had been an active member of the workers' unions most of his life, refused to believe that the Polish workers would take without protest such an attempt to split up their own ranks. Adam Czerniakow, who now had for all practical purposes become the mayor of the ghetto, could not bring himself to believe that the average decent Polish citizen was going to stand for this introduction of an institution typical of the spirit of the Middle Ages. Professor Balaban was willing to believe that many Poles were outraged. But he doubted that they would do anything about it, for he realized too well that although many of them were opposed to Nazi methods, they had no sympathy either for the Jews who lived among them.

Relations between the Poles and the Jews had always been somewhat complex, ever since the time when the Jews had first fled there to escape the growing persecution in German countries at the time of the Crusades and the Black Death, and later when they were driven from Spain by the Inquisition.

At that time Poland became for them a haven of religious tolerance.

Since the country was economically undeveloped in those days, the Jews, most of them merchants and artisans, found ample economic opportunity. The kings and princes welcomed them and protected them, and thus the Jews succeeded in building up a community life of their own based on religious autonomy. Later the Church and the steadily growing Polish middle class began to oppose the Jews. But by that time the Jews had become an integral part of the Polish nation, sharing its fortunes and misfortunes through the centuries, fighting side by side with the Poles, sticking with them through the many partitions that were the lot of that unhappy country.

During the time when most of Poland was under the domination of the Russian Tsars, the Jews suffered greatly from the cruel persecutions and pogroms carried on by the oppressors. When Poland was liberated after World War I, they thought their worries were over. Poland had declared that she would take good care of her minorities, the largest group of which were the Jews. In fact, Poland was responsible to the League of Nations for giving the Jews equal rights. True, there was still a certain amount of anti-Semitism in Poland, but it was mostly part and parcel of the economic opposition of the growing Polish middle class to the presence of Jews in business and the professions.

When Hitler came to power and started to persecute the German Jews, Polish anti-Semites thought their moment had come. Anti-Semitic incidents became the rule in the Polish universities; extreme political leaders tried to import Nazi race theories into Poland, and the Nationalist Radical party (Nara) even went so far as to incite the population of certain communities to commit acts of violence against the Jews. And the Polish government let the League of Nations know that it no longer felt itself bound by the minority treaty.

Still, this influx of Nazi ideas could not destroy the strong ties created by common life, work, and struggle of Jews and Poles over many centuries.

When Hitler attacked Poland, Jews were among the most determined and loyal soldiers in the Polish Army, and the "Aryan" Poles did not feel that the difference in race made for a different kind of shooting and dying. When Warsaw was besieged and the mayor called on the citizens to defend the city, thousands of Jewish workers thronged around the City Hall clamoring for weapons. And many of them died defending the city, before it finally fell into the hands of the Germans.

Stephan Starzynski, the heroic mayor of Warsaw, was no enemy of the Jews. He recognized no difference between races. In October 1939, shortly after the occupation, the Nazis suggested that he bar the distribution of food to Jewish districts of Warsaw, but Starzynski refused to heed such a suggestion. The Germans therefore arrested him and took him to a concentration camp inside Germany, where he died soon afterward.

Or take Prince Zdzislaw Lubomirski, a fine elderly gentleman who looked every inch a prince, with his aristocratic features and his small gray beard. He had been a member of the Emergency Committee during the siege of Warsaw. The Jewish representatives had been in constant contact with him during the three weeks of the siege. When the prince first learned about the plan to establish a ghetto, he used all his influence to convince the Germans that they could not do such a thing. It seemed utterly senseless as far as he was concerned. For he could not see any difference between Jews and non-Jews.

Other prominent Poles did, however. There was Franciszek Nowodworski, the president of the Polish Bar Association and leader of a rightist party, who had never made a secret of his anti-Semitic feelings. But even that did not mean that he had any intention whatever of co-operating with the Germans in persecuting the Jews. He was asked by the Nazi authorities to bar Jews from the association, a move which would automatically have barred them from all Polish courts. The Nazis barred them anyhow, but for propaganda reasons they would have preferred to have a Polish citizen arrange the move. Nowodworski refused to do any such thing. His answer is almost a classic, showing as it does the muddled mind of a man struggling between his hatred for the Nazis and his dislike of the Jew: "If we decide to bar the Jews from our courts, we will do it ourselves," he declared. "But if the Germans order us to do so, we'll fight."

There was nobody among the Poles who really wanted to collaborate with the Nazis or could be forced into such collaboration, no Quisling, as these types were called later on. And that made it impossible for any of them to aid the Nazis in their war against the Jews, no matter what their own personal feelings about them might be.

This was equally true of the Catholic clergy, some members of which had in former times disseminated anti-Semitic propaganda. The only man of God who went over wholeheartedly to the Nazis was Metropolitan Dionizji, the head of the Orthodox Church in Poland. He had been pampered and flattered and decorated by Polish governments. But when the Germans entered he immediately blessed them—a thing which the representatives of neither the Protestant nor the Catholic church stooped to do. From that time on he worked in every way possible for Hitler, associating himself with reactionary White Russians in the hope of profiting by Hitler's conquest of Russia.

But the majority of the Catholic priests, even those who had never liked the Jews, now came to find an understanding with them, an understanding born of mutual suffering. This was a comparatively early development, because the persecution of Catholic priests began soon after the invasion of Poland. In October 1939 the Gestapo of Kalish humiliated—or so they thought—Catholic priests by forcing a group of them to meet, embrace, and kiss a group of rabbis in front of the City Hall. The old men did meet, did embrace and kiss. They did not, however, feel humiliated. They felt comforted by each other's presence, and the knowledge that they all were suffering because they believed in a common God and wanted to be free to pray to him in their own fashion made them strong and kept them determined not to falter in their fight against the antichrist.

Some Poles had really been violent anti-Semites, and some had followed suit, repeating anti-Jewish slogans without thinking much about the matter one way or the other. Some of the original anti-Semites never changed—indeed, they thought the Germans were doing a grand job by taking the Jews off their hands . . . if only the Germans, too, would disappear. The members of the Nara felt that way. But these men formed an infinitesimal part of the Polish people. The large majority—those who might have repeated anti-Jewish slogans in the past without thinking twice—began now to think twice.

It was one thing to curse a Jew but another thing to see a Jew beaten up in the street. It was all right to repeat stock epithets about "dirty Jews," but they soon found that they could not easily banish from their minds the dreadful pictures of the sufferings of these same Jews. The Poles saw the suffering Jews and recognized their brothers.

The gates were closed. The Jews no longer spoke of the ghetto with irony directed against themselves. They began to understand that the Nazis had indeed "turned the clock back" several centuries. They understood that the Nazis had decided to ignore the fruits of the fight for enlightenment and liberation, which the best heads of every nation, the Jews with them, had fought during these centuries.

The Nazis were proud of their achievement, so proud that one of the first things they did after the Warsaw Ghetto was established in November 1940 was to call in German newspapermen and take them on several personally conducted tours through the Jewish quarters.

It was cold that winter, and there was no coal to be had in the ghetto. So the Jews had to feed their stoves with tables, chairs, and wardrobes. The snow fell steadily. The faces of the people in the streets were blue with cold. As much as possible, the Jews stayed at home, burying themselves under the bedcovers in a futile attempt to keep warm. Many froze to death. One could see mothers cuddling their babies who had died hours ago, trying to put warmth into their little dead bodies. One could see children trying to awake their mothers who seemingly had fallen asleep at a street corner and who would never awaken again.

The gentlemen of the press whom the Nazi authorities called into the Warsaw Ghetto came with pleasure. They were given a special car from Berlin to Warsaw. They were representatives of papers in Berlin, Leipzig, Munich, Hamburg, Cologne, Dortmund, and Nuremberg. They had rested well in their sleepers; they were given an excellent breakfast by the representatives of the Propaganda Ministry in Warsaw, and then they were loaded into cars to be driven through the ghetto. They leaned back against the cushions and watched. They felt very superior; they had slept well and eaten well, and now they were being handed a good story. They felt fine. Was it not wonderful to be a German journalist? A German journalist had nothing to write about but German victories. A German journalist could always write about the superiority of the German race. Was it not as clear as water that the Germans were superior to all other people? Look how fast they had beaten the Poles and the Norwegians and the French, not to speak of the smaller nations. And look at these Jews. . . .

But the chief reason why the German newsmen felt so fine was that they did not have to think. They did not have to worry their heads about what to write. They had been told what to write.

Some of them had to give a pseudo-scientific discussion of the problem of the ghetto, to explain why the ghetto had to be created. Perhaps they did not know themselves, but, never mind, there was always the handout of the Propaganda Ministry to fall back on.

The handout said that there were: (1) Considerations of health: "The Jews, who show no concern about the hygienic conditions of their persons and dwellings, are the chief carriers of disease." (2) Economic considerations: "The effective carrying on of war industries requires the exclusion of Jews from economic life." (3) Political considerations: "Jewish influence has a detrimental effect on the loyal attitude of the Poles to the German administration."

Other scribes were less "scientific." They could not be bothered with the niceties of explanations and "considerations." Their public was used to stronger food. Their public was soon to applaud a speech of Alfred Rosenberg, head man of the *Voelkischer Beobachter,* who had always declared that the Reich and Europe must be cleared "speedily" of all Jews. "In this work of purification," he was to state (on March 28, 1941), "Roosevelt and his Baruch and his Hollywood culture will not disturb us."

So the reporters wrote: "Wherever we looked we saw Jews. And what figures! Filthy, ragged, and with an expression in which a perpetual grin mingled with hesitation and uncertainty."

They looked around a bit more and wrote: "The stores in the streets resemble caverns and holes. They are thick with dirt. The deeper we went into the ghetto, the more dismal it became."

Naturally the German reporters did not pause to reflect that it was the master race that had forced human beings to live like that. Such ideas could not be found in the handouts of the Propaganda Ministry. All the German newsmen knew was that they were more favored than these Jews, and that therefore, by the same token, they must be better. And they wrote:

"The streets grew narrower; the dirty houses, with their filthy windows without curtains, became smaller. In the rooms which were on the ground floor the Jews had hung cardboard or newspaper over the windows so that one could not look into their filthy stables."

Yes, things were bad in the ghetto. About two hundred thousand people had lived in that district before the war. That meant that an average of three to four people had to live in one room then. Now the Jews of Warsaw who had formerly lived elsewhere, as well as the Jewish refugees from other Polish towns and villages—about five hundred thousand in all—were quartered there. The official figures were somewhat smaller, though, because many of the refugees in the ghetto were living there illegally, hiding from the Gestapo for one reason or another.

Yes, things were bad. The German journalists saw it with pleasure and jotted down their notes about the rags the Jews were wearing, the goods they were offering for sale, such as old shoes and worn suspenders and secondhand jackets and half-broken dishes. "Here a couple of Jewesses haggled over a few potatoes. There some Jewish boys fought over a cigarette butt. Wherever we looked, we saw miserable, fallen creatures."

And the final word of these gentlemen of the press: "Let them choke in their filth . . . it's all right with us."

But the Jews did not choke in their filth. For the first few weeks they had been stunned; but then, rallying, they determined to endure the unendurable and immediately set to work to make the best of things.

Adam Czerniakow, president of the Jewish Council and mayor of the ghetto, showed an unbelievable amount of energy. He surrounded himself with a group of men and women who were as determined as himself to make the best of things, and in an astonishingly short time he succeeded in bringing some kind of order out of the chaos. He worked day and night, often snatching a few hours of sleep in his office to save time.

One of the first things Czerniakow and the Jewish Council did was to create a number of departments to take care of the most urgent problems. First there was a Tax Department. Every Jew had to pay taxes. The amount was established by employees of the department. Only the poorest were exempt from taxation. There was also a Department for Burials, which, alas, was kept extremely busy. There was a Cultural Department which organized schools and, for grownups, lectures and other means of recreation and relaxation, even concerts and theaters. Among those shaping this department was Professor Balaban—who, of course, was no longer permitted to teach at the University of Warsaw—and his friend and pupil, Dr. Ringelblum. Out of nothing they created not only kindergartens, elementary and high schools, but a large number of specialized schools in which boys and girls between fifteen and twenty years of age could study what in normal times they might have studied at universities. There were schools for engineers, chemists, doctors, painters, et cetera. Many of these schools had to be run behind false fronts, for the Nazis had decided that it was not necessary for young Jews to have any higher education. There was also a Department of Health which furnished medical supplies in so far as possible. Later there was also a Police Department, established when the Germans, for reasons of their own, decided that the ghetto should have a special Jewish police.

The most vital organization within the entire setup created by the Jewish Council was the Food Department. It ran soup kitchens, gave other aid to poor, hungry, or stricken families, and supervised the rationing system. Since the Germans allowed only very scanty amounts of food to come into the ghetto, the Food Department entered into negotiations with the Nazis in order to obtain additional supplies in exchange for labor. It sent workers to work in factories and on the roads for the Nazis, and received in return a certain amount of food which it was allowed to distribute.

From the very beginning food was the main problem. Three quarters of the population depended entirely on soup kitchens for nourishment. The Food Department soon organized additional feeding projects for children. Social workers went from house to house to see that no child went without food. Self-help was organized on a large scale, under the direction of house committees which collected contributions from everyone in the house. There were more than twenty thousand such house committees active in the ghetto.

All this was only part of an enormous social effort, of a plan developed by the Jews, and it was a magnificent testimonial to the almost unbelievable energy which drove them on, to the strength of their determination not to perish just because the Nazis willed it so.

The Germans did not interfere with the activities organized by the Jewish Council. A Dr. Auerwald, who had been appointed special commissar by Governor General Frank to serve as liaison officer between the ghetto and the German authorities, was in constant contact with Adam Czerniakow. He was rather glad that the Jews were working out their own problems. The Nazis still had hopes of convincing the world of their cultural mission. In any event, Dr. Auerwald was interested only in getting as much manpower out of the ghetto as was humanly possible. There were more than forty thousand skilled Jewish craftsmen, and at least an equal number of men who could do hard labor. As long as these men labored for the Hitler machine there seemed to be no reason for the Nazis to interfere with life in the ghetto.

That was what the Jews believed—or at least what they wanted to believe. Czerniakow wanted to believe it. He wanted to find some *modus vivendi* with the Germans, even under these dreadful and subhuman conditions. He hoped, and encouraged the others to hope also, that by making a supreme effort to maintain discipline and self-help, and by careful obedience to German orders, they might somehow manage to hibernate till the war was over, till Hitler was beaten and they were finally liberated.

This was what they hoped for, and it was this hope which kept them going for a long time. As long as they could cling to this hope they could endure anything. Perhaps it was the memory of this false hope which prompted them later on, when speaking of the first eighteen months they spent in the ghetto, to refer to that time, somewhat ironically, though truly, in comparison with what followed, as the "idyllic period."

Chapter IV

The Idyllic Period

Toward the end of 1940 Hitler had made himself master of Poland, Czechoslovakia, Denmark, Norway, Belgium, the Netherlands, and France. The Balkan countries, too, had been brought completely under German economic domination.

England was still holding out. Goering sent the Luftwaffe over the Channel against a numerically small force of the RAF. The Nazi fliers came back and back again, throwing their bombs on English ports, on English towns, on London. How long would the English be able to take it? When would Hitler enter London to begin his reign over Europe, or perhaps over the world? To most people all over the world Hitler seemed unbeatable. But never, even for a moment, did the Jews in the Warsaw Ghetto believe that Hitler would win this war. They knew such a victory would have meant their end—the end of all Jews throughout the world, whom Hitler had sworn to annihilate. But it could not happen. Again and again throughout their long history the Jews had been faced with the threat of extermination at the hands of their enemies, fully as formidable as Hitler. And always a miracle had happened to stop their would-be conqueror.

One of these predecessors of Hitler was Haman, who, about 400 B.C., was about to do away with all the Jews. But a miracle had happened to frustrate him and his sinister plans. And in memory of their salvation the Jews ever since then celebrated the Purim holiday. The Nazis had never liked this holiday of the Jews because it kept alive the story of what God had done to punish the enemies of His chosen people. In 1933 Goebbels had closed a German-Jewish newspaper just for printing the story of that holiday.

In 1941 Purim fell on March 13. The Nazis installed many additional guards in the ghetto to see to it that the Jews did not attempt to assemble in common prayer during that day.

But the Jews found ways of meeting in cellars and in back rooms, where they said the prayers ordained for the Purim holiday.

"In the days of Mordecai and Esther, in Sushan the capital, when wicked Haman rose up against them, and sought to destroy, to slay, and make to perish all the Jews, both young and old, little children and women, on one day, on the thirteenth day of the twelfth month, which is the month of Adar, and to take the spoil of them for a prey—then didst Thou in Thy abundant mercy bring his council to naught, didst frustrate his design and return his recompense upon his own head; and they hanged him and his sons upon the gallows.

"For all these things Thy name, O our King, shall be continually blessed and exalted for ever and ever."

In a few cases the Nazi guards discovered where the Jews were praying. They drove them out of the houses with whips and forced them to wipe the dirt off the streets with their prayer shawls. But the Jews did not feel the sting of the lash, because they were thinking of Haman, who had been the Hitler of his time, and of what had happened to him in the end.

Only a few hundred feet from the place where the Jews were wiping up the streets with their prayer shawls a priest stood in his pulpit and spoke these words to the men and women who thronged the church to hear him:

"Blessed are those that mourn, for they shall be comforted.

"Blessed are the meek, for they shall inherit the earth.

"Blessed are those who hunger and thirst after righteousness, for they shall be satisfied.

"Blessed are the merciful, for they shall receive mercy.

"Blessed are the pure in heart, for they shall see God.

"Blessed are the peace makers, for they shall be called the children of God.

"Blessed are those who have endured persecution for righteousness' sake, for theirs is the Kingdom of Heaven."

These words were spoken on the day of Purim in the beautiful Gothic Church of All Saints, which stood within the ghetto walls on the Place Grzybowski.

On July 24, 1940, the Nazi authorities had introduced the Nuremberg Laws into Poland. Everybody who had one Jewish parent or grandparent was considered a Jew. Every converted Jew was, of course, considered a Jew, and all of them were ordered into the ghetto by January 1, 1941. Thus more than two thousand Catholics and more than one thousand Protestants lived in the Warsaw Ghetto. The Church of All Saints was filled twice every day by ardent Catholics wearing the yellow badge and the Star of David.

The man who preached to them and blessed them was Father Jan Puder. He, too, wore a yellow badge, for he, too, was of Jewish origin.

Father Puder was known all over Warsaw. He used to preach at the oldest church in town in Freta Street. His sermons were fiery, and he knew well how to keep his followers engrossed in his subject. One day in 1937 a group of reactionary Polish students, led by some agents of the Nara party, entered his church while he was preaching and shouted, "Down with the Jews!" When the Father ignored them they attacked him bodily, beat him and tore his robes. Puder's followers, many women among them, came to his aid, and a free-for-all fight ensued, in which umbrellas and fingernails played an outstanding part and which ended with the students ignominiously retreating.

This was Father Puder. He had gladly gone to the ghetto to comfort the Catholics who had suddenly found themselves counted as Jews. They needed his comfort, too, for they were in an even more desperate situation than the orthodox Jews. Their entire world had come tumbling down about their ears. They had been reared as Catholics; they had never known that their mothers or perhaps their grandmothers had been of Jewish origins. All their friends were Catholics. Now they felt forlorn, deserted. Many of them had lost their "Aryan" husbands, wives, fathers, or mothers, all of whom had to separate themselves from them according to the law. Economically they were even worse off than the Jews. They had no friends to fall back on inside the ghetto. They could not hope to establish even a moderate business, since they knew nobody and nobody knew them. Most of the Jews tried to help them, but there was so little they could do. The Catholics in the ghetto tried to listen to the Jewish language, which they had never spoken, tried to get used to the Jewish way of life, which was unknown to them. They felt utterly hopeless and in complete despair.

But Father Puder spoke to them:

"Blessed art thou when people abuse you, and falsely speak evil against you on my account. Exult and be exceeding glad, for great will be your reward in Heaven, for that is the way of the prophets who went before you." And they were comforted.

Spring came, but little of it could be felt in the ghetto. Those who lived near the walls could see the trees outside becoming green and flowers opening up. The narrow, crooked streets of the ghetto hardly allowed the rays of the sun to enter. There were no parks, no trees in the ghetto. The children lay around in the filthy courtyards. They began to fall sick with typhoid; they contracted tuberculosis. Soon there was hardly a room where you could not hear the strange, labored breath of a consumptive. Then it became hot, very hot. There was no relief. There was no place to swim. The narrow ghetto was like an oven.

The Germans had a passion for taking moving pictures in the ghetto. Every once in a while a crew of cameramen would appear, always accompanied by a few Gestapo men who saw to it that they had no trouble getting the pictures they wanted. For some time they seemed mainly interested in filming scenes of misery such as ragged, half-naked beggars imploring passers-by for a crust of bread, or children digging into refuse boxes for something to eat. It did not make sense, at first, that the Nazis wanted thus to preserve documents of the unhappiness and need they themselves had created. But later their purpose became clear. They were out for pictures of contrast. They wanted to show the world that while a part of the Jews were starving, others were having the time of their lives.

The German cameramen would enter one of the better houses of the ghetto and build there the setting of a night club. They would bring in a number of Jewish men and women whom they had seized in the streets and whom they now forced to sit at the tables, to converse, laugh, and drink champagne.

Or they would bring in smartly dressed women—unmistakably prostitutes—and photograph them together with respectable-looking Jews in especially arranged poses. They even entered the house of one of the members of the Jewish Council, bringing with them champagne and ladies of doubtful reputation, and staged an orgy which they then proceeded to film.

Finally they broke into the ritual bathhouse on Zeglana Street. They ordered a number of young girls and some elderly orthodox Jews with long flowing beards to strip and dance naked in the pool. This scene was later shown in German theaters under the caption "Glimpses of Jewish Religious Life."

To be sure, there were still a few well-to-do people in the ghetto. They were Jews who had some jewels, clothing, or other valuables saved from better times, which they could sell now. You did not see or hear much of this class of better-situated Jews. Many of them used what was left of their riches to get faked papers of some kind to help them make their getaway. In the meantime they gave their money or their jewels piece by piece to the Gestapo in order to be left alone . . . and stay alive.

Some of these people still lived rather comfortably during the first few months in the ghetto. They frequented the few cafés which were opened in Sienna and Leszno streets. Their women still tried to dress well or even fashionably. Somehow they kept in touch with the newest Paris fashions and somehow they found tailors and shoemakers who fitted them out. Small, high hats, long jackets without collars in gray and wine red, shoes on high cork heels were the fashion of those days. There were only a relatively small number of people rich enough to fool themselves that everything would go on just as it always had. And they did not fool themselves for long.

But there were other "rich Jews," whom no one had ever heard of before and who certainly had not been well off before the Nazis came. They had made their money since the occupation and, in almost every instance, in collaboration with the Gestapo. Some of them had not lived in Warsaw before, having been imported by the Gestapo from other cities so that the Gestapo could make money through them. This was the Jewish underworld.

What then did these people do to make themselves so valuable to the Gestapo? They smuggled food into the ghetto. There was an enormous amount of smuggling of foodstuffs going on day and night, with the connivance of certain members of the Gestapo, who arranged that there should be no interference with this activity. They gave what is known in this country as "protection." And they got their cut, quite a nice cut. But this was not their only source of income. The Jewish friends of the Gestapo also worked as informers. They "put the finger" on Jews who still had some money—which was illegal—or jewels, so that the Gestapo could confiscate whatever they had.

The Jewish underworld lived in the better houses in the southern part of the ghetto, in Sienna Street and thereabouts. They frequented a few restaurants where, thanks to the Gestapo, they could get plenty of good food, even caviar. They sat in the one or two cafés and drank champagne and danced with the gay ladies who frequented those places.

This Jewish underworld succeeded in corrupting some young Jewish men, sons of good families; even, in a few cases, sons of fathers who worked for the Jewish Council. These young men were given plenty of money and taken to good restaurants where they were made drunk. They soon began to think themselves important personalities. The agents of the underworld did everything to flatter these playboys of the ghetto, for they needed them to find out about the measures the council or any of the committees or departments were about to take. They sought all kinds of information which they could sell to the Germans.

The young men had, so they thought, a good time. When they found out what they were doing, it was too late.

The vast majority of the Jews kept away from these young men, as they kept away from their newly rich friends. They never entered cafés where there was dancing or drinking. Most of them still believed that life would go on indefinitely in the ghetto and therefore devoted most of their time to their shops or businesses, in an effort to make an honest living, and were deeply ashamed that there were Jews who would take advantage of the misery of their brothers.

There was almost no transportation in the ghetto. No taxis were allowed to enter, and only one street railway line was running. The streetcars in the ghetto carried the Star of David. Later even this line was discontinued.

Several enterprising Jews soon introduced a means of transportation which had been discarded everywhere in Europe around 1914: busses drawn by horses—a kind of stagecoach. They too had to carry the Star of David as insigne. Since the horses at the disposal of the bus company were rather old and badly fed, the busses had to make many more stops than was foreseen in the itinerary, and travel was accordingly slow. But this bus line did a thriving business, notwithstanding, even though the men who organized it did not make much profit, since they had to give most of their earnings to the Gestapo officials who otherwise would never have granted them the necessary license.

The Jews also introduced another means of transportation which so far had never been used in Europe: the ricksha. From old wheels taken from cars no longer used they had built small open carriages with room for one or two persons, which they used chiefly to transport the old and infirm. Poor Jews were employed to pull these rickshas. The Germans soon decided that this was a wonderful way to demonstrate their superiority over the Jews, and so every day one could see rickshas filled with Gestapo passengers, lustily swinging their whips over the backs of the Jewish "horses." The Jewish underworld, too, made use of these new taxis.

The only relaxation for most of the Jews—those who could afford it, that is—was the theater. There were in the ghetto a large number of Jewish or half-Jewish singers and actors who had formerly been with the Polish National Opera and other theaters. In fact, most of the best actors in Poland were now in the Warsaw Ghetto. They played in wooden barracks, in half-ruined apartment houses, in vacant factories.

There was the Eldorado, which presented light musical comedies and dramas in Jewish. There was the New Azazel Theater, where Jewish classics were shown. Then there was Femina, which played in Polish. It had a choir and a ballet and was considered the representative theater of the ghetto. In July a second Polish theater opened, the New Studio Theater, devoted mainly to modern plays of more intimate character. The Zionist Youth organization founded still another theater which played in Hebrew. There was also a marionette theater for the children.

The theaters played from two to five in the afternoon, because there was a curfew in the evening. But they were always crowded. People might go hungry, but they would not miss a show. Here was the only relief from drab and unhappy reality. Here for a few moments they could dream, could share in the joys and sorrows of those on the stage, be torn by conflicts which belonged in another world. Here there was no hunger, no slavery or humiliation; or, if there was, the crime was always followed by punishment. And, happily, theater tickets were not rationed.

Finally, there were a great number of variety shows, some of high artistic standing. All of them produced shows of social and political significance. There would be a song full of double meanings, and everybody in the public understood that everything which was said against a certain non-existent person was meant to be applied against Adolf Hitler or some other prominent Nazi. There would be recitations of certain parts of the Bible containing curses against the Egyptians or other enemies of the children of Israel, to the accompaniment of muffled drums or a gong, and all those who listened knew that it was not the Egyptians or the Philistines who were meant, but the Germans. Or there would be very funny sketches satirizing the Jewish Council and its prominent members, making fun of their weak spots or of the bureaucracy which had swamped certain departments.

Even in their precarious situation, with the future so uncertain, the Jews could always fall back on one of their greatest talents: to make fun of everything around them, including themselves. It was a good relaxation, this making fun. And in a way it was also a weapon, the only weapon they could use against their oppressors. But if ridicule could kill, many of the Nazis would have fallen dead in the streets of Warsaw during those days.

This talent of the Jews for making fun of themselves and of their enemies created an unbelievable and seemingly inexhaustible number of new jokes which the people in the ghetto told each other. Many made fun of the Fuehrer himself.

There was, for instance, the incident which was supposed to have occurred in 1933 in a German school which Jewish children were still allowed to attend. The teacher asked: "Hans, what would you be if your father was the Fuehrer?" The answer was: "I would like to be a general." "And what would you want to be if your father was the Fuehrer, Karl?" And the answer was: "I would like to be an admiral." "And you, Abraham, what would you want to be if your father was the Fuehrer?" And little Abraham answered spontaneously: "In that case I'd love to be an orphan."

Or there was the story of the Pole, the Ukrainian, and the Jew who were arrested by the Gestapo and asked: "Where do you want to be buried after the execution?" The Pole wanted to be buried in the military cemetery in Warsaw. The Ukrainian wanted to be buried in Lwów, near the grave of the famous poet, Iwan Frank. The Jew said: "I would like best to be buried near our beloved Fuehrer, Adolf Hitler." The Gestapo man almost had apoplexy. "How dare you? Don't you know that the Fuehrer is alive?" Whereupon the Jew added, "Oh, I'm not in any hurry. I can wait."

There was the story of the Fuehrer who, after having tried in vain to subdue England, was finally persuaded to seek the advice of a famous rabbi as to how he could manage to cross the Channel. The rabbi was brought to him and after a moment's deliberation declared: "There is only one thing for you to do. You must get hold of the rod which Moses used to divide the Red Sea so that the children of Israel could walk through it without even getting their feet wet." Hitler asked impatiently, "But how can I get this rod?" "Oh, that's easy," the rabbi answered, stroking his beard. "You'll find it in the British Museum."

The ghetto was a big city. Half a million people, even if you put them in a cage, are still half a million people, with all kinds of interests, hopes, ideas, frustrations, with different behavior, appearance, means of expression. There were people who had always lived in big cities and those who had never left their native village before the Nazis drove them out.

In a way, this ghetto was a small universe. Every type of human being was represented. Every level of human society could be found there. There were the very orthodox Jews, who never in their lives had even thought a wrong thought; and there were the cynical criminals who worked hand in glove with the Gestapo. There were the intellectuals, the writers, lawyers, and doctors, and there were the peasants and the workers. There were those who had seen better days and could not but believe that all this was a nightmare which would soon be over, and there were those who all their lives had been poor, dependent on the charity of others.

All these people lived together in a small space, and they were all equal, in a way, as they were to find out later: the same death awaited them. But they did not see it that way, not yet. They still clung to their hopes and to the illusion that they were the same people they had been all their lives. They tried to express this conviction by keeping up the same kind of standards as before, a pitiful pretense of their former social level.

They had not yet become a mass.

Outside the ghetto walls the war went on, involving more and more countries, killing more and more people.

On June 22, 1941, Hitler started his most gigantic effort, the invasion of Russia.

On June 22, 1941, the "idyllic period" of the ghetto ended.

Chapter V

Hunger

ADAM CZERNIAKOW, the mayor of the ghetto, was hardly ever seen by the average inhabitant of the ghetto. Only on rare occasions did he go out to inspect a school or a hospital. Those who saw him were impressed by his pale and serious face. It was said of him in the ghetto that nobody had seen him smile since the Nazis had come into Warsaw.

He had little reason to smile. For it was he and only he who had to conduct negotiations with the Nazis, with Captain Batz and Gruppenfuehrer Mende. When he left the ghetto for a conference with the Gestapo he usually came back in a state bordering on exhaustion, his face even more drawn, his shoulders sagging. He hardly answered the greetings of his employees, but rushed into his office and buried himself in work. He was still trying to make the best of it. He was still fighting.

Gruppenfuehrer Mende had a peculiar sense of humor. He thought, evidently, that the ghetto was not sufficiently crowded yet. And he had a splendid idea of how to increase the population. One day—it was shortly after the ghetto had been closed in November 1940—he told Czerniakow that there would be more Jews arriving, whom he would have to take care of. Soon afterward they came. They numbered more than two thousand, and they were the incurably insane, from an asylum in Tworky. The Nazis dumped them on the ghetto market near Muranow Place, and Czerniakow was notified that something had to be done about them.

Yes, something had to be done about them quickly. For these unhappy people stood there, filling the market place and the neighboring streets with their strange mad laughter. Some of them began stripping off their clothing in spite of the bitter cold; others stopped passers-by to tell them mysterious stories or divulge "secrets" of great importance, or they attacked them as persecutors of long standing.

Czerniakow did not even have a hospital in which to put them, since the few at the disposal of the Jews were all filled up. He finally arranged for the most dangerous cases to be sent to the Pawiak prison, but soon the prison, too, was overcrowded; there were prisoners, too, who had to serve their terms. So some dangerously insane persons had to be brought to private homes and put into rooms which were already crowded with four or five other inhabitants. They terrorized everybody who came near them.

But Mende continued to dispatch the inhabitants of insane aslyums into the ghetto. He sent them from Wadovice near Cracow, from Austria and from Czechoslovakia. And Czerniakow worked day and night to solve the problem of the overcrowded ghetto.

For almost every day new people were coming in. Whole villages appeared with nothing but a few rags. They were given no time to collect their belongings when they were evacuated by the Germans. They were assembled in the market place and not even allowed to return to their homes for a bundle of clothes or a bit of food or a few zlotys. There they stood now, in front of the Jewish Community Building. They had to be put into barracks, hastily erected without any comforts or any sanitary facilities. Twice a day they were fed a kind of watery soup. Many of them died from exhaustion, many from typhus and other contagious diseases which they had brought along.

The inhabitants of the ghetto had at first felt sorry for those unfortunates who had been driven from their villages and towns. But by now they had become accustomed to the constant new arrivals, and they began to resent them. After all, there was not room enough for themselves and their children. They felt that they all would suffocate if any more were allowed to come in.

Adam Czerniakow was dismayed at this reaction. What was going to become of the Jews if they began to fight among themselves? He decided to make an appeal:

"Do not forget, Jews, that we are people with a warm heart, and with pity for sufferers. Open your houses to your exiled brethren, and meet them with the unforgettable words of Ruth to her mother-in-law Naomi: 'Whither thou goest I will go; your people shall be my people, thy God, my God.' "

But little by little the housing problem which seemed so difficult at first slowly began to solve itself. The starvation rations, the unhygienic conditions, the insufficient medical care began to produce results. Soon people were dying in great numbers.

Still the ghetto had to be considered a relatively safe haven for the Jews of Poland. Whatever they suffered in Warsaw, even the indignities, the hunger, the impossible housing conditions, could hardly be compared with what the Jews in other parts of Poland had suffered ever since the Germans had invaded Poland. Ever since then Warsaw had been full of stories told by the frightened refugees about the German terror against the Jews. For some time Adam Czerniakow had been inclined to discard some of the rumors as exaggerations. It was a year before the Jewish Council was able to secure definite figures contained in reports made out by dependable Poles not given to spreading panic.

The figures were terrifying. From the very first day the Nazis had come into Poland they had killed Jews wherever they found them. During the first week thousands had perished, and those who were allowed to live had been put in camps or told to flee for their lives. And the Germans had, of course, confiscated all their property. Jewish soldiers taken as war prisoners were separated from the non-Jewish Poles, beaten up, and often killed. After the Nazis occupied Poland and the war was officially over, the extermination of Polish Jews took a less dramatic form. Ghettos were formed everywhere, and for a while it looked as though the Nazis were willing to let them stay in these ghettos and slowly perish by starvation and epidemics.

This at least was the opinion of Professor Balaban up to June 22, 1941. On that day the Warsaw newspapers came out with headlines about the German invasion of Russia. They declared unanimously that Germany was "protecting" civilized Europe against the "aggression of Bolshevism." Everywhere in the ghetto the Jew smiled. Nobody believed the official German explanation; everybody was hoping that the war might bring them a step nearer to liberation.

Balaban did not smile. "I'm afraid this will mean more slaughter of Jews," he told Czerniakow. "We will have a repetition of what happened at the beginning of the war."

He was right. Only a few days later the first news reached the Jewish Council that the Germans were killing thousands of Jews throughout eastern Galicia.

Czerniakow said, "We must do everything to keep this news from leaking out. It would create a panic."

"But sooner or later the Germans will continue their murders right here in the ghetto," Balaban remonstrated. "What is the use of keeping our people in the dark?"

Czerniakow shook his head. "I don't believe it. I can't believe it. They cannot kill half a million people. It just can't be done. Not even the Nazis can do it."

"The Nazis can do anything if it comes to murder."

There were many things on which Czerniakow and Balaban disagreed. One of them was the institution of the Jewish militia, on which the Nazis had insisted. It was a police force headed by a certain Colonel Szerynski, a baptized Jew who had been chief of the police of Lublin before the war. Next in command was a certain Jacob Lejkin, a small man with a swarthy face and twinkling eyes, who had been a shyster lawyer of decidedly bad reputation. Balaban met him almost daily when Lejkin came to the Community Building.

"I don't trust this man," Balaban told Czerniakow. "I don't like the whole institution of the Jewish police corps."

The Jewish policemen wore blue uniforms with the yellow Star of David as their badge. They were under authority of the police commissioner of Warsaw and, of course, under the Gestapo. They had to regulate traffic, see that everybody had his proper identification papers, and, after the war with Russia began, were charged with organizing the anti-aircraft defense. Besides this they had to watch the inner gates of the ghetto. They had to disperse Jews who assembled near the gates, for the Germans had ordered them to shoot anyone who might approach the gates or even the walls nearer than fifty yards without permission.

Czerniakow shrugged. "There is nothing we can do. The Nazis ordered us to create a police force."

"And if we had refused to carry out this order? Or if we had let it be known in the ghetto that the Jewish Council does not expect any Jews to volunteer?"

"We are in no position to sabotage the orders of the Nazis," Czerniakow said tersely. "We have no right to challenge them and to risk the lives of those who trust us."

Even after the Jewish Council had published the appeal for volunteer policemen, in accordance with the Nazis' demands, Balaban hoped that no Jew would be willing to serve as a policeman policing his own people under the direction of the Nazis. The Jewish Council had made an appeal for a thousand voluntary policemen. More than three thousand applicants came to the Community Building, though it was understood that they would not receive any money for their services. The only remuneration was a loaf of bread a day and soup from the kitchen of the Jewish Community. But the main attraction of the job was that the policeman was something a bit better than the rest of the people; he had a certain standing. A Jew who was a policeman was someone who not only could not be pushed around, he could do some pushing himself.

The applicants were mostly former lawyers, teachers, engineers—in short, they came from the more educated classes. It soon became evident that it had been a great mistake to hire this type of person. The police force never became a part of the ghetto, and the policemen never felt close to the Jewish working class, which made up the largest part of the ghetto population. Most of them, coming as they did from well-to-do and long-assimilated families, could not even speak Yiddish, the language of the Jewish masses.

Every Jew in the ghetto had to pay thirty groszy (about six cents) a month to cover the expenses of the police. But it was not for this reason that they resented the police. They resented the fact that their own people were helping the Nazis to push them around.

Balaban said, "It seems grotesque and humiliating that we Jews should furnish helpers to carry out the laws of our oppressors."

Czerniakow did not answer. He did not even know about the resentment of the Jews against the Jewish policemen. Almost submerged in ever-growing work, he scarcely saw anyone except the men who worked with him. If an outsider wanted to see him, he had to pass a half-dozen secretaries and wait at least a couple of weeks. By the time Czerniakow could see him, the applicant no longer was there: emergencies that arose in the ghetto could not wait to be solved. Thus Czerniakow lost his touch with the average Jews. He no longer knew what they wanted or how they felt. He became a lonesome man, trying to do his best, knowing all the time that he was attempting the impossible, but still considering it his duty to try again and again.

Perhaps many Jewish policemen would have given up their jobs after a short time if it had not been for the loaf of bread. Thus at least they could protect their families from going hungry. For there was less and less food in the ghetto.

The official food rations for the Poles were a pound of bread daily, one egg and two pounds of marmalade made of beets and carrots a month. There were also one hundred pounds of potatoes and one hundred pounds of coal every year. Later the bread ration was cut in half.

In theory the Jews were entitled to the same rations. In reality, during 1940, they received a pound of bread every sixth day. But after the gates of the ghetto closed, the rations of the Jews existed on paper only. They could consider themselves lucky if they got even a few pounds of bread per month.

There were certain foodstuffs which could be bought freely without any ration points, if one had the money. There were pushcarts in the street with rotten carrots and cabbage and little fish which smelled to high heaven. They were quite expensive, though—a pound cost one zloty. There were also a few shops where chicken and other poultry could be bought, but a pound of chicken cost twenty zlotys, and other meat was even more expensive.

In order to relieve the food shortage the Jewish Community had encouraged the manufacture of foodstuffs, such as artificial honey and marmalade, which looked somewhat like the original but were only a miserable ersatz which tasted quite different. Even these ersatz products were beyond the means of most inhabitants. There were also factories where the afore-mentioned little fish were canned or made into spreads. Others manufactured synthetic candy. For some time horse meat was made into sausages which looked like salami. They, too, cost twenty zlotys a pound and more.

The Jewish Council did its utmost to feed as many of the people as possible in soup kitchens. But it was difficult to find even the basic foodstuffs which went into the soup. The council charged thirty groszy for a dish of soup which consisted mainly of hot water with some faded vegetable or potatoes swimming in it. A more substantial soup with some oatmeal in it cost one zloty. By the end of 1941 the council was feeding almost the entire population of the ghetto once a day—the luxury of two meals a day was one unknown by then to any of the Jews in Warsaw.

The children suffered most from the scarcity of food. They swarmed the streets, their little bodies mere skeletons, their legs so thin that it seemed they might break any minute, their faces and abdomens swollen. They sat on street corners crying. They cried because they were hungry.

Even the arrival of food packages from abroad did little enough to relieve the general misery, for although Jewish organizations in the United States, Portugal, and Switzerland spent large sums for food relief, they could not, of course, begin to feed as many as five hundred thousand people regularly. And many packages never arrived. The Nazis liked the food too.

Whoever was known to get food packages from abroad was watched closely by the other less fortunate ones, and when he walked down the streets carrying a package it not infrequently happened that he was assaulted and the package snatched away from him.

Those who did forced labor were at least allowed the minimum of food to enable them to go on with their work. The others had to try to smuggle in food from the outside. By the fall of 1941 more than half of the population of the ghetto was involved in one way or another in food-smuggling transactions.

Bribes which had to be paid to the Nazis lest they stop the influx of smuggled foodstuff raised the price of food to fantastic heights. By the end of 1941 the price of bread in the ghetto had climbed from five to 17½ zlotys per pound. (Before the war one pound of bread had cost twenty-five groszy—five cents.) By the summer of 1942 one pound of bread cost fifty zlotys, while sugar cost two hundred and butter four hundred zlotys respectively, as against one zloty and three zlotys before the war.

There were different ways of smuggling. First of all there was the Gestapo-sponsored type of smuggling carried on by the Jewish underworld in the ghetto. Large amounts of food came in that way, but it was too expensive, because of the huge cuts the Gestapo took. Then there was the smuggling which was arranged by private persons who dealt with Polish business associates on the other side of the wall. They met each other in the Church of All Saints or the Court Building. This type of smuggling could be successful only when guards were regularly bribed to look the other way while the food was actually being brought into the ghetto. The guards were not quite so expensive as the Gestapo, but expensive enough to make food dearer and dearer.

Then, finally, there was the smuggling which was carried on, without any connection with business from either the ghetto or the Polish side, by hundreds of kindhearted Poles who would come to a certain spot at the wall, specified beforehand, and throw a sack of flour over. The Jewish friends would wait on the other side and carry the flour off. Aryan mothers would come to the Church of All Saints and secretly hand their half-Jewish children something to eat. Wives would meet their husbands there and give them what they had saved from their own meager rations. Food was also smuggled into the ghetto through the cellars of the bombed houses which had exits to the ghetto as well as to the part of Warsaw beyond the walls.

The Gestapo tried to stop all smuggling in order to have a monopoly on food. But even the threat that anybody found trying to bring food into the ghetto would pay with his life did not end the smuggling activities. The only consequence was that the bribes went higher than before. New methods of smuggling were devised constantly. People even went so far as to dig tunnels in order to get food into the ghetto.

But even all the food obtained thus was not enough, not half enough, to feed the population of the ghetto. The people soon began to show the effects of their undernourished condition. Their faces were drawn and pale, their bodies emaciated. They staggered feebly about the streets, collapsed, and died. Yes, they actually starved to death, hundreds of them, thousands of them.

At first their families gave them religious burials, with prayers and ceremonies. But as the victims of starvation became more numerous with every passing day, with the rest of the family knowing that it was only a matter of weeks, perhaps days, before they, too, would go the same way, death lost the dignity it had once worn. It was now a daily occurrence, and you had to harden your heart against it if you wanted to survive, even for a little while.

Every night hundreds of corpses were thrown out by members of their own family to lie, almost naked, on the sidewalks. Thus the clothing of the dead persons could be spared, and also the ration card could be used to buy some food for the survivors for a little while longer. Sometimes the ration card was all a dead mother had to leave to her family. Anyhow, the expenses of a burial were much too high for most of the inhabitants of the ghetto.

In the morning employees of the Jewish Community would patrol the streets with their pushcarts, picking up the corpses and piling them one on the other until they could carry no more. In the afternoon the dead were buried in a few mass graves. A rabbi said a prayer. Some of the family members came to the cemetery but kept as far in the background as they could. They tried not to cry. They did not want to be recognized. They were afraid that they might lose the ration points of the dead person.

From January to June 1939, when Poland was still at peace, the Jewish birth rate in Warsaw had been 8.8 per thousand. From January to June 1941, when the Jews were in the ghetto, the birth rate sank to 3.8 per cent.

The Jewish death rate from January to June 1939 was 10 per thousand. From January to June 1941 it was 86 per thousand.

And this was still the "idyllic period."

Professor Balaban often talked to Dr. Mileikowski about this state of affairs.

Dr. Israel Mileikowski had been a well-known physician in Warsaw before the war. A small, slim, energetic man, he gave much of his time to treating workers who could not afford to pay for medical care. In October 1939 he was caught by the Nazis during one of their daily raids. They completely disregarded the Red Cross badge he wore and beat him up severely. Then they asked him to sing and dance.

"And what did you do?" Balaban asked.

The little doctor smiled apologetically. "I could have showed character and refused, in which case the Nazis would have killed me. That would not have been too pleasant for me, and, in the long run, even worse for my patients, who need me. I figured that if I swallowed my pride, I could at least attend to them. So I danced."

Dr. Mileikowski was indeed a much-needed man, even more so after the Jews were imprisoned in the ghetto. It was due mainly to his efforts that the Health Department functioned so well and that the epidemics did not claim more victims.

"But how much longer can we hold out?" the little doctor said. "The situation is quite desperate. In the first place, we haven't enough doctors—we need three, four times as many to take care of all the sick people. If the Polish doctors could help us . . . But of course the Nazis have forbidden non-Jewish doctors to treat Jewish patients. They say that otherwise a non-Jew might eventually catch the disease of a Jew." He smiled bitterly. After a while he continued: "Of course there are no Jewish doctors any more. According to one of those Nazi decrees, we are now just 'supervisors of the sick.' Well, that doesn't bother me too much. If we only had enough supervisors. If we only had enough hospitals and the right food for the sick people, and drugs."

Balaban had heard all this many times. He knew all the sad stories about health conditions in the ghetto. He did not want to hear any more—and at the same time he wanted to hear more and more. There was always this burning curiosity in spite of himself, this feeling that he had to know, that he had no right to hide his head in the sand, that somebody had to know. . . .

He cleared his throat. "Is there no way out? After all, not even the Germans can be interested in having an epidemic in the ghetto."

"You are wrong. They like it. It seems to prove something to them. German newspapers delight in telling their readers that there are more cases of contagious diseases inside the ghetto than in the rest of Warsaw; for instance, that 98 per cent of all cases of typhoid fever spotted in Warsaw were located in the ghetto. Does this not prove, they say, that the Jews are an inferior race?"

"The German doctors cannot possibly believe such rubbish."

"Speaking of Nazi doctors . . . they sometimes help us," Dr. Mileikowski said. "You know that the Nazi authorities do not allow Jews to be inoculated against typhoid. But Dr. Deuhler, a German physician who is now the head of the Institute of Hygiene in Warsaw, has been good enough to sell me some serum anyhow. In fact, he sells me any quantity I want. He charges high prices. He must have made quite a fortune on the stuff."

Balaban nodded and then went on. He had no special place to go. He just went down the street, around the corner, and into another street. Here he came to a hospital. There was a sign outside: "No beds available." He entered and talked to the superintendent. "Mostly typhoid fever," he was told. "And more than three fourths of the patients are children."

Balaban turned to go, but the man seized him by his coat lapel and went on talking to him: "It's heartbreaking, but you know, what can we do? A few hours ago a woman came with her little boy in her arms. Typhoid fever. She begged us to take the child in. The little one was in a coma. He had a high fever. But what could I do? The woman finally just put the boy here on the floor and rushed out. She stood on the other side of the street so that she could see what we would do. . . . There wasn't anything we could do. The boy died almost instantly. It's heartbreaking. I wish I were dead myself."

Balaban slowly went out. The man was following him. "Why are you going? I'd like to talk to you. There's nobody I can talk to." The man seemed frantic. "Do you know how many of us have died this month? Eight hundred . . . one thousand . . . nothing to eat. Typhoid fever. And it will be worse . . . much worse . . . you'll see."

Again Balaban turned to go. The man followed him out into the street still talking, as though he could not allow the old man to get away.

Balaban walked on. His face was gray with pain and pity. To be able to help . . . But what could anybody do to help? Or even to let the world know what was happening? He was cut off; they all were cut off from the rest of the world. For the first time he missed his students at the University of Warsaw. If he could talk to them; if he could tell them what was going on! But he was alone; he had nobody to talk to.

Dusk fell. Balaban stopped in front of a house. There was a corpse lying just in front of the house, covered with newspapers. There were many corpses lying in the street. Soon a pushcart would come to take them away. If he only knew a way to tell these things to the world. But there was no way. And since he was alone and unable to tell the world what was going on, why should he continue to torture himself? Why did he have to stand here and look at the corpse of somebody he had never known and feel unhappy?

Still he did not move. He felt it was his responsibility to remain here and to see things no matter how much it hurt him. Somebody had to see. Somebody had to know of these things.

Soon afterward two men came down the street with a pushcart, put the corpse on it, and moved away. It had begun to rain. For a moment Balaban remained where he was. Then he slowly followed the push-cart. He followed all the way to the cemetery. It was raining harder now, and it was getting dark. A grave had been prepared for all those nameless people whom the collectors found in the streets that day. They buried them as fast as they could because they wanted to get home before the curfew began. Somebody murmured a prayer, then went away. Only Balaban remained till the last one was buried.

And while he was looking on, his old eyes filling slowly with tears for those whom he had never seen or known, he knew what he was going to do. He was going to write down everything he had seen and heard. He was going to write the history of the ghetto of Warsaw.

It was dark when he left the cemetery.

Once more the Jewish New Year had come. The Nazis finally gave their permission to reopen a few synagogues, but at the same time let it be known that the Jews would do better not to assemble for prayer, otherwise there might be incidents. But the Jews could not be frightened off. They went to their places of worship and they prayed:

"We celebrate the mighty holiness of this day, for it is one of awe and terror. Thereon is Thy dominion exalted and Thy throne established in mercy, and Thou sittest thereon in truth. Verily it is Thou alone who art Judge and Arbiter, who knowest and art witness. Thou writest down and settest the seal, Thou recordest and tellest. Yea, Thou re-memberest the things forgotten. Thou unfoldest the records and the deeds therein inscribed proclaim themselves; for lo! the seal of every man's hand is set thereto!"

The Jews never believed, not for one moment, that God would for-get them. But the world, they were certain, had forgotten them. No-body was coming to their help. Nobody was trying to liberate them from their prison. The world was going to let them perish.

And just then they were given proof that the world had not forgotten them. Some of the Jews still had radios hidden away somewhere which they sometimes tuned in after they had locked the doors. That night they heard a secret Polish station broadcasting a New Year's greeting to the Jews in the Warsaw Ghetto.

"We Poles of whatever party or religion are mourning together with you Jews in this, the darkest hour of our history. We are waiting for the time when our and your tragedy will have finished and a new Poland will arise from the ashes. We see the sun rising for a better morning—even for you, within the walls of the ghetto. Together we will destroy our common enemy, the Nazis."

During the same night a group of Polish workers approached the walls of the ghetto near Chlodna Street and threw flowers over the wall. There was a little card, too, which said that this was a New Year's greeting from the Polish workers of the Wola factories.

From then on the radio of the Polish underground spoke every night to the Jews in the ghetto. It told them of what was happening in Poland, of the mass deportations of Polish workers into Germany, and of the mass deportations of Polish women to German brothels on the Russian front.

But the Jews who listened, at such grave danger, to the Polish broadcasts heard better news too. They learned that Hitler's war on the Russian front was not going quite so well as the Fuehrer had expected. The Germans had made spectacular progress, but when Hitler declared on October 5 that the Russian armies were crushed and that the final victory had been won, he indulged in too much wishful thinking. For it was on this very day that the Russian armies, far from being crushed, began their counteroffensive and forced Hitler's men to fight on all during the winter, and many of his men froze to death.

And one night they also listened to a story of which they had vaguely heard before: the story of two men meeting on a warship somewhere on the Atlantic Ocean early in August 1941: President Roosevelt and Prime Minister Winston Churchill. They were told that before these men parted they had composed a document which they called the "Atlantic Charter." This document set forth clearly the main reasons and the main goals for which all free men in this world were fighting.

The Jews in the ghetto of Warsaw wanted to learn all about this document, and they listened with great intentness while it was read to them; they held their breath in order not to miss a word.

They learned about "hopes for a better future of the world," about the wish of the men who had written the document for "the fullest collaboration between all nations in the economic field with the object of securing, for all, improved labor standards, economic advancement, and social security." They heard about "the final destruction of Nazi tyranny," and they learned that the men who had composed the document hoped to "see established a peace which will afford to all nations the means of dwelling in safety, within their own boundaries, and which will afford assurance that all men in all lands may live out their lives in freedom from fear and want."

After the document was read, the Jews in the ghetto of Warsaw were silent for a long time. Finally one of them asked, "Is this meant for everybody? Is this meant for us Jews too?"

Chapter VI

A Visitor from Berlin

In the middle of March 1942, Heinrich Himmler arrived at the Warsaw airport on a special plane. The visit was in the nature of a surprise, German authorities in Warsaw having been notified of it only at the last minute. Reichsamtsleiter Dr. Fritz Fischer, governor of the city and district of Warsaw, was present at the airport to welcome the distinguished visitor.

Himmler and Fischer drove immediately to the latter's offices, the former Ministry of Foreign Affairs, a beautiful modern building in chromium and black situated on a square now called Adolf Hitler Platz. Gestapo men on motorcycles preceded and followed the car, sirens screaming.

Himmler stayed only about fifteen minutes at Fischer's office. Then the two drove together to the Commandantur, only a few hundred feet away, past the grave of the Unknown Soldier where the eternal light had been extinguished when Poland fell, past some of the more fashionable restaurants where German officers were sitting chatting and laughing with elegant ladies, until finally they came to the Commandantur, a famous three-story building of baroque architecture, now the headquarters of the German General Staff. By that time the news of Himmler's arrival had made the rounds. Everybody in Warsaw knew that the Police Minister of Germany, the head of the Gestapo and all other police forces, the chief of the Elite troops had arrived. But why, they wondered, had he come?

The German authorities in Warsaw, Dr. Fischer and Dr. Auerwald, as well as Obergruppenfuehrer Batz, should have known what it was all about. They should have known that it had to do with the Jews. For some time now anti-Semitic propaganda in Germany had been increasing again by leaps and bounds. Anyone who read German publications during the months preceding March 1942 might well have thought that never before had the Nazis had any anti-Semitic feelings, that only now had they discovered that the Jews were a bad lot and solely to blame for everything that was happening to mankind in general and to the Germans in particular. They had begun the same old arguments all over again, as though there was still some need to convince themselves and their followers.

Dr. Goebbels led the parade. On November 16, 1941, he wrote in *Das Reich:* "The Jews are a parasitic race which has attached itself like a corroding mildew on the culture of healthy but undynamic nations. There is only one remedy—to cut them off and throw them out. How futile are the stupid, thoughtless, sentimental arguments of the few remaining friends of the Jews, in view of the world problem with which mankind has had to deal for thousands of years! They would probably stare open-mouthed if they could but once see how their beloved Jews wield the power. But then it would be too late. And therefore it is the duty of the national leadership to take care of it now by appropriate means, so that such a situation shall not come about. . . . There is a difference between man and man, as there is between animals. The fact that the Jew still lives among us is no proof that he belongs to us, just as a flea cannot be considered a domestic animal, even though it lives in the house."

Such now was the general tenor of the German press and radio. This was the lead thousands of German writers were following toward the end of 1941 and the beginning of 1942. Of course the Jews were not the real issue. They had been driven from their homes and their jobs in every country that Hitler had invaded and occupied. There was not the slightest danger that they might "wield power"—if there had ever been such a danger in connection with such a hopeless minority. Dr. Goebbels and his stooges knew this perfectly well.

But Hitler had not won the war in Russia. German soldiers had had to fight there all during a most terrible winter. They had not been prepared for such a fight; the General Staff had not supplied them with winter clothing since it was assumed that the Russian campaign would be over before the cold set in; the oil in their tanks and in their planes froze; their losses had been fearful. In fact, at the turn of the year the leading German generals knew that the war in Russia could not be won, if, indeed, it was not already lost, for Germany. The generals declined to take any further responsibility and the Fuehrer himself was forced to take over the High Command.

Eighteen months had now passed since the day on which the Fuehrer had promised to be in London and to make peace. The United States had entered the war. Peace seemed more distant than ever. People inside Germany were none too happy about this state of affairs. That is why something had to be done to distract them from the grim reality. They had to be given some sort of escapist entertainment. They had to be shown that it was in their power to end all threats to their future forever. That is why they were told that the Jews constituted this threat. That is why more Jews had to die.

Heinrich Himmler did not hold the position then that he was to achieve later. To the world in general he was known only as the brutal and ruthless chief of the Gestapo. But even then he was the third most important man in the Third Reich, coming right after Hitler and Goering. But those who believed him to be just a kind of executioner, who simply carried out what the others decided was necessary, greatly underestimated the man. Himmler had long been an almost unknown quantity, a person who preferred to work backstage and leave the limelight to others. But he had actually been the real force in Germany ever since 1934. It was Himmler who arranged for the blood purge of June 1934 which did away with the clique of Captain Roehm and his Storm Troopers, the assassination of Gregor Strasser, who only a short time before had been Hitler's right-hand man. It was Himmler who, during the following years, built up the Elite troops into a private army for Hitler which made the latter independent of his military leaders and also assured a completely quiet and subjugated home front. It was Himmler who, during the years of the rearmament, reorganized the police system in such a way that the world at large was unable to find out what was going on in Germany. It was Himmler who supervised the concentration camps and whose agents spread all over the world, intimidating all those who attempted to call attention to the Third Reich and its preparation for war. And it was Himmler who, whenever Hitler invaded a country, took his police force into the new territory, where he arrested patriots and beat down any attempt at resistance with no regard for human lives.

They called Himmler brutal and cruel. But he was merely matter-of-fact. When he killed Captain Roehm and Gregor Strasser he eliminated the two men who had made him, who had started his career, and who were presumably his only personal friends among the higher-ups of the party. He eliminated them because he knew that it was necessary to do so if Hitler was to proceed with his plans. Everything Himmler did was necessary in this sense. His machine worked with utter disregard for any moral or humane standards. His orders were cruel and brutal in the extreme. He had things done which were so horrible that onlookers could not believe their eyes and ears. His men behaved more like beasts than men. Observers could not understand how a man so mild-mannered and almost gentle, as Himmler was in his private life, could be so fanatical and could hate so deeply. But he was not really a fanatic, and most probably not even a hater. He was simply a realist. If the Third Reich was to continue to exist, if Hitler was to continue to conquer the world, it was necessary to exterminate all possible resistance. It was necessary to be brutal and to arrange for continuous blood baths. And to do that was his job.

Perhaps Himmler did really dislike the Jews. We will never know. The point is that he came to Warsaw, not because he hated them, but because it was the moment to do something about the Jews.

That moment had arrived some time ago. Why had nothing radical been done about the Polish Jews during the last six months? Himmler wanted to know. He made a statement, shortly after his arrival in Warsaw, which was sent to his collaborators. This statement read:

"There are too many Jews in Poland. They must be exterminated completely. The Jews are the scum of the earth, the excrement of all living beings. They must be utilized as such. In the Fuehrer's name I declare that the Jews must cease to exist. Their liquidation must start in the Warsaw Ghetto."

Himmler held a short conference with Obergruppenfuehrer Batz. He told him that Berlin was not at all satisfied with the way the Warsaw Ghetto was being run. Batz did not understand. Had not everything been carried out according to orders? The Jews were starving and dying from their diseases. He gave a vivid picture of how the corpses were put into the streets at night by their relatives. "It's only a question of time until they'll all be dead," he declared.

"A question of time," Himmler said. "That's just it. There is not so much time. We cannot wait for years and years till the last Jew has finally perished. Things must go faster."

And then Himmler said something which made the usually red face of Captain Batz become deadly pale. When he left the room he looked like a man who had just heard his own death sentence. Those who worked with him and under him immediately understood what it was all about. Captain Batz was through. He had received orders to report to the Russian front.

In the afternoon Himmler had a conference with Dr. Auerwald. He told him, too, that he was quite disappointed. Things were moving too slowly. If the Jews adapted themselves to the conditions in the ghetto, if they managed to survive where Berlin had figured on their dying in vast numbers from the very start, it only proved that other measures would have to be taken.

Other measures? Dr. Auerwald was astonished. Had Berlin not given notice, time and time again, that there should be as little open shooting of the Jews as possible? Had he not been given to understand that the mass slaughters in eastern Galicia at the beginning of the Russian war had made a bad impression abroad?

Himmler became impatient. "These times are past. We no longer care about the impression we make abroad." If Berlin had put a stop to the earlier wholesale shooting, if Berlin had insisted that such shooting should at least not take place in cities like Warsaw or Lodz, which were watched by the world more than the little towns and villages were, there would have been a good reason for their insistence. Before the attack on Russia many highly placed Nazis, Foreign Minister Ribbentrop himself among them, had hoped that in the case of a war against the Communists, England might come in on the side of Germany. In England, the Nazis felt, the Jews had some influence. As long as the Polish Jews were allowed to live, the English Jews might want to help them and advise a more pro-German policy in London. More important, in the mind of the Nazis, was what the American Jews might do. Many of them had come originally from Poland and still had relatives there. If the Polish Jews, or at least the greater part of them, were kept alive, one might blackmail the American Jews into a less anti-Nazi attitude.

But for once the Nazis had been badly mistaken. The English Jews, whether or not they had any influence in Downing Street, had not advised the government to stop fighting Hitler or influenced public opinion in this direction. The American Jews had not ceased to warn the public that the Axis sooner or later would attack America too. And since Pearl Harbor there was no longer any possibility of blackmailing the Jews in the United States. Therefore there was no longer any reason to be soft toward the Jews in Warsaw.

In the evening Dr. Fischer, Dr. Auerwald, and a few other high Nazi officials in Warsaw met with Heinrich Himmler. The Gestapo chief declared to them:

1. Hitler had said to him (Himmler) personally that the Jews had commenced the war and should, therefore, be punished.

2. The Jews were the scum of the earth and must be converted to dust.

3. Every Jew must die, but before his death he should go through agony and all kinds of suffering.

Himmler left the next day. In a last conference with Dr. Fischer and Colonel Tebens of the Transportation Department, he issued formal orders concerning the Jews in Poland. Only qualified workers necessary for the German industries should be exempted from these orders.

The village of Treblinka is situated near the Warsaw-Bialystok railroad line in a sandy area surrounded by woods. Its population consisted chiefly of peasants and forest laborers. In 1940 the Germans had built near the village a concentration camp for Poles, which they called "Treblinka A." It was used mainly to punish peasants and farmers who had failed to supply the Germans with the demanded quotas of grain or other agricultural produce. The discipline at the camp was very strict. The Nazis shot their prisoners for the slightest offense.

Only a few days after Himmler had left Warsaw the Germans began to build another concentration camp near Treblinka, which they called "Treblinka B." The work was done by the Poles imprisoned in Treblinka A and by Jews from the neighboring villages. This new camp was situated on sandy hills. It stretched over about 12,500 acres and was surrounded by a green fence and barbed wire. In the four corners slightly elevated observation points were built for the guards, and strong searchlights were installed there which could light the entire place during the night.

To the west the border was formed by a rail embankment. Through it ran a sidetrack connecting the camp with the main railroad line. On the north the camp bordered on a forest.

Just where the railroad ended in the camp a square, large enough to hold about three thousand people, had been left free. The square was flanked by guardhouses and fenced in with barbed wire.

In the middle of the camp, and to be approached only through paths which led through a small forest, was a strange building of brick construction. Inside it were three chambers about forty yards square and six feet high. There were no windows in these chambers, and the only exit was through a door which led into a corridor. The walls of the chambers had valves installed in them. Next to this building was a smaller one which contained nothing but a steam room. Here there was a huge kettle in which steam was produced and sent through pipes into the chambers of the adjoining building.

The building with the chambers was called Death House I. Later another building of the same kind was started, about fifty yards long and twenty yards wide. It was to contain ten chambers. It was to have been Death House II, but it was never finished.

Not far from these buildings a large number of small barracks were built to house the gravediggers. The remaining area of Treblinka B, more than half of it, was left free. It was to serve as a cemetery.

Part Two: The Extermination

Chapter VII

Hands across the Wall

Sometimes the gates of the ghetto would open and a group of men would pass through them into the crowded narrow streets. Sometimes they appeared in the morning, sometimes in the afternoon or evening. Sometimes they rode in on motorcycles, sometimes in cars, sometimes they came on foot. They were armed with sub-machine guns or tommy guns or sometimes revolvers. And they shot. They did not look for a particular person to shoot at; they had not made up their minds whom they were going to shoot before they entered the ghetto. They simply left it to the moment and to their inspiration just when and whom to shoot. But they shot to kill.

These were the *Vernichtungs-Kolonnen,* the annihilation squads. Some of the members of these squads were Germans, mostly members of the Gestapo. But you saw other uniforms too, uniforms which had never been seen inside the ghetto or inside Warsaw till their wearers came on their murder mission. Most of them were Latvians, but there were also many Lithuanians and Ukrainians and a few Estonians among them. These were the people who had been "liberated" by the Nazis when they started their war against Russia. The Germans told them that now was their opportunity to show how grateful they were to the Fuehrer. It was also their opportunity to prove to themselves and to others that they could actually shoot. Several thousand of them volunteered for the annihilation squads. New formations of these squads exercised on the Mokotow Field in Warsaw, under the supervision of German experts.

They came and shot. They did not care whom they killed, so long as they killed. They would ride into the ghetto, cruise awhile, and suddenly their guns would go off. The victims would fall on the pavement and stay there. And the annihilation squads would go in quest of new prey. There was no visible strategy or purpose in it all. They did not know the people they happened to kill. If they had come a minute earlier or later they would have killed somebody else. All they wanted was to kill. Because all they had been told to do and trained to do was to kill.

It took the people in the ghetto a while to comprehend what was going on. Only a short time before they had despaired because they felt they had been forgotten in the ghetto and left there to rot. Now they were getting too much attention. But what did it mean? What did those men in the strange uniforms want? At first the Jews came out of their houses and shops, curious to find out what it was all about. Then, when the shots began to ring out, they hustled back to shelter as fast as they could. They were bewildered. They had been imprisoned in the ghetto; they had been humiliated, robbed, and they were being starved. They were treated worse than dogs, but aside from the incidents of the first months after the German occupation, they had not been attacked. Since they had been sent to the ghetto, it seemed as though the Nazis had abstained from any shooting or killing in Warsaw. In a way the Jews had come to regard the ghetto of Warsaw almost as a haven in which they were comparatively safe—at least safe from being murdered. Like their leader Czerniakow, they had convinced themselves that what happened to Jews in other Polish towns and villages could not happen to a community of almost half a million people.

So when they heard the shots of the annihilation squads they could not imagine what was going on. What had those who now lay dead on the pavement done to arouse the ire of the Nazis? For whose crimes had they been punished?

They never found out. Because the Jews had committed no crime except that of still being alive. That was a state of affairs which the annihilation squads had come to change. They wandered and drove through the streets. They stopped. Here was an old Jew. Hello, old Jew! Still alive? Well, we'll see to that. There was the report of a gun, a groan, and a man sank down. That was all. The annihilation squads wandered on. They saw a woman carrying her child in her arms. What a nice child, isn't it? Well, we'll take it. Now don't you cry, little mother, just go on your way! You want to know what is happening to your child. . . . For God's sake. Now we have dropped your precious little Jewish babe. Now it is dead, his precious little skull crushed on the pavement. Now don't you cry, or we'll have to shoot you too, understand?

Let's go on. What's that? A group of Jews talking to each other. . . . What can they be talking about? Perhaps it is a conspiracy against the Fuehrer. Perhaps they are plotting to disturb the war effort. They are all capitalist-communist traitors anyhow, who get their orders from London and Moscow. Let's shoot at them. Isn't it funny how they run and try to reach the safety of a house? At least, those who can still run. . . . What's that? We almost fell. Why, it's blood, dirty Jewish blood. Even in their death they try to make us fall in their slippery blood and dirty our nice clean uniforms. . . . And the sight of superintendents forever scrubbing the pavement in front of their houses, trying to remove the stains of blood, became a permanent part of the ghetto street scene.

The world knew little and cared little what was happening to the Jews in Poland. There was only one exception right from the time when Hitler invaded Poland: Palestine. Palestine was the logical heaven for the persecuted Jews of Poland. Had not the English promised the Jews during the last war, when they needed Jewish help so badly, that Palestine would be acknowledged as their national home? Did they not have the Balfour Declaration, which stated all this in clear and simple words? Had it not been Jewish farmers who had developed the country, Jewish money that built the cities, Jewish spirit that created industry and business in Palestine?

Yes, all this was certainly true. But it was also true that the gentlemen who ran the British Colonial Office in London could not see their way to giving the Jews the rights and privileges which Mr. Balfour had promised. They wanted to appease the Arabs, even if that meant breaking their pledge to the Jews. They favored the Arabs in every way and hampered the Jews wherever they could. They gave weapons to the Arabs and took them away from the Jews.

When Hitler came to power the question of a Jewish homeland became much more than a matter of politics. Now it became a matter of saving lives. The civilized world believed that now the gates of Palestine would be thrown wide open. Was it not in the interest of the Empire to get a large number of Jews into Palestine to balance the Arabs, who, ever since Hitler took over, had proved themselves willing listeners to the Fascist and Nazi propaganda which was so violently anti-British? But the Colonial Office did not see it that way. The more anti-British the Palestine Arabs became, the more the gentlemen in London tried to appease them by cutting down what was left of the rights of the Jews. The more dangerous life became for the Jews under Hitler's heel, the more difficulties the British put in the way of their immigration into Palestine. And by the time the war began it had become next to impossible for any great number of European Jews to enter the homeland that had been promised them.

The Jews in Palestine did not take all this lying down. It was too bad, they felt, that the Colonial Office was playing thus into the hands of Hitler and was helping him, no matter how unintentionally, to carry out his pledge to exterminate the Jews. But the Palestine Jews were determined not to remain passive, while this went on before their eyes. They made up their minds to get as many Jews as possible out of the Hitler-occupied countries and into Palestine, legally or illegally, it mattered not which. They chartered ships. They bought passports, wherever they could get them, or they had them manufactured. They sent funds into neutral European countries to tide refugees over. They sent their agents right into Hitler's own back yard. And they sent arms and ammunition there, too, and bought machine guns and rifles right under Hitler's nose.

This was the work of Dagani.

Dagani's headquarters were neither in Haifa nor in Jerusalem. They were located on a collective Jewish farm in a beautiful valley not far from Nazareth. On this farm there was a concrete tower, which served at once as a water tower and as a watch tower from which the Jews could sight any Arabs who might be coming down to attack and kill the farmers and their families. In this tower Dagani had installed his office. Here was centralized all the activity of the Jews in defense of their unfortunate brothers in other lands. It was to this spot that the various intelligence that issued from every corner of Europe was directed. Here the most daring plans to save the endangered Jews of

Poland were formed, and the grand strategy of an extensive underground fight against Hitler was devised.

Dagani—his real name cannot yet be divulged—was a tall, slender man with a stern, determined face and a military bearing. There are no pictures of him floating around; he has always shunned publicity and his few visits to Poland were always unheralded.

Dagani had formerly been an intelligence officer in the British Army, one of their best. He was with Marshal Allenby when the English invaded and took Turkish-owned Palestine during World War I. Later he retired from the army and settled in Palestine, where he became the military instructor of the young Jewish farmers who streamed to that country after the war. He told them that there was no sense in farming if they were not prepared to defend their land. He taught them to use a gun with one hand and the plow with the other. He built up the self-defense organization called "Haganah."

When the Arabs struck against what they so fondly believed to be unarmed and unprepared Jews in 1929, it was the pupils of Dagani who finally repelled them. From that time on Haganah developed into a real military machine, a semiofficial underground organization which was to come into the open in times of emergency.

But Dagani's activities and those of his collaborators extended far beyond Palestine. They had a hand in preparing the Jewish youth of various European countries for their work in Palestine. These young boys and girls were members of an organization called "Chaluzim" (The Pioneers). In Poland there were numerous camps of these Pioneers near cities, both large and small, where boys and girls were trained to become farmers in the co-operative settlements of Palestine. That much was known to the Polish authorities. What they did not know was that the Haganah also had a hand in training this youth, training which included not only agricultural studies, but the use of arms and ammunition for self-defense. It was for this purpose that Dagani made his trips to Poland and, of course, to other countries where groups existed. He was quite proud of the results he achieved, particularly in regard to many young boys and girls who seemed to do better in shooting than farming. While on a trip to Poland, in the summer of 1939, he spoke with warmth about the new spirit of the Chaluzim youth throughout Poland. "We must find ways and means to get them to Palestine soon," he said. "War is coming, and no matter what happens in the end, the Jews will be the first victims. These youths are too good to perish at the hands of the Hitler gang. Illegal immigration to Paletsine . . . well, why not? The Jews have won a right to call Palestine their own country, if not by charter, then by blood and tears and sacrifice."

At the time of the Nazi invasion of Poland, thousands of Jewish youths were in the numerous Chaluzim camps there, preparing for their emigration to Palestine. The German army units which passed these camps left them alone. The commanding officer probably considered most of the boys and girls mere children and utterly harmless. Furthermore, they preferred Jews working on farms to Jews living in cities and presumably living by the work and sweat of non-Jews. Finally, the idea of a great number of Jews emigrating to Palestine appealed to the average army officer. If the Jews left Poland, the Germans would no longer have to be bothered by them.

This was, of course, the point of view of the army men. The Gestapo had not yet got around to the Chaluzim.

Dagani decided to take advantage of the situation. If the Chaluzim camps were left unmolested—at least for a time—they could continue to be training camps for those who wanted to emigrate to Palestine. But perhaps they could serve another purpose, too. In the back of Dagani's mind was the idea that not all of the Chaluzim might want to emigrate and that some might want to stay and resist. Such resistance might be possible later when the Germans would have to fight on other fronts or if perhaps the war would be brought back into Poland. But the idea of resistance was still a vague one and Dagani was not yet ready to discuss it.

He had made some long-range plans even before the Germans moved into Poland. He had arranged for some of his most trusted Chaluzim to leave Poland and find refuge in neighboring neutral countries. Now, when he saw that the Chaluzim were not in any immediate danger of being murdered or put into concentration camps, he called on these boys and girls to make their way back into Poland, either to help finish the training of those who had remained in the training camps or to go to the cities and towns to help the Jews there, and, above all, to establish some kind of connection between the numerous Jewish communities which had been isolated by the Nazis.

Among those who were called back was a young woman who called herself Zivia. She had joined the Chaluzim as a young girl and at the age of twenty had been sent to one of the training farms. She was almost ready to go to Palestine when the war began. She was then about twenty-five. Receiving an order from Dagani to save herself, she joined the Polish refugees who were fleeing into Soviet-occupied territory. Later another message from Dagani came to her, telling her to go back into Nazi-occupied Poland. She immediately complied and began to appear in ghettos. She talked to the desperate Jews there; she inspired them with new hope; she brought them medicine, sometimes food. She also brought foreign money with her to bribe German officials. Thus she helped many Jews to escape across the frontier.

She became a saga. Nobody knew where she came from or who had sent her, but her name and fame were well known to the people in many ghettos. They called her "the Mother," because she was always willing to listen and to help, never thinking of herself, always caring for others as though all the Jews, even those who were so much older than herself, were her children.

There was also Samuel Breslaw, formerly a member of the Jewish scout movement. He was not quite twenty when the war broke out. After the fall of Warsaw he succeeded in reaching Wilno. He stayed in Lithuania all during 1940 and the better part of 1941, reorganizing the Jewish youth movement and improvising new farms or centers of activity in towns and villages, with the aim of preparing the youth both for emigration and for the coming fight inside Poland. When Dagani's message reached him he went back into Poland and immediately began to reorganize a number of deserted training farms for the same purpose.

Then there was Tosia—or so she called herself. Her real name was Tania Altman. She was a tall, blonde, extremely beautiful girl only a little more than twenty years of age, and a member of a very wealthy family. She had been an early Chaluz, but only in her late teens had she been seized by the spirit of self-sacrifice which the movement demanded from its members. Then she had developed into one of the outstanding Chaluzim, and Dagani and others regarded her as one of the destined leaders of the movement in the not too far distant future. When the war broke out she was about to leave for Palestine, but when Dagani let her know that she should stay, she obeyed at once. For some time she worked in a neutral country, living under another name, protected by a false passport, and directing emergency operations to aid in the escape of persecuted Jews from Poland. Later, after a certain order from Palestine had reached her, she made her way back into Poland.

Like Zivia, she appeared in many different places; traveling as she did with false passports and under assumed names, she was able to go about quite openly. This made it easier for her to serve as a liaison officer between the different ghettos, arranging for money or false papers for Jews whose lives were in danger.

Nobody ever suspected her of being Jewish, least of all the Nazis themselves. German officers frequently made a play for her. She always seemed to be only too glad to accept their offers to accompany her. To be with a German officer made it so much easier for her to travel about. More than once during those missions it happened that she invited one or the other of these officers for a walk in the woods. The man in question accepted readily, full of hope. But he never came back from the promenade. Tosia's friends, Chaluzim, who had been hiding in the forest, took care of that.

It was not long before the Gestapo was looking for her. A description of her was sent to all German agents, and they were asked to keep a constant lookout for the beautiful girl. But Tosia proved faster and cleverer than any of the German bloodhounds. She outwitted them at every turn. At night she disappeared into the ghettos, getting in by climbing a wall or finding a passage through a house with exits to both sides, or gaining admission during broad daylight with forged papers. By the time the Germans had learned of her whereabouts she would be gone. While they were looking for her she disappeared into a wood armed with new papers, and soon she was hundreds of miles away, engaged in carrying out a new assignment.

The most important of the agents whom Dagani now sent back into Poland was a tall, blond man with the face of a child and clear blue eyes, a man who looked rather like an overgrown boy, though he was twenty-five years of age. His name was Mordecai Anilewicz. He had grown up in a small town in eastern Poland, had joined the youth pioneer movement, and, like all the others, had prepared to go to Palestine. When Dagani called on him he came back from a little town beyond one of the frontiers and for more than two years traveled from place to place preparing the Jewish youth everywhere to be ready to fight the Nazis. During that period, too, he edited a Jewish daily *The Flame,* a kind of political bulletin depending for its contents largely on what he and his friends gathered from the shortwave broadcasts that came from England.

Toward the end of 1941 Mordecai went to the city of Czestochowa, where the Pioneers had a training farm of more than seven acres. There an important conference took place to which all other training farms sent delegates, and in which the further course of action to be taken was formulated. What was going to happen to the Jewish youth of Poland? Were they to continue their training? Was it not better to send as many of them as possible to Palestine now while there was still time?

Mordecai got up and made a speech. Yes, he was for continuing the training of the Jewish youth. But he was not for sending them to Palestine. Poland had become the front line in the war which the Jews had to fight. The boys and girls should be trained—to fight the Nazis right here, in the middle of Poland. Thus Mordecai voiced what had been in Dagani's mind for a long time.

Others objected. What was the sense of fighting a hopeless battle? Mordecai was passionate. It was not the Jews who had started the fight. Not to accept it was dishonorable—no matter how hopeless the situation was. But perhaps it was not that hopeless. The Nazis were now fighting the Russians. Therefore the Russians had become the allies of the Polish Jews.

There were new protests. The Polish Zionist youth movement had always been opposed to Soviet Russia because the Russian Communists opposed the idea of Zionism and had persecuted the Zionist leaders in their country. Mordecai declared that it was more important to beat the common enemy, the Germans, than to clarify the Zionist issue at the present time.

It was Mordecai's day. He could convince the others. From then on he was regarded as the leader of the Jewish youth movement.

As soon as Dagani and his men of the self-defense movement in Palestine, Haganah, saw that the Germans were driving at the extermination of the Polish Jews, they decided that the Chaluzim inside Poland needed auxiliary troops. A secret circular was sent to all the members of the Haganah:

"We need volunteers, both men and women. They are to be sent to the inferno of Europe. They will be supplied with 'Aryan' papers and passports of neutral countries. They will have to help our people in Hitler-dominated countries. They will have to do everything to get as many of them as possible into safer regions. Few of those who volunteer can count on coming back."

Dagani needed three hundred agents. More than a thousand volunteered. Dagani himself interviewed each applicant. Only those who looked "Aryan" enough not to be suspected of being Jewish, and those who could be depended upon to have enough personal initiative to be able to act decisively in an emergency, could be taken.

At length the selection was made. The three hundred received training in guerrilla tactics from Dagani himself. They were taught a code. They were given addresses in every European country which they had to learn by heart. Then they were furnished with papers and money and sent in many roundabout ways to the places of their destination.

These agents appeared all over Europe—in Belgium, Austria, the Balkans, even in Germany itself. And slowly, step by step, they made their way into Poland. They seemed to be everywhere. They crossed borders with as much ease as though they were employed by the all-powerful Gestapo. In many cases they even presented passes signed and stamped by a Gestapo man. And how could the guards who looked at these passes know that the man who had presumably issued them had been dead even when they were being issued?

The three hundred agents were untiring. They knew that they must not lose a second, because even that much time meant the death of several more Polish Jews. They gathered together the fugitive Jews and brought them by night into a safe shelter or into a still neutral country. They even managed to enter into prisons and liberate many of their people, shooting their way out and then disappearing again into the night. They wandered over mountains, across rivers, and through valleys. And everywhere they built up the theaters of resistance, encouraging the Jews to believe that everything was not lost yet, that help was coming.

These men and women took no thought for themselves. In their own eyes they were merely tools. As one of them wrote in the summer of 1942: "At times I think of myself as a can of oil, the last can of oil that is still burning. And I pray to God that I may be spared to burn long enough to kindle in men's hearts a desire for love, for truth, and for justice."

That is how all of them felt.

Slowly and steadily those who had been placed in neutral countries and in western and northern Europe converged on Poland. And wherever they passed they trained new Jewish leaders, set up underground railroads, and organized Jewish resistance against the Nazis. But all of them knew that the main battle was to be fought inside Poland.

They kept in constant touch with Dagani. Their messages and their reports to him found their way out of an almost hermetically sealed Europe, mostly by way of several "post offices" in Switzerland and Portugal, though sometimes they had to go as far as New York before they could safely be sent on to Palestine.

Their code was simple enough. In their communications the agents used Hebrew words with Slavic suffixes, so that the words looked like names of persons. On the face of it the messages said only that a certain person had arrived or was leaving. If the Nazi censors had known Hebrew, they would soon have found out that the uncle who had arrived in Lodz called himself "Hunger" or "Starvation," that the friend who was traveling through Poland answered to the name of "Epidemics," and that the cousin who had come to the Warsaw Ghetto for an indefinite stay was "Cousin Murder."

"Cousin Murder" had indeed come to stay. And the Nazis killed fast. The Jews had to have arms if they were to stop them, so the agents reported to Dagani.

Jews in Palestine arranged to have arms sent. But only a very few of them reached the youth who were training on the Chaluzim farms. Dagani's agents therefore decided that something drastic had to be done. They found that many German soldiers were willing enough to sell arms and ammunition if they were paid a high enough price for them. As a result a regular black market came into existence. The agents sometimes paid as much as two thousand marks for a revolver, five thousand marks for a rifle, or twenty-five-thousand marks for a machine gun. They set up printing shops where they manufactured false passports which they used to bring more Jews out of Poland. They set up tailor shops to make the German uniforms which they needed when they staged their surprise visits to prisons and concentration camps. They asked for more and more money from Palestine to bribe high Gestapo officials to help them carry out their plans.

Their lives were in constant danger. They never knew in the morning whether they would still be alive that evening. They knew that they must not be caught. If they were surrounded or surprised they fought to the last. And if they were unable to escape they swallowed arsenic, which they carried with them wherever they went. Dagani had given it to them when they started out on their dangerous mission, saying, "If you fall into the hands of the Nazis take it—quickly. You will have no chance, then, of escaping with your life anyway, and the Nazis have ways and means of torture so terrible that no human being can withstand them long. You would give away some of your secrets no matter how hard you tried not to."

And the annihilation squads continued to invade the ghetto of Warsaw, to shoot at passers-by, killing them by the dozens, destroying once and for all the fond illusion of many of the Jews that at least in the ghetto they were safe from assassination.

The Jews disappeared into their houses, they hid in their closets or cellars whenever they heard the annihilation squads approaching. But a city of many hundreds of thousands cannot go entirely into hiding. The annihilation squads always found some victims. You heard the reports of their guns all during the day and later also during the night. And sometimes you heard the cries of the victims.

The Germans in the squad were easily recognizable, even if they had not been clad in their Gestapo uniforms. They were so much more systematic than the others. They wanted to keep track of their achievements. Many of them carried a piece of chalk with them, and after they had killed their victims they would record a number on the corpse. When they left an apartment where they had hunted the victims they would chalk the number on the door. Sometimes they had to pause a moment as though to be sure that they made no mistake in adding.

The Jews, trapped, hunted, threatened with being shot at any time of the day or the night, the poor defenseless Jews, would have gone mad if they had not had recourse to a mental defense. Even in this nightmare they could not fail to see what a macabre comedy was being played by these murderers who were so concerned with keeping the books straight. In the process of being strangled they still could utter a horselaugh. The assassins could murder them, but they could not escape being ridiculous in the eyes of their victims. Even these horrible hours in the ghetto gave birth to jokes. Strange jokes which made you shiver, jokes which gave proof of the superiority of the victim over the murderer—such as this one: An SS man was told to make order in a home for aged and infirm Jews in the ghetto of Warsaw. There were sixty persons living in a space where hardly thirty should have been. Therefore he was to kill half of them. He came to the room where the old people slept and, walking down the rows of the beds, shot every second one. Then he had the dead bodies carried out. He remained in the door to count them. He counted: "Twenty-eight, twenty-nine, thirty . . . thirty-one." Suddenly he began to sob. "What have I done?" he cried out. "I have killed an innocent person!"

Reality dealt in larger figures than the jest. One morning in the beginning of May 1942 a Gestapo man named Fritz Krause wrote on the door of a Jewish apartment a figure indicating the number of people he had killed thus far. The number was 488.

Chapter VIII

Underground

Early in May 1942 a few Soviet bombers flew over Warsaw. Sirens sounded and anti-aircraft guns roared. In the ghetto Jewish policemen rushed the inhabitants into the cellars. The Jews thought these precautions superfluous. After all, why should the Russians bomb the ghetto?

Then suddenly the Russians dropped their bombs. Some of them fell into the ghetto, and started many fires. The Jews were frantic, for they had no fire-fighting apparatus. Some Polish firemen arrived to help put out the fires, which by now had destroyed a few houses. The Jews brought water in big kettles and all kinds of containers. But almost before they had begun to fight the fire, the Poles left again, called back by the German authorities. What was the idea of saving Jewish houses? they asked harshly.

The Jews themselves somehow managed to put out the fires. But after they had finally got them under control they began to ponder. What is the use of saving our houses? they thought. Some of them are vacant already. Soon all of them will be empty. But the Jews were bitter, nevertheless. Why did the bombs have to fall on their houses? Why was it that even the enemy of their mortal foe had to help destroy the Jews? Why had the bombs not fallen on the section around Ujazdow Alley, where the Nazis lived and worked? It almost seemed as if heaven and earth had entered into an alliance to annihilate the Jews of Warsaw, if not by one means, then by another.

But soon the Jews changed their attitude. They were no longer bitter about this bombing. They began to see in the bombing of Warsaw a sign from Heaven, a fiery warning. They were confident that any day now a hail of fire would fall on the criminals themselves. The Nazis had been triumphant for too long. God in his heaven had lost patience with them. The first bombs had fallen on Jewish houses so that they might know God had not forgotten their plight.

Ten days later the Soviet fliers returned. This time they had the corrected map of Warsaw with them. Now their bombs fell into the German-occupied part of Warsaw. More than five hundred German officers and soldiers were killed on the spot. On the same day Lodz, Skwernewiec, Malkin, and other towns where the Germans had concentrated their forces were also bombed.

During the raid on Warsaw the pilots dropped leaflets, some of which fell on the streets of the ghetto and were picked up by Jews. They read:

"Brother Poles! We are sorry that we have been compelled to bomb Warsaw. We are not trying to get you, but the Germans. We are bombing our enemy, which is also the worst enemy you have ever had. To you we are the messengers of your allies and friends, the peoples of the Soviet Union. Our cause is your cause. Our victory is your victory. Poles, arise and fight our common enemy!"

The Jews looked at each other in amazement. There was something they could not understand. These leaflets were directed to the "brother Poles." But many of them were printed in Yiddish. What did this mean?

Some of the people in the ghetto of Warsaw understood: the members of the Jewish underground.

The Polish Jews—no matter to which political party they belonged—had been fighting Fascism and Nazism ever since Hitler came to power. The Jewish Anti-Hitler Committee which was founded in 1933 had included representatives of all political parties and professional groups. Even during those years the Polish Jews had been obliged to fight Hitler by underground methods. For Poland had signed a treaty of friendship with the Fuehrer early in 1934, and therefore the government fought every attempt on the part of the Jews to demonstrate against the Third Reich, to boycott German goods, etc.

It is certain that the Gestapo had a long blacklist of Polish Jews who had been politically active during that period and were therefore able to arrest many of them and put them into concentration camps or shoot them after the occupation of Poland by the Germans in 1939.

Only a very few of the leaders escaped. Most of them settled in the ghetto of Warsaw under assumed names. But even there they were not safe from the persecutions of the Gestapo. Most of them had to change their addresses frequently.

In spite of the constant danger in which they lived, these Jewish leaders were eager to continue their anti-Nazi work. But what could they do? How could they oppose the Nazis?

A number of meetings were held. It immediately became apparent, however, that there was no common line on which the representatives of the various Jewish organizations and parties could compromise. There were too many groups, too many different political philosophies, too many conflicting principles involved. There were the various Zionist parties, the socialists organized in the Jewish Workers' party "Bund," the Communists whose members had suffered so greatly from persecution at the hands of the Germans, and a great many other organizations with no definite political color.

There was great confusion of opinion as to the most advisable procedure. Some thought it most important to reorganize and re-establish contacts, to wait and see. Others, like the Chaluzim, wanted to build up a fighting machine so that they would be ready for any eventuality. Still others, like the Communists, proclaimed the necessity for making active resistance as soon as possible.

The representatives of the Chaluzim soon became disgusted with the inability of the others to create a common front for what they considered the certainty of the fight against the Nazis. They therefore decided to do whatever they could themselves without waiting for help from other groups in the ghetto. They continued their efforts to build up new armies in the different camps, at the same time trying with every means at their disposal to awaken the Jews in the ghetto to the seriousness of the situation, to make them understand that there was no sense in pursuing the policy of appeasement toward the Germans which Adam Czerniakow had undertaken.

The leaders of the "Bund" were equally disappointed. For them the issue was less a Jewish one than one of class struggle. Hitler to them was not so much the world's greatest Jew baiter as the foremost representative of capitalism which was striving to deprive the workers of their rights and enslave them forever.

From the very beginning the Jewish workers inside the ghetto had been treated much better than the other Jews. Because the Germans depended on their labor in essential war plants, they at least received sufficient food to enable them to do the work. They were even given a certain amount of pay. And when the killings began, the Nazis took care that nothing happened to these workers.

But the leaders of the workers were not fooled by all this. They knew that in other parts of Poland the Germans had already begun to treat workers—Polish as well as Jewish ones—as veritable slaves. Early reports from Oswiecim gave a clear picture of what was in store for the workers under Hitler: dormitories where four hundred of them had to sleep, without any heat and with no blankets to cover them during the winter. Even during the coldest season they had to work outside without warm clothing. The working hours began at five in the morning and extended to seven in the evening, Sundays and holidays included. They were not allowed to talk during these hours. If they so much as spoke a word they were immediately shot. The food ration consisted of a slice of bread and a plate of watery soup per day. Most of the workers could not stand the treatment for more than a few weeks. When they were no longer able to work they were taken away and shot.

There were numerous reports telling of equally bad or worse working conditions in other places. They made it clear to the leaders of the Jewish Workers' Organization, and particularly to the leaders of the "Bund," that they had to fight Hitler actively.

But when they tried to do something definite about it, they found to their surprise that they were hampered in every possible way by those who were in charge of running the ghetto. These Jews, who suffered much more under the new restrictions than did the workers in Warsaw, seemed unwilling to fight these restrictions. For some time—all during the year of 1941, in fact—the workers' organizations found it practically impossible to print their pamphlets or to organize whispering campaigns, stymied as they were at every turn by Czerniakow and the Jewish militia. It was for this reason that they and their leaders thought it infeasible to co-operate with the rest of the Jews in the fight against Hitler.

The man who was to lead them in this fight was Michael Klepfisz.

Klepfisz was born and reared in Warsaw. His father had been a teacher in a public school, and his mother headmistress of another school and a director of the Association of Jewish Teachers. Young Michael grew up in a revolutionary atmosphere. Both of his parents were members of the "Bund" and had been active participants in the fight of the Jewish workers against the dictatorial government of the Tsar of Russia. (Warsaw and most of Poland belonged to Russia until 1917.) Later the "Bund" fought the encroachment of reactionary Polish circles on the rights of the workers, which grew steadily as their influence on the government of Poland increased.

Michael Klepfisz joined the Socialist Youth movement at the age of fifteen. He took part in many fights against Polish anti-Semitism. When the Spanish Civil War began he immediately recognized that this war was more than an internal affair. He understood that General Franco represented only the advance guard of the Fascist army which was poised to strike at any moment. Some of Klepfisz' closest friends went to Spain and fought there as members of the International Brigade. Klepfisz himself was active in organizations which provided the Loyalists with men and money.

He studied engineering, graduating with honors at the age of twenty-five. That was in 1939. A few months afterward Poland was at war. Michael Klepfisz was among the soldiers who succeeded in retreating into Warsaw. He took an active part in the defense of the city, organizing the Socialist Youth groups for this purpose. When Warsaw surrendered, he escaped. Soon afterward he appeared in Soviet Russia, where he stayed for more than a year. Nobody in Warsaw knew what had become of him. Later it was said that during his sojourn in Russia he had received training in the tactics of guerrilla warfare.

Then one night, in the middle of 1941, he came back to Warsaw. Polish workers who knew him offered to hide him, but he refused. He had not come back to hide out. He had come back to do a job. The very night of his arrival he managed to smuggle himself into the ghetto. He entered the house of his parents. He told them why he had come back: He was going to fight.

The passionate young socialist had become a determined man. But he still looked like a boy. He was of medium height, with the wiry body of a trained sportsman. He was good-looking, too: a straight nose, tender mouth, and large, soft, expressive eyes, set wide apart. But there was a cold, appraising look in his eyes, a purposefulness in all his movements and in the way he carried himself, that told his parents and friends that Michael Klepfisz, no matter how boyish he looked, was now a man, and a man who knew what he wanted and was going to get what he wanted.

What he wanted first was to get acclimatized, to get the feel of the ghetto, the feel of the Jewish working masses. He found a job at a small electrical shop, not far outside the ghetto, which belonged to a German subcontractor for big munitions factories. Both men and women were employed there and quite a few children, as young as twelve and thirteen.

To most of his co-workers Klepfisz was just another one of them. Only occasionally would he utter an opinion, always warning them against a dark future, always urging them not to believe in German promises. But he did more watching than talking. He wanted to find out what the others thought and felt, and whether or not they were willing to act.

He soon found that they were not. The psychological moment for such a step had passed for them. In the beginning they would have followed their leaders in any resistance they might have initiated against the Nazis. Now, during the year of 1941 and the beginning of 1942, the situation had somewhat changed. The Jews in the ghetto were suffering, but the workers were not so badly off as the rest. They were forced to work hard, but they were also protected by the German owners of the factories in which they worked, and who were interested in keeping them alive and working.

Many of the leaders freely admitted that they no longer had any control over the workers, and that they could not bring them into line. Klepfisz did not share their pessimism. "What the Nazis want to do ultimately," he declared in one of the many secret meetings he held with these people, "is to enslave the working masses of Europe forever. No matter how privileged the status of the Jewish workers in the ghetto is today, sooner or later the Nazis will treat them as they did the rest of the Jews. This will arouse them from their lethargy. We have only to see to it that the awakening does not come too late."

It may seem strange that in the midst of the inferno of brutal sadism and mass murder Michael Klepfisz could view the situation in such a detached fashion; that he could use, in discussing it, the same words and expressions he had used ever since he had first become conscious of being engaged in a class struggle. Undoubtedly it was his political education, first in the house of his father, and later through the "Bund" and the unions, that was mainly responsible for the fact that he was able to think and speak with so much clarity in the midst of the confusion in the ghetto.

"If Fascism succeeds in establishing itself in Europe," he said once, "we will lose everything we have gained in the battle of more than half a century. It is for this reason that the workers must hit back everywhere—even when they find themselves in as hopeless a position as ours in the ghetto of Warsaw."

Klepfisz was not the man to wait patiently for the day when the workers were going to awaken. He was already preparing for the fight which he felt was important far beyond the Jewish issue, and which, too, he realized was inevitable. In his opinion it was of primary importance that the Jewish workers should escape from the isolation into which they had been forced. He and his friends tried therefore to establish contact with the Polish underground movement.

Certain contacts existed already. Many Polish underground leaders had established lines of communication with the Warsaw Ghetto during the earliest days of its existence. Among these underground leaders was a man named Joseph Junosza, formerly an electrical engineer, who played a large part in organizing the Warsaw underground and served as a liaison officer between different Polish groups. In 1941, when the Gestapo was about to arrest him, he escaped to London and later came to the United States. He and other leaders of the Polish underground were not slow to realize that what the Nazis did to the Jews they would later try to do to every Pole, if they were not stopped quickly. They met leaders of the "Bund" party and other members of Jewish groups and organizations which had gone underground, their chief meeting places being the Church of All Saints and the Court Building with the two exits, as well as certain other houses which were strategically situated. A steady contact between the two was also maintained through the medium of Polish motormen on the streetcars which came into the ghetto, and through employees of the waterworks and other utilities who also had to have access to the ghetto.

Numerous conferences took place between the two groups around the end of 1940 and the beginning of 1941. But it was only after Klepfisz had come back that the collaboration was intensified and a common policy and strategy was decided upon, to be followed not only in Warsaw but throughout all of Poland. It was Michael Klepfisz who had made the Poles realize that one of the most important primary tasks they had to accomplish was to fight with every means at hand the German attempt to split the Poles from the Jews by disseminating anti-Semitic propaganda. "If the Germans want us to hate each other," he declared, "so much the more reason for us to close our ranks."

The Poles took the cue and created the League to Fight Anti-Semitism, an underground organization which devised a large-scale program for the enlightenment of the Polish masses. Right under the nose of the Gestapo they conducted a campaign of counterpropaganda throughout Poland. The Gestapo learned about the existence of this League, and began to hunt down all its members. By the end of 1941 it had liquidated them. The League was dead, but it had achieved the purpose for which it was founded, for by that time the vast majority of Polish people realized that it was not the Jews whom they should consider as their enemies. They understood that Poles and Jews alike had one common enemy: the Nazis.

The Polish underground made countless appeals to its followers to protest against the existence of ghettos and the discrimination against the Jews. One such appeal said:

"There are no degrees in slavery and there are no 'better' or 'worse' categories of slaves. The Polish people understand the meaning of the game the Nazis are playing, trying to separate the Poles and the Jews, and reject with contempt the proposition made to them by Hitlerism to accept the role of 'better' types of slaves, simply because they are not enclosed in ghettos. In the face of the brutalities of the invaders the Polish people recognize only two classes: those who submit to and compromise with the oppressors and those who fight against them."

Michael Klepfisz had been right. The workers inside the ghetto, no matter how privileged their position, did not stand aloof for a long time. They saw the suffering of the other Jews and they forgot that these Jews had stopped them from acting against the Nazis in the beginning. Klepfisz had also been right as far as the Nazis were concerned. They were afraid of the Jewish workers. They needed them for their production, but they did not want to take any chances with them. They watched them carefully and occasionally clamped down on them to demonstrate their superiority.

They would invade factories which hired Jewish workers, under the pretense of looking for someone who had committed a crime or was living under an assumed name. They would line up men, women, and children against the wall and make them kneel down with their hands folded behind their heads, covering them with a machine gun. They would search the factory and also the Jewish workers, looking for weapons or perhaps forbidden newspapers. When they did not find anything, they would hit a few of the Jews over the head and leave.

Such incidents became more and more frequent. Klepfisz looked on, noted the rising ire of the Jewish workers but remained silent.

In the beginning of 1942 he was instrumental in having two Jewish representatives sent into the executive committee of the Polish underground. These representatives not only served as liaison officers to arrange for giving information concerning Jewish matters to the Poles and information concerning Polish matters to the Jews, but they also had a voice in the supreme council which shaped the Polish underground strategy. They lived outside the ghetto, with Aryan papers provided by the Polish underground. On the other hand, Polish leaders who were in danger of being arrested by the Gestapo disappeared into the ghetto where they lived under Jewish names just out of reach of the Gestapo.

Polish underground papers were smuggled into the ghetto in great numbers. Some of them were even printed in the ghetto, because it was found out that this was safer than to print them in Warsaw. For a relatively long time—till the beginning of 1942—it never occurred to the Gestapo to look for Polish underground literature in the ghetto. At that time there were no fewer than eight underground papers and pamphlets edited and printed by the Jewish underground inside the ghetto. They were distributed both there and among the Poles in Warsaw by specially trained underground couriers, concealed inside the pages of either the *Gazeta Zydowska,* the official ghetto newspaper permitted and supervised by the Germans, or the *Nowy Kurjer Warszawski,* the official Warsaw paper. There were also weekly information bulletins with news from abroad obtained by monitors on secret radio sets. There was a magazine printed in Polish dealing with questions of the Polish-Jewish relations. And there were papers edited by and for members of the Bund and, of course, Zionist papers.

When the Gestapo finally found out about the ghetto underground press, they sent a large number of agents into the ghetto to discover the hidden printing presses and the clandestine broadcasting station. Specially equipped cars cruised all day long through the streets. Countless searching parties invaded houses and basements. But only in a few cases did the Gestapo succeed in finding what they were looking for. Wherever they did make an arrest an execution followed within the hour.

A German agent had purported to "discover" that the bakers, who were among the richest people in the ghetto, had been compelled by the Jewish underground to contribute considerable sums to be used in publishing leaflets and newspapers. The Gestapo rounded up sixty of the more prominent bakers and shot them, though there was not the slightest proof that it was these sixty bakers who had given the money. As a matter of fact, most of the men who were killed had nothing whatever to do with illegal newspapers.

The night after the mass murder Michael Klepfisz met with a few of the Bund leaders in a room where the Yiddish underground newspaper *Storm* was set, printed, and handed over to those who had to distribute it. This room, which was located behind a shop, presented during the day the outward appearances of a stock room, and that is what it was. The printing presses—little, outmoded, hand-operated machines—were carefully hidden. The paper on which the newssheet was printed had to be smuggled into the ghetto through underground channels. But it could not be stored in the room where the printing was done, because of the danger of discovery in case the Nazis chose to search the room. So all the men who worked on the sheet, and who later distributed it, had to bring the paper for each number with them just before it was to be printed.

A few of those present that night, visibly shaken by the mass murder of the bakers, brought up the problem of whether the printing of illegal newspapers should be continued. "We know what we are doing and the risk we are taking," they said. "If we are caught and killed we die in a battle which we have taken up. But what about those innocent people who do not even know about our fight? Have we the right to risk their lives?"

"What do you propose to do?" Klepfisz asked impatiently. "Are we supposed to give in to German blackmail?"

"Do you seriously believe that the Germans will not kill Jews—guilty or innocent—whenever they so desire?" a tall, blond young man asked softly. "Do you really believe that there is anything that can stop the Germans from killing except to kill them first?"

Klepfisz looked at the speaker. He knew the man was Mordecai Anilewicz, the leader of the Chaluzim. He had heard about him, and friends had pointed Mordecai out to him. But he had never met him personally.

"I am glad you are here," he said, extending his hand to Mordecai.

"I have wanted to meet you for a long time," Mordecai said, and shook the proffered hand. "That is why I asked a friend to bring me here tonight."

That is how Michael Klepfisz and Mordecai Anilewicz met.

It seems strange that the Chaluzim and the Socialists got together at such a relatively late date. But then the Zionist youths and the men of the "Bund" were worlds apart in their outlook and their general ideas—almost as far apart as both groups were from the conservative Jews around Adam Czerniakow. The Chaluzim were looking at Poland purely from the Jewish point of view. They wanted to help the Jews, to save as many as possible. Michael Klepfisz, on the other hand, was first of all a socialist, a man who wanted to fight against oppression in general, no matter whence it came or who its victims. He regarded the strictly Jewish angle of the problem as merely the corollary, so to speak, to the larger, more embracing problem.

Klepfisz was not interested in Zionism; he even disapproved of it. He felt that Jews were Poles like other Poles, Frenchmen like other Frenchmen, Englishmen like other Englishmen. He regarded the Zionists' desire to go to Palestine as an admission—nay, an acceptance—of defeat in the struggle to be accepted on equal terms.

"Let us not quarrel about Zionism in general," Mordecai told him. "You look upon yourself as a worker. That is your right. But the Nazis look upon you as a Jew. The Nazis want to enslave the people of Europe—you are quite right about that. But they do not want to enslave us Jews. They want to wipe us out entirely. I say that they want to wipe us out as a nation. If it makes you feel any better, you can say that they want to wipe us out as individuals. Whichever way you put it, the fact remains that they are exterminating us on a scale unprecedented in history, and certainly not comparable to what they do to other people."

The two young men understood each other immediately. For no matter how far apart they were in their basic outlook, they both spoke the same language—the language of resistance.

"Resistance," Mordecai said, "is our only recourse. Thousands of young Jews throughout Poland are being prepared to fight the oppressor." He gave Klepfisz a picture of the organization of the Chaluzim camps which Dagani's agents had built up. "We have a number of groups right here in the ghetto, too," he added.

"How about weapons?"

"We have some. . . . But of course they won't get us very far."

"We, too, have some," Klepfisz said.

One day, after they had inspected the stocks of arms hidden away in the ghetto, Mordecai said, "It is at least a beginning. But we must find more. A hundred times more."

"I think I know where I can get more—perhaps even a hundred times more," Klepfisz said. "But I want to wait. The time to strike is not yet ripe. We are too few."

Both men knew that the overwhelming majority of the inhabitants of the ghetto was exhausted, hungry, sick, frightened, and utterly demoralized.

"Can we ever arouse in them the spirit of resistance again?" Klepfisz asked.

"We must. We must find a way to make them understand that there is nothing left for them but to fight." From then on Mordecai and Klepfisz united their efforts to convert the Jews, telling them by way of written and spoken word that they must no longer believe in the promises of the Nazis and that they must strike, and strike soon, or else all of them would be killed.

That they must strike soon . . . it seemed impossible to convince the Jews of that. There was nothing left in them but gloomy resignation. They could not imagine that there was any sense in opposing the oppressor. The Germans had so much of a head start.

It was a hard uphill fight for Mordecai and Klepfisz. Theirs seemed to be a hopeless endeavor. But they went on talking, writing, appealing, threatening. There was little time left for them to do the job. But they never thought of giving up.

Chapter IX

S.O.S.

THE ANNIHILATION SQUADS continued to appear in the ghetto and shoot at people as though they were clay pigeons. Czerniakow went to Dr. Auerwald to protest against this outrage. The Nazi seemed quite astonished. He said that he had no idea what it was all about. The annihilation squads had certainly not been sent by him. Evidently they were under the authority of one of his colleagues, but he would gladly investigate and let Czerniakow know.

He telephoned the next morning. But he did not speak of the annihilation squads. "We are very disturbed," he said. "We have found a number of silly anti-Nazi sheets printed in the ghetto. Of course we had to make some arrests. We have taken a hundred Jewish printers."

"You mean to say that they found out that a hundred of our printers were involved in printing illegal newspapers?"

"Of course not. But we shot them anyway. It will teach the guilty ones a lesson."

A few nights later Czerniakow received another telephone call from Dr. Auerwald. The Nazi ordered him to have the Department for Burials prepare a number of graves at once.

"How many graves?" Czerniakow asked tonelessly.

"Oh, I don't know. A few hundred will do."

"Why? What has happened? What are you going to do now?" Czerniakow's voice had taken on a frantic tone. But Dr. Auerwald had rung off.

The next day the Nazis shot two hundred inmates of the prison in Gesia Street. These two hundred were charged with smuggling food into the ghetto. From then on similar executions took place every night. The annihilation squads entered the ghetto by night, penetrated a number of houses, took the people out of their beds, and shot them in the courtyards.

No reason was given. Perhaps there was no reason. They were Jews—that was enough.

Only now, in the spring of 1942, the truth of what had happened to the Jews in eastern Galicia at the time of Hitler's invasion of Russia was beginning to reach the Jewish Council. Balaban talked to many refugees who came from that part of the country, studied notes taken down by monitors who listened to illegal broadcasts, studied the reports sent by envoys of the underground all the way from London. The overall picture left no doubt: the Nazis had exterminated the Jews of eastern Galicia.

Balaban said to Czerniakow, "They followed more or less the same pattern all the time. They drove boys and men between the ages of fourteen and sixty together into one place, the market place or preferably the cemetery, and mowed them down with machine guns or blasted them to bits with hand grenades. Usually they were ordered to dig their own graves first. The women were killed in their own houses. Even children in orphanages were not spared. The sick in the hospitals were shot in their beds."

Thus the Nazis killed thirty thousand Jews in Lwów, fifteen thousand in Stanislawów, five thousand in Tarnopol, four thousand in Brzežany—to name just a few of the places. And that was only the beginning. Later, in October and November 1941, they killed fifty thousand in Wilno, nine thousand in Slonim, fifteen thousand in Równe, and six thousand in Baranowicze. In most of the smaller towns not a single Jew was left alive.

Czerniakow remained silent as Balaban quoted these figures. There was nothing he could say. There was nothing any of the members of the Jewish Council could say. It all seemed so hopeless. If only they could help the people who were being murdered! But they could do nothing for them. They just had to sit there and listen to what was going on, to what was happening to their brothers, without being able to raise a finger. And those who had been killed were perhaps even more fortunate than others who were sent to concentration camps to be tortured, subjected to all kinds of unspeakable indignities, and treated worse than animals, and who eventually also died—not the sudden death of a bullet through the heart, but the slow and painful death of exhaustion, starvation, desperation.

And what was happening to the Jews in Lublin? Lublin was a town of a hundred thousand inhabitants to which the Germans had been sending Jews from other occupied countries—from France, Belgium, Austria, Holland. Thus, they had declared, they were going to "solve the Jewish question." Lublin was soon overcrowded. The Jews could not even find any room in the neighborhood of the town. Lately trains filled with Jews went on to the town of Belzec near Lublin. Some of the Jews were left there or in the open country with no food, with no possibility of building barracks or huts for themselves. And then the trains destined to go to Lublin or Belzec no longer arrived there. The Jews in these trains simply disappeared from the earth, leaving no trace. There were all kinds of horrible rumors of what had happened to them.

Czerniakow had tried to find out. He had sent secret couriers out of Warsaw. Three of these couriers had not returned. The fourth, a former officer in the Polish Army, finally made his way back into the Warsaw Ghetto. He had been away for only ten days, but he had aged twenty-five years in that time. He seemed unable and even unwilling to speak, and when he finally did tell his story it was only after he was alone with the mayor of the ghetto.

He had learned that thousands of Jews, perhaps tens of thousands, from every European country and also from every corner of Poland, had been sent to an especially prepared camp where they, their wives, and their children were killed by a new kind of gas or by electricity. The corpses, the courier said, were used by the Germans to make soap.

Czerniakow listened to the gruesome story without interrupting the narrator. Lublin no longer seemed far away to him. Galicia no longer seemed far away to him. Now he was certain that everything that had happened to the Jews in other parts of Poland would happen to the Jews in Warsaw too. How soon would the Nazis become tired of those small-scale raids of the annihilation squads?

"There is one thing we can and should do," Balaban once remarked. "We should let the others know what is going on. We should tell everyone in the ghetto of Warsaw what is happening to the Jews in Poland. They have a right to know."

"We can't do that," Czerniakow replied. "There would be a panic. They would go mad with fear; they would make some sudden, desperate move that would give the Germans the perfect excuse for coming in here and killing them off."

"As if the Germans needed any excuse to kill us, if they wanted to!"

"The lives of the people in the ghetto are my responsibility," Czerniakow declared firmly. "I cannot risk any of those lives in demonstrations which, after all, would not produce any practical solution. We must not give up hope. Perhaps we can save at least some of those among us."

His voice had become sad and tired. He was full of doubts. He no longer could believe that he would be able to save the lives which he felt were entrusted to him. He wondered how long it would take till everything was over.

Some of the Jews of the ghetto were able to make an escape. Help came to them from the Catholic Church.

Pope Pius XII had, toward the end of 1941, created a special division in the Vatican for the purpose of aiding Jews in occupied countries to escape from Nazi persecution. This division was particularly active in Poland. In Warsaw a committee was formed to carry out the pope's suggestion. Papal Prelate Marcelli Godlewsky was head of the committee.

This prelate had formerly been a strong nationalist. He had therefore little difficulty in convincing the Nazis he was not in sympathy with the Jews and that they could make him head of all the ghetto churches without taking any risk. Thus he could enter and leave the ghetto at will.

Godlewsky, a tall man with long gray hair, had his headquarters in the Church of All Saints. Here he met Jews and arranged for them to get all kind of "Aryan" documents and papers. From time to time it then happened that whole Jewish families disappeared from the ghetto. Some of them escaped abroad with papers furnished by the prelate. Others simply went to live as Catholics in Poland with other Catholics. How many of them were actually saved will not be known until years after this war is over.

The Nazis were duped for quite some time. But they were bound to find out in the end. Then they took Prelate Godlewsky to the Oswiecim Concentration Camp.

Balaban lived in a spacious room on the third floor of a house in Walicow Street which he shared with a number of other people. There was a young woman with a child born in the beginning of 1940. This woman had come as a refugee from a neighboring town which had been occupied by the Germans. Then there was a young man, a rabbinical student, twenty-two or twenty-three years of age, thin, pale, suffering from consumption. Finally there was an old couple, the man formerly a well-to-do shopkeeper whose business in Warsaw had been taken away from him. He never could get over it. He spoke constantly about the shop he had lost and the money which someone else was making with his goods now. His wife, a white-haired woman with a frightened face, tried to calm him. She did not want him to speak; she was afraid somebody might listen and report him to the Gestapo. She saw Gestapo agents everywhere.

It was in this room that Balaban began to write what he had seen and heard, the history of the Warsaw Ghetto. The old historian missed the quiet atmosphere of his study, where he had been able to work without any interruption. Here this was impossible. He could hardly concentrate. The little child would cry; the young student would cough; the old businessman was always wanting to talk about his shop, and his wife would implore Balaban not to listen to her husband and, for God's sake, not to repeat what he was saying to anyone. The mother of the little child would suddenly start to weep, almost tonelessly, her shoulders shaking.

Balaban would get up, exasperated, with a feeling of frustration. Why couldn't they leave him alone? After all, he had work to do. He had to put down what he knew and what he learned. It was important, it was absolutely necessary, that he should finish this work of his.

He would walk the streets thinking of the reports he had read, of the witnesses he had interviewed, trying to digest the material, putting it into order in his mind so that he could write it down. He wondered how much of all this was known to the world outside Poland and how that world would react to these unbelievable stories. Perhaps there would not be any reaction at all for some time to come. There was no reason to fool oneself, Balaban felt. The world was still fascinated, almost hypnotized, by the spectacular successes of the Germans and their steady advance in Soviet Russia and by the accomplishments of the Japanese in the Pacific. Bataan had surrendered; Corregidor had surrendered; the American fleet seemed to be nowhere. General Rommel advanced in North Africa with no one to stop him. There seemed to be no hope of stopping the Nazis anywhere. Hence, Balaban concluded, there was no hope that they could be prevented from annihilating the Jews in Poland.

Planes roared overhead. Balaban looked up at them. In an hour or so, he calculated, they would be at the front. In just an hour. The world had become so small, and still so many things went on in this small world which were not known to the people in it. And even if they did know, did they care? The world had become so small. But it was still everyone for himself. If something happened to one's neighbor—why, that was too bad for him. But it was the neighbor's business, and that was all there was to that. Hitler could have been stopped so easily if people had minded their neighbor's business ten years ago. But everybody had thought: Maybe I will not be touched; maybe, somehow, the deluge will go the other way. The world had become so small. People read in the newspapers what happened inside Germany after Hitler took power. But they did not do anything about it. They merely shrugged their shoulders. First it was the Communists and the Jews. Later it was the Austrians and then the Czechoslovakians. Then it was the Poles. Yes, the world was small, but people still believed that they could stand on an island inside this world and say, "This piece of land is neutral. Please don't step on the grass."

The planes had gone. It was quiet now. The world had become so small. But, Balaban thought, did this not mean that there was no longer such a thing as my business or your business? Did it not mean that everybody was responsible for what was happening in this small world—that everybody had to do something about what was happening to his neighbor?

Shots were fired. As he turned the corner Balaban saw some drunken Gestapo men aiming at a window. There were a few young boys with them, Hitler Youths, children no more than thirteen or fourteen years old. They, too, were armed. "Come on! Kill a Jew!" they were admonished by one of the Gestapo men. The boys began to shoot, their faces pale with excitement. They were having a wonderful time.

Balaban stared at them for a long time, oblivious of his own danger, incapable of making a motion. Then slowly, like a man in a trance, he turned and went back home. The world had become small. Everyone was responsible for everybody else. Everybody had to help everybody else. Balaban was thinking now of the people he was living with in his room. He felt the despair of the young mother as though it were his own despair. He suffered for the old businessman as though somebody had taken away from him, too, the thing he valued most. He went on faster. His old face was full of compassion. He must not allow himself ever again to become exasperated by the actions of the people with whom he lived. Their worries were his worries. How could he write about the sufferings of those in the ghetto if he did not suffer with them?

The Jews had sent the first S.O.S. into the world. Specially trained messengers left Warsaw, crossed the country, and smuggled themselves across the border. Some of them got caught on the way and were killed by the Germans, but a few of them managed to get through and finally reached England. They told the story of what was happening to the Jews throughout Poland and gave the first figures concerning the number of Jews who had been killed already. For the most part these messengers were met with disbelief. A few English newspapers printed their reports, but even they condensed them into a few insignificant lines, hidden away on a back page. The editors simply did not believe that such things could happen. Nor did American editors.

The world was not yet ready to believe the horrible truth. The first S.O.S. faded away—unheard.

Chapter X

The Decree

"Well, that's about the size of it," said Dr. Fischer, governor of the district and city of Warsaw. He had asked Dr. Auerwald and Gruppenfuehrer Mende to a conference, a confidential conference, as he remarked several times. He had given them a complete picture of the strategy he was going to employ in his fight against the Jews from now on. He had been speaking for more than an hour, wandering restlessly across the large office he occupied in the former building of the Polish Ministry of Foreign Affairs. Now he dropped into the chair behind his desk, sprawling there with an air of complete exhaustion.

"If only it weren't so hot," he complained. "And those damned flies . . ."

The other two rose from their chairs. Dr. Fischer waved them back. "Better stay awhile," he said. "I am going to dictate the entire decree now. You can listen. If you have any suggestions to make . . ."

"Gladly," replied Dr. Auerwald, and both men sat down again. The governor picked up the telephone. "I want a stenographer—right away," he barked. Then they waited. Mende lighted a cigarette. After a minute or so a young girl entered the room. She was blonde, rather large, and wore nose glasses.

"Take a memorandum, Fräulein," Dr. Fischer said. He thought for a minute or so and then said: "Okay. Here goes. . . .

"All Jewish inhabitants of Warsaw, irrespective of sex or age, will be resettled in the East. The following categories are exempt from resettlement:

"a. All Jews employed by German authorities or enterprises who are able to submit proof of such employment.

"b. All Jews who are members or employees of the Jewish Council as of the day of the publication of this decree.

"c. All Jews employed by firms belonging to the German Reich who are able to submit proof of such employment.

"d. All Jews fit for work but not yet employed. These are to be isolated in the Jewish quarter.

"e. All Jews enrolled in the Jewish police.

"f. All Jews belonging to the personnel of Jewish hospitals as well as those who work for the Jewish Department of Health."

Dr. Fischer looked up from his notes. "I suppose that covers it. Any suggestions?"

Dr. Auerwald spoke: "You'll have to do something about the families of the men you want to keep in the ghetto. You can't separate them, I don't believe."

Gruppenfuehrer Mende was amused. "Our good doctor is sentimental."

Dr. Auerwald said: "No, it's not a matter of sentiment. It's just that

I don't want to make a mess out of it, as some of my colleagues sometimes do." He looked sharply at Mende, but the latter made no reply, and Auerwald continued after a moment: "It stands to reason that many of the men you want to keep here will simply try to join their families if you evacuate them. You are bound to have a lot of disorder."

"I suppose you are right," the governor murmured. "God, it's hot. And those flies . . . Come to think of it, we also have to make some provision for the people in the hospitals. . . . Fräulein, where were we?"

"f. All Jews belonging to the personnel of Jewish hospitals . . ."

"Yes, yes, I know. Go on from there, Fräulein:

"g. All Jews in the immediate families of the persons enumerated under a to f. Only wives and children are considered members of the immediate family.

"h. All Jews who on the first day of the resettlement are patients in one of the Jewish hospitals and are not fit to be released. The unfitness for release must be stated by a physician designated by the Jewish Council.

"i. Every Jewish deportee is permitted to take along fifteen kilograms of his property as traveling luggage. Luggage above this weight will be confiscated."

"I have a suggestion," said Mende. "How about putting in something about money and valuables? It will save us time when we search their houses later on."

"A very good idea," the governor agreed. He laughed. "I should have thought of it myself. Take it down, Fräulein. . . .

"All precious objects—such as money, jewels, gold, et cetera—may be taken along. Food for three days is to be taken.

"The resettlement will begin . . . What is today, Fräulein?"

"July eighteenth, Governor."

"Very well. The resettlement will begin July 22, 1942, 11 A.M."

Dr. Fischer moved restlessly in his chair. "I can't stand this heat," he wailed. "Fräulein, get us some nice cold beer, won't you? I'll go on with the dictation in a little while."

The girl nodded and went out. Mende got up and went to the window. On his way he stopped in front of a picture of Minister Hans

Frank, Governor General of Poland. It was dedicated to Dr. Fischer. Mende read: "Poland has never before been governed so frankly and honestly as now." The words were a quotation from a speech Frank had made in Cracow, in which he had enumerated the accomplishments and improvements brought about in the occupied countries under Nazi rule. Mende wanted to say something but checked himself. Fischer was a close friend of Frank.

Dr. Auerwald sat in gloomy silence. When a young soldier brought the beer he hardly touched it. "I wish all this was over," he finally confessed. "I don't feel any too happy about it."

The governor looked sharply at him. "What's the matter, man? Nerves?"

"Perhaps it is my nerves. Anyhow . . . you don't believe there will be incidents?"

Mende turned around. "Incidents? What kind of incidents?"

Auerwald said, "I was just thinking. You see, I have to go to this damned place all the time. It won't be very comfortable in the ghetto, you know."

Mende went over to him. "You aren't afraid, are you?"

Auerwald tried to laugh. It did not come off too well. "No. Not a bit afraid. I was just thinking."

There was complete silence in the room. All of them were thinking now of Reinhard Heydrich. He seemed to have Czechoslovakia in the palm of his hand. And then, just about six weeks ago, they had blown him up. It would never be found out who did it. It did not matter, anyhow, as far as the men in this room were concerned. They knew there were many men in every occupied country who were waiting to spring another Heydrich on them. There were plenty of such men in Poland.

They were still silent when the stenographer entered again. She sat down, her notebook open and her pencil poised. Only then did the governor speak:

"Well, now, let's see where we were. . . . I am now going to dictate a statement to the Jewish Council." He took out his notes and began:

"The following instructions for the duration of resettlement are given to the Jewish Council for the carrying out of which the members of the Jewish Council are responsible with their lives:

"1. The Jewish Council receives orders concerning resettlement from the Delegate for Resettlement Matters or his deputy only. For the duration of the resettlement the Jewish Council may elect a special committee for resettlement matters, whose chairman is the president of the Jewish Council, and deputy chairman, the commandant of the Jewish police.

"2. The Jewish Council is responsible for producing the Jews designated daily for resettlement. In order to accomplish that task, the Jewish Council is to use the Jewish police (one thousand people). The Jewish Council is to see to it that six thousand Jews are delivered daily, not later than at 4 P.M., to the assembly place, beginning July 22, 1942. The assembly place for the duration of the evacuation is the Jewish Hospital at Stawki Street. On July 22, 1942, six thousand Jews are to be delivered directly to the loading station at the Transfer Point. For the time being the Jewish Council may draw the daily quota of Jews from the general population. Later on the Jewish Council will receive definite instructions as to the parts of streets or housing blocks to be emptied.

"3. On July 23, 1942, the Jewish Council is to evacuate the Jewish Hospital at Stawki Street and to transfer the patients and staff to another suitable building inside the ghetto, so that on the evening of July 23, 1942, the hospital may be ready to receive daily the Jews to be resettled.

"4. Furthermore, the Jewish Council must see to it that objects and property left by these Jews, unless infected, are taken and registered in special assembly points to be designated. For that purpose the Jewish Council should use the Jewish police and a proper number of Jewish laborers. This activity will be supervised by the Sicherheitspolizei, which will issue special instructions to the Jewish Council. Illegal appropriation of these objects and property will be punished by death.

"5. The Jewish Council must also see to it that Jews employed in German enterprises or by German authorities continue their work during the action. To carry out this order the Jewish Council will issue proper announcements to the Jewish population supported by heaviest penalties. The Jewish Council must also see to it that there is no pause in the functioning of such Jewish supply enterprises as will be required to secure the feeding of the Jews gathered at the assembly point as well as of the remaining Jews.

"6. Moreover, the Jewish Council is responsible for burying on the day of death Jews deceased during the resettlement period. . . .

"I put that last paragraph in because I rather think there will be quite a lot of suicides, once we get our little . . . ah . . . evacuation started."

"I hope they will be content with killing themselves," said Dr. Auerwald after a while. He still didn't look very happy.

"I am not afraid of Jews," commented Gruppenfuehrer Mende. "You know, there is something funny about Jews. They don't believe in murder." He laughed. "They are just a stinkingly decadent race, that's what I think."

The governor remarked hurriedly, "You may go now, Fräulein. Type this out. I'll call you as soon as I want to continue." He waited till the girl had closed the door, then he turned sharply to Auerwald. "Do you expect any difficulties? After all, you know the ghetto better than we do."

"Well, I can't put my finger on anything definite. But don't forget there are still more than four hundred thousand people in the ghetto. If there is a panic, nobody can tell where it will end."

Dr. Fischer cleared his throat. "Gentlemen, without giving any details, I can assure you that any action on the part of the Jews that would necessitate the use of a large number of German soldiers would be inopportune at this moment, most inopportune indeed."

"All the more reason," Mende interjected, "for proceeding with the deportations as quickly as possible. If we can get rid of six thousand Jews a day, we'll have at least half of them out of the way in a month or so."

They discussed this for a while. Mende mentioned the fact that, after all, more than half a million Jews from other occupied countries had been disposed of without any difficulties. The main thing was to deprive them at the earliest possible moment of their leaders, both actual and potential. "We must see to it," he said, "that the Jewish intelligentsia disappears as rapidly as possible. Take away the lawyers, the doctors, the journalists, and all those who can exercise a certain influence on the others, and mere numbers don't mean a thing. A few hundred thousand people with nobody to tell them where to go will just run around and bump their heads against the wall. That's what the Gestapo found out in the other countries."

"There's another thing that's bothering me," the governor said after a while, finishing his beer. "It's the Poles. Don't let us fool ourselves. We have been relying on the fact that the Poles are anti-Semites. At least that's what we were told when we moved in here. Now they may have been anti-Semites before, or at least some of them may have been. But they aren't any longer. And, strictly between ourselves, gentlemen, none of the Poles believes a word of our anti-Jewish propaganda any more."

The others knew that the governor was speaking the truth. The Poles had changed considerably. They felt pity for the Jews. They tried to supply them with food. They even tried to help them escape whenever they could. Most Poles were good Christians. One could not be a good Christian and not be revolted at the treatment the Jews were enduring. And then, besides, there was another reason for this new feeling of sympathy on the part of the Poles. Most of them understood instinctively that the Jews were but the first victims. The Poles themselves would come next. The enemy of the Jews was the enemy of the Poles, too. There was only one enemy.

Dr. Fischer and the men in his office knew it only too well. And there was nothing much they could do about it. "Except," Dr. Fischer said, "to keep as quiet as possible our plans for the Jews. The less the Poles know, the better. As long as they believe that we are really planning to resettle the Jews they will keep quiet. So this is our line, gentlemen," he concluded.

Dr. Auerwald then suggested that it might be a good idea to use the same tactics with the Jews too. "Let us appeal to their instinct of self-preservation. Let us explain to them that resettlement is nothing to be afraid of, that they will be placed in territory on the other side of the river Bug, or somewhere inside Russia. Later we can furnish some letters from those already 'resettled,' telling their friends in Warsaw how nice their new homes are and all that sort of thing . . . you understand."

The others understood. They, too, thought it might be a very good idea.

A tall man in black SS uniform entered. It was Captain Reinhard, the new chief of the annihilation squads. He had been stationed until just a short time ago in Lublin, and had done excellent work there, according to Heinrich Himmler. In fact, Himmler himself had made him the chief of the annihilation squads in the ghetto. He knew that certain Gestapo men were making a lot of money by smuggling food into the ghetto and by being friendly to Jews who could pay for it. He wanted to stop all this. He thought that Reinhard would do the trick.

"I am just dictating the decree, Captain," the governor said. "If you'll wait outside . . ." He did not like Reinhard, and neither did the others. They did not mind the man himself so much as the fact that he seemed close to Himmler. It was never too healthy to work with somebody who was too close to Himmler. Furthermore they resented the fact that Reinhard had been sent there to stop their little business affairs. It was really too silly, this meddling in their affairs. For Reinhard himself was the worst of them all. Where they made a few thousand marks he made a fortune. He confiscated and sold everything he could lay his hands on. He sold bed sheets and shoes, jewelry and coal, flour and shirts, whole forests and cows, watches and eggs. He owned several houses in Poland. He also owned several businesses, or rather his mistresses owned them. He was doing all right for himself. But there was nothing you could do about him. Not even the governor could do anything about him. For Himmler liked him.

"It's just such men as Reinhard," Dr. Auerwald said, "who might prove to be the match in the powder magazine. He is overdoing it. I wish he were not here to conduct the evacuation."

The governor shrugged. "You know, Reichsfuehrer Himmler . . ."

"I have a suggestion to make," Gruppenfuehrer Mende said. "Why don't we use the Jewish police more in this evacuation? Let us use them as much as possible. This will give the Jews a bit more confidence. After all, they will trust the Jewish police. And if they find out what it is all about later—well, then they can curse the Jewish police."

The others thought this was an excellent idea indeed.

"By all means let us use as many of the Jewish police force as possible," Dr. Fischer decided. "Let us use them wherever possible." He took up the telephone again. "Stenographer." He began to study his notes.

The girl entered. "I have typed what you dictated so far."

"Never mind. I want to finish first. . . . These damned flies . . . Where were we?"

"6. Moreover, the Jewish Council . . ."

"Oh yes. . . . Well, let's go on:

"7. The Jewish Council will post the following announcements to the Jewish population of Warsaw:

"On the order of the German authorities all Jewish inhabitants of Warsaw will be resettled in the East . . . et cetera—from point one to four.

"8. Penalties:

"a. Every Jew who does not belong to nor has so far the right to belong to group two, points a and c, and who leaves the Jewish quarter after the start of resettlement, will be shot.

"b. Every Jew who undertakes a move which may circumvent or disturb the carrying out of the resettlement orders will be shot.

"c. Every Jew who assists a move which may circumvent or disturb the carrying out of the resettlement orders will be shot.

"d. All Jews not belonging to categories enumerated under group two, points a to h, who will be found in Warsaw after the conclusion of the resettlement, will be shot.

"The Jewish Council is warned that should its instructions and orders not be carried out fully, a proper number of hostages will be taken and shot."

The governor got up. "Fräulein, let's have some more beer. It's so damned hot." Then he turned to the others. "I suppose that about covers it?"

The others nodded. "Yes," they said, "that about covers it."

Chapter XI

THE DECISION OF ADAM CZERNIAKOW

DURING THE NIGHT OF JULY 20, 1942, the annihilation squads intensified their raids to a hitherto unprecedented degree. Captain Reinhard supervised the actions in person. Several hundred people were killed. Throughout that long night nobody in the ghetto could sleep.

At the same time about sixty Jewish intellectuals, doctors, lawyers, and teachers, many of them members of the Jewish Council, were arrested and sent to the Pawiak prison. No reason was given for their arrest, but it was plain that it could mean only one thing: the Nazis wanted to deprive the Jews of their leaders.

Why?

Czerniakow tried in vain to obtain an explanation from Dr. Auerwald or Gruppenfuehrer Mende. The Germans simply said that they had no authority to divulge anything.

Early on the morning of July 21, Dr. Auerwald informed Czerniakow by telephone that one of the few remaining hospitals, located in the northern end of the ghetto on Stawki Street, would have to be evacuated immediately. The mayor of the ghetto remonstrated: the hospital not only housed many of the cases of contagious diseases in the ghetto but also contained the only well-equipped pharmacy that was left for the Jews. Dr. Auerwald let it be known that he had arrested the manager of the hospital as a hostage and that the evacuation would have to be completed within the next twenty-four hours.

"Twenty-four hours . . . that is impossible! We don't know where to put the sick people. We have no facilities, anyhow, to move a whole hospital."

"That is your worry. I said twenty-four hours. If the hospital is not vacated by 4 P.M. tomorrow, our soldiers will throw all the Jewish patients out into the street."

Czerniakow forced himself to remain calm. "But why? If it is space you need, maybe you could find another building which we could evacuate for you."

"We need that building on Stawki Street."

The ghetto was to learn to its sorrow, within a very few days, just why the Germans needed that particular building on Stawki Street.

Czerniakow got in touch with his Health Department and began to make plans for the evacuation. The serious cases would have to be sent to the other available hospitals in the ghetto. As for those patients who were too ill to be taken to the other hospitals—nothing whatever could be done about them.

All during that afternoon, and throughout the whole night and the next morning, there was a mad rush. Every conceivable means of transportation was used to transfer the patients, their beds, the most necessary apparatus as well as the drugs and supplies. Dr. Auerwald was finally prevailed upon to allow some of the Aryan Poles to furnish private cars and trucks to aid in the move.

As was to be expected, a number of the patients died while they were being transferred from one hospital to the other, and many others succumbed during the following day. The facilities in the new and much smaller hospital were completely inadequate. It had only 278 beds. Now more than eleven hundred patients had to be accommodated. There was no room to put up that number of beds, even if they had been available. Most of the sick had to lie on the floor.

All during July 21 and 22 Adam Czerniakow had his hands full arranging for the evacuation of the hospital. He made and answered countless telephone calls. He signed hundreds of passes and letters and dictated dozens of orders to those who were assisting with the transfer. All during the night he worked on, keeping himself awake by bathing his face in cold water from time to time.

No outsider, not even any of the other members of the Jewish Council, could gain entrance to his office. Thus the mayor of the ghetto was completely oblivious of the fact that hundreds of frightened Jews came running to the Community Building, demanding to see somebody in charge in order to learn whether there was any truth in the strange rumors that were spreading throughout the ghetto. But since there was no one there who could tell them anything they remained in the neighborhood of the building, blocking the streets, waiting, milling around, afraid to go home before they knew the truth. Some of them stayed on even after the curfew hour, shrugging off the risk involved: it was no longer easy to frighten them.

One rumor spread through the ghetto to the effect that the Nazis intended to liquidate all the old people over sixty. Another said that every child of less than ten years was to be killed.

The young refugee woman who lived in the same room with Balaban told him about this rumor. "They won't take my baby away, will they?" she asked anxiously.

"Of course not," Balaban said, stroking the child's hair absent-mindedly.

"Why shouldn't they?" the old man who lived with them exclaimed. "First they took away my business; now they are going to take away my life." He tried unsuccessfully to laugh.

"Don't speak so loud," his wife admonished him. "Somebody might hear."

"There is really no reason to get upset," Balaban told them. But he wasn't so sure of that himself. He left them to find out.

The streets seemed deserted on that morning of July 22. The few goods and the small amounts of foodstuffs that had been in the shop-windows had disappeared. Many of the shops had closed down altogether. One of the few people whom Balaban met in the streets said that something was in the wind. The walls of the ghetto were surrounded by heavy forces of German police, fortified by Ukrainian, Lithuanian, and Latvian militia.

As he went on he was called to several times by people who this morning did not dare leave the protection of their houses: Did he know anything? they asked him. What was going to happen?

"Is it true that the ghetto is to be evacuated?" an old woman standing in a doorway asked.

Balaban shook his head. "What do you mean, evacuated? I haven't heard anything about it. Why should they evacuate the ghetto?"

The old woman merely looked at him, unbelieving.

More and more people asked him if there was any truth in the rumor concerning the evacuation of the ghetto. Once or twice Balaban tried to ask who had told them such things. Nobody seemed to know where the report had started. But it was spreading fast. By noon everybody had heard about it. Was there anything in this rumor? Why were they to be evacuated? Where were they to be sent?

Professor Balaban listened to many frightened and hysterical questions. He looked at the anxious-faced men and women, and he saw their despair, even as they still listened for some word from him that might give them new hope. His heart was full of pity for them, but what could he tell them? He did not know anything. And they would not believe that he did not know.

He could not find out anything at the Jewish Community Building. Czerniakow was still tied up. None of the employees who worked there seemed to know anything, though all had heard about the rumor.

Balaban returned to his room, where he found the other occupants waiting for him. They looked up eagerly as he came in, mutely begging him to tell them what he had found out.

"These are just a lot of silly stories," he said, trying to make his voice sound casual. "I do not believe . . ."

Their faces showed disappointment. They, too, did not believe him.

"They are going to kill all of us," the consumptive student whispered. "Nobody will stop them. Nobody will ever stop them. They will kill all of us. But one day they will be punished. One day they will all perish. For has not God told us that all our enemies will disappear from the face of the earth?" He began to cough.

"Yes. One day they will be punished," Balaban said quietly. In this moment he knew it, not only with the faith of an orthodox Jew, but with the faith of a wise historian. He knew that domination of the world such as the Nazis aspired to had never been achieved by any nation for any length of time. It was something which could not succeed because it was contrary to all the laws that govern human nature, and therefore contrary to all historical developments. It was something impossible because it was mad. No matter how long the Nazis would go on winning battles, they were bound to lose the last battle—in five years, perhaps, or in twenty-five or even in fifty. No, they could not win. For a moment Professor Balaban was about to say all this, to assure his fellow roomers that what the Nazis were attempting had been tried many times before without success in the history of mankind. He could furnish them with many historical parallels. He could talk to them about the downfall of the Persian Empire, of the Roman Empire, of the Spanish Empire . . . but he did not say anything to them, after all. What good would it do them to know that sometime in the future, be it near or far, the Nazis would inevitably meet their downfall? It would be no comfort to these poor creatures to hear such things, for they would be dead by then. Long before the tide could turn they, like himself, would have perished, victims of their oppressors. No, there was no consolation for those whose tragic fate it was to be living at a time when the sinister forces of tyranny seemed triumphant, to be assured that ultimately those forces would be destroyed. All he could tell them was that they had come into this world either a little too late or a little too early. Not that that would make any difference to history. But it did make all the difference to those who happened to be alive here and now.

Late that afternoon Professor Balaban went a second time to the Jewish Community Building. This time he was able to see Czerniakow. He found the mayor more excited than he had ever seen him before. He, too, had heard the rumors.

"I cannot imagine what it is all about," he declared as he paced the floor of his office. "We have not been notified of any new measures that the Gestapo might be contemplating. There must be some irresponsible rumormongers in the ghetto."

"The Germans have done a great many things to us Jews without notifying us beforehand," Balaban remarked calmly.

"Is that any reason for believing anything you hear?" Czerniakow stood still looking at Balaban. "Is that any reason for driving people crazy with fear?"

Balaban remained silent.

Czerniakow began again to walk up and down. "Perhaps some of the members of the annihilation squads have dropped a word or two . . . and our people, always ready to believe the worst, have made a big thing out of nothing at all."

"Aren't you ready yet to believe the worst?"

The mayor sank into his chair. "Yes . . . no . . . I don't want to believe it. I know things look bad. But perhaps at least some of the people in the ghetto can be spared. They can't kill them all. They can't let them all starve!"

Balaban went over to the desk and put his hand on Czerniakow's shoulder. "Do you really believe it?"

Czerniakow looked up. He said nothing.

Neither Czerniakow nor Balaban left the Community Building that night. They wanted to be on hand in case something new should develop. During the night they learned that the Nazis had freed a number of the Jewish intellectuals whom they had arrested forty-eight hours before. Those of them who were members of the Jewish Council came straight to the Community Building. They looked tired, unshaven, and bewildered. They were completely in the dark as to the reason for their arrest or subsequent release. The Nazis had not told them anything.

Professor Balaban said, "This is what the Germans call psychological warfare."

Early in the morning Dr. Auerwald telephoned Czerniakow and ordered him to assemble the members of the Jewish Council. He himself arrived at the Community Building shortly afterward. The meeting took place in the large room in which the Jews had first learned that a ghetto was to be established—back in 1939.

Dr. Auerwald said, "I've come to bring you good news. A number of people will be evacuated from the ghetto."

Czerniakow and Balaban exchanged glances. The rumors had been true, after all.

"Evacuation." Czerniakow pronounced the word slowly, as though to taste it. He paused a moment. "And what will happen to the people who are evacuated?" He was about to ask whether they would share the fate of the Jews who had been sent to Lublin and Belzec.

"As things are now, the authorities intend to evacuate only a limited number of people. The daily rate has been fixed at four thousand. They will be put into trains and resettled somewhere in the East. They will be given barracks to sleep in and a certain amount of food. And, of course, they will have to work."

"Of course," Balaban said. "We have heard about a planned evacuation. People seem to be afraid of it. Small wonder. The last time they had to evacuate their dwellings and come to the ghetto they lost almost everything they owned. And since then they have had the experience that every change in their lives has been a change for the worse."

Dr. Auerwald countered, "You have complained constantly about the crowded conditions in the ghetto. Now we are trying to make some room for you, and you still find fault."

Czerniakow replied, "We have tried hard to co-operate. We have done so because we thought it would be in the interest of those for whom we are responsible. But we no longer feel that co-operation is justified, because we no longer see that the Jews will derive any advantage from it."

"I don't think you have any choice," the Nazi snarled. "If you do not wish to co-operate, I will have to arrest you. The evacuation of the ghetto will take place anyhow."

He got up. "You will make all the necessary arrangements. Four thousand people daily. Men and women. You will see to it that the Jewish police delivers them promptly. The place they are to assemble, and from which they will be transferred to the East, is the square north of Stawki Street, where the railroad tracks are. The Resettlement Office where our men will write out the papers required for the transfer is the hospital which you so kindly evacuated for us."

He was already at the door when he turned around once more. "I forgot. The first contingent of four thousand will have to be at the Transfer Point at four o'clock sharp this afternoon."

Then he was gone.

Everybody began to talk at once. Four o'clock this very afternoon! It was impossible. How could four thousand people be found who would be able to pack their most necessary belongings and appear at the Transfer Point within the few hours that were left?

For the first time Czerniakow was incapable of pulling himself together and taking measures. He sat helplessly in his chair. After a while he murmured, "Of course the ghetto really is overcrowded."

Professor Balaban shook his head. "You don't believe them, do you? They don't care whether the ghetto is crowded or not."

Czerniakow looked up. "No. They do not care. They always lied to us."

During the morning a poster with the decree giving all the details of the scheduled evacuation and signed by Governor Fischer appeared everywhere in the ghetto. While Dr. Auerwald was still in conference at the Jewish Community Building, Mende appeared at the headquarters of the Jewish militia to give the necessary orders. The Jewish militia was to supervise the evacuation and see to it that the required number of Jews would appear every day at the Transfer Point on Stawki Street.

If there were not enough volunteers—and Gruppenfuehrer Mende thought that it was quite likely that there would not be enough volunteers after the first few days—the militia would have to take the required number of Jews to the Transfer Point—by force, if necessary.

The sick and the aged people were to be taken away first; then those who had no definite source of income, peddlers and the like, and persons dependent on their families; and last, those who worked in trades non-essential to the German war effort—artisans, tailors, shoemakers, and shopkeepers.

The Jewish militiamen stood listening to him. Only a little more than a year ago they had been proud to be allowed to wear a uniform and to have a job which gave them certain powers over the other Jews. They had worn their uniforms, these former lawyers, bookkeepers, and doctors. They had eaten the bread and the soup which they had been given as meager remuneration for their work. They had felt comparatively happy then, but now they no longer felt so. The Germans, in their sadism, forced them to be present when the annihilation squads performed. They had to look on while their people were being killed. Now the Germans would force them to take their own brothers and sisters away—where?

"Transfer Point." The words meant nothing to the Jewish policemen. But they had a strange feeling every time they heard them spoken. There was something sinister, almost frightening, about the sound of the words, something that made them shiver, although they could not say precisely what it was.

But what could they do? They could not quit. They would not be allowed to quit. Then, too, they hoped that if they stayed in the militia their own lives and those of their families might possibly be spared. And some of them hoped also that they might be able to help others. After all, they still wore uniforms.

And so they set out to do the work that most of them hated. And most of them hated themselves for doing it.

Somehow the first contingent of four thousand men and women was brought to the Transfer Point on Stawki Street in time. Czerniakow had asked for volunteers, telling the people that they were to be given food and work somewhere in the East. Some of the Jews who felt that whatever awaited them in the East, it could not be any worse than it had been in the ghetto, volunteered at once.

But all kinds of rumors continued to circulate in the ghetto. Transfer Point. What did it mean? Where were they being transferred to? Many Jews who had considered volunteering now decided to wait and see.

Late in the afternoon Auerwald telephoned to Czerniakow to complain about these rumors. "You have got to do something about it," he demanded.

"What can I do?" Czerniakow countered. "It is not my fault that the Jews no longer trust anything you do."

Auerwald shouted, "I'm sending you an appeal which you are to sign. We'll have posters everywhere in the ghetto."

Shortly afterward the appeal of which Dr. Auerwald had spoken was put on Czerniakow's desk. The mayor began to read:

1. In view of the false information circulating in the Jewish Quarter in Warsaw concerning the resettlement, the Jewish Council in Warsaw has been empowered by the authorities to announce that the resettlement of the part of the population which does not produce for the German war effort in the Jewish Quarter will take place in the Eastern territories.
2. It is in the interests of the population itself that the resettlement be carried out within the time indicated. The Jewish Council in Warsaw asks the persons subject to resettlement not to hide or avoid resettlement, since that would make the task more difficult.
3. In the interests of the bulk of the Jewish population of Warsaw it is indicated that persons subject to resettlement, who live in the progressively designated houses, shall report voluntarily to the assembly point at 6/8 Stawki Street. According to assurances we have received, families that report voluntarily will not be separated.

Czerniakow read the document twice. The ink dried in the pen which he was holding ready to sign. But he did not sign.

He sat at his desk for many hours without stirring. He did not answer the telephone when it rang. Nor did he answer his secretaries when they came in to ask him something. He simply sat there staring off into space.

It was toward midnight when he came to life again. With a determined movement he took the telephone and asked that he be connected with Dr. Auerwald. It was some time before the man on duty located Dr. Auerwald in one of the Warsaw night clubs. When he finally came to the telephone, Czerniakow could hear violins playing soft dance music. "I called to tell you that I am not going to sign the appeal which you have sent me," Czerniakow said.

"You are not going to—— What did you say?"

Czerniakow repeated his statement.

"I order you to sign immediately," the Nazi shouted. "I'll have you arrested if you don't."

"I don't think you will arrest me," Czerniakow said quietly.

Dr. Auerwald laughed. He had drunk too much. "Of course we won't arrest you. It was just a joke. You know it was just a joke, don't you? We have been getting along fine so far, haven't we? Look! You are not going to make any difficulties. We don't want any trouble just now. We want things to go smoothly. Now if you are afraid that you might be evacuated yourself——"

"I assure you, I am not afraid. If I were I would never have taken on the job of running the ghetto. I would have gone out of the country while there was still time."

"Of course, of course. It is just that we don't want any trouble just now, don't you see?" The music had become louder, and Dr. Auerwald had to shout to make himself heard. "I can do a lot for you. I can arrange for you to live outside the ghetto if you so prefer. After all, we want to treat the people well who are helping us."

"But I don't want to help you!" Czerniakow was shouting too. It was one of the few times that this usually calm and composed man lost his serenity completely.

"I don't understand. What is this? You seemed quite reasonable this morning."

"Nothing has happened except that I think I know now what it is all about. You told me that you wanted to resettle our people so that they could work for you. At the same time you instructed our police that the infirm and the old should be taken before the others. The infirm and the old—the only ones who could not do any work. But you don't want to make them work. You want to murder them. You want to murder all of them!"

"Lies!" Dr. Auerwald was frantic. "Typical Jewish lies!"

"And what happened in Lublin?" There was no answer. "It's no use. You are going to kill them, all of them, sooner or later. Today it is four thousand. Tomorrow it may be more. I know. I think I have known for a long time, only I did not dare to admit it even to myself."

"But I assure you! I give you my word of honor as a German officer . . ."

Czerniakow replaced the receiver without another word.

He continued sitting at his desk, oblivious to everything about him. Slowly he tore up the appeal which he was supposed to sign. Yes, he had known for some time that there was no way of saving the Jews. Perhaps he should have said so a long time ago. Perhaps he should have raised his voice to warn his brothers. Perhaps he should have forced the Nazis to kill him, and thus made it plain to everybody in the ghetto that the Jewish Council was not willing to play the game of the Nazis.

But would it have helped? Would anything have been changed? Could any lives have been saved? Was there any way of resisting the Germans?

At last he got up. He went through the offices where a few employees were still working. He said that he was tired and was going to try to get some sleep. Slowly he walked up the one flight of stairs to his private quarters, where he sat down and prepared to write two letters, one to a friend, another to his wife.

He wrote that he no longer could be a party to the crime that was being committed against his people. He had stayed at his post as long as he possibly could. He had tried in every possible way to collaborate with the Nazis—in the hope of being able to help those who had trusted in him.

Now it was clear that he could not save them. Now he knew that all his attempts to get along with the Nazis, to play their game in order to save the lives of innocent ones, had been in vain.

So Adam Czerniakow swallowed the poison which he had carried with him constantly since he had taken over the leadership in the ghetto. It was the only way he could take.

Dr. Auerwald was notified of Czerniakow's suicide early the following morning and he immediately reported it to Governor Fischer. There was quite a scene. The governor was afraid that the mayor's death would create precisely the effect Czerniakow had wanted it to create: it would warn the Jews of their impending fate and drive them into a panic. Certainly it would make things much more difficult for the Nazis, who had hoped that the Jews would let themselves be taken away like so many cattle.

Dr. Fischer decided that something had to be done fast. A new head of the ghetto had to be found, a man who was more dependable than Czerniakow from the Nazi point of view. This man, the perfect collaborationist, was Mark Lichtenbaum, who succeeded Czerniakow in office. The appeal which Czerniakow had refused to sign should be posted in the ghetto immediately, with the signature of Czerniakow affixed to it. Perhaps people would fall for it.

"I doubt it, though," Fischer remarked. "I wish he had not killed himself. It makes things so much more complicated."

Since there was nothing else to do, Fischer had Czerniakow's widow arrested as a hostage. She and her son were killed soon afterward by the Germans.

During the very hours when Czerniakow was arriving at his decision to do away with himself a mass meeting was taking place in Madison Square Garden, New York, to protest against the treatment of Polish Jews in the hands of the Nazis.

One of the messages read during that mass meeting was signed by Franklin D. Roosevelt. It said in part:

> . . . Citizens, regardless of religious allegiance, will share in the sorrow of our Jewish fellow citizens over the savagery of the Nazis against their helpless victims. . . . The American people not only sympathize with all victims of Nazi crimes but will hold the perpetrators of these crimes to strict accountability on a day of reckoning which will surely come.
>
> I express the confident hope that the Atlantic Charter and the just world order to be made possible by the triumph of the United Nations will bring

the Jews and oppressed people in all lands the four freedoms which Christian and Jewish teachings have largely inspired.

Another message was sent by Prime Minister Winston Churchill:

. . . The Jews were Hitler's first victims, and ever since they have been in the forefront of resistance to Nazi aggression.

All over the world Jewish communities have made their contribution to the cause of the United Nations, and on behalf of His Majesty's Government in the United Kingdom I welcome your determination to help as gladly as I acknowledge the eager support which the Jews of Palestine above all are already giving. Over ten thousand are now serving with British forces in the Middle East; more than twenty thousand are enrolled in various police formations in Palestine and, as in this country, great numbers are employed in that front line constituted by pursuits and industries essential for the prosecution of war industries and in various services for civil defense. . . .

The following day was Tishah b'ab, the ninth day of the month of Ab, which the Jews celebrate as a day of fasting and mourning, in memory of the destruction of the Temple of Jerusalem by Titus, son of the Roman Emperor Vespasian, almost two thousand years before.

On this day of Tishah b'ab in 1942 the Jews of Warsaw had more reason than ever to think of the long-ago destruction of their temple at the hands of the Romans. They met in cellars and in back rooms, and wrapped themselves in their prayer shawls and prayed:

"Mark, O Lord, what has befallen us!
Look upon us, and see our disgrace!
Our heritage has been turned over to aliens,
Our homes to foreigners.
We have become orphans, without a father;
Our mothers are like widows.
Our drinking water we have to buy;
Our wood comes only by purchase.
With a yoke on our necks we are persecuted.
We toil without rest."

On this day the Nazis once more arrested half of the members of the Jewish Council. They posted notices all over the ghetto, announcing that every Jew would be deported except those who were employed in German factories or in the office of the Jewish Community Council or as members of the Jewish police force. They had given up any attempt to mask their intentions. For they realized—as the Nazis everywhere in the world realized—that the time had passed when their lies had any effect. People everywhere had begun to wake up. People realized now that Hitler was not just another enemy against whom one could fight just another war. They realized at last that Hitler and the Germans were determined to exterminate millions of human beings. They wanted to do something to stop it.

But they were too late. The mass murder had already begun.

Chapter XII

The Street

Gruppenfuehrer Mende had sent for Professor Balaban. When the professor arrived at Gestapo headquarters, Mende pointed to a chair. Balaban ignored the gesture. He looked at the Nazi, wondering what he wanted.

Mende smiled slightly. "As you wish, Herr Professor. I just thought you might be tired."

"You are very considerate."

"I am not sure that I like your tone."

Balaban did not answer.

Mende got up, went to the window, and looked out. Without turning around he said, "After all, there is nothing you can complain about, Professor Balaban. You have not been touched."

"You have a strange way of putting things, Herr Gruppenfuehrer."

Mende decided to face the other man. "You are looking quite well. I mean, considering the circumstances . . ."

The professor stroked his long white beard. "You mean your men have not cut off my beard yet. I suppose I have to be grateful for that." The professor was referring to the document which he and all the other members of the Jewish Council carried with them, a document made out and signed by the governor, which said that the members of the Jewish Council must not be touched.

"You be grateful that you are still alive!" Mende's voice betrayed his irritation. "Herr Professor, don't let us misunderstand each other. I am not at all in favor of everything that has happened in the ghetto. I do not approve of cutting off the beards of old men. But you know our soldiers must have some fun."

"I suppose it also comes under the heading of fun that they kill people and take them away, God only knows where?"

"I am not the one who gives the orders."

Again there was a slight pause. Then Balaban asked wearily, "May I ask why I have been sent for?"

"Herr Professor, I have taken the opportunity of making myself a bit familiar with your works." Mende glanced at a paper that lay on his desk. "You are quite a famous writer, Herr Professor. You have written some very important books on the history of Poland."

Balaban made no comment.

"And how is your new book progressing, Herr Professor?"

"My new book?"

"Yes, your new book. I am informed that you are working on a new manuscript."

Mende played with a pencil on his desk. He was smiling.

"Your spies seem to be everywhere. I did not think that it made any difference to you that I write or what I write."

"My dear professor, you underestimate yourself. I can well imagine that such a famous historian as yourself could write a very exciting book on these exciting times through which we are living."

"Perhaps. But you would hardly like to read it, Herr Gruppenfuehrer."

Mende decided to ignore Balaban's last remark. "An exciting book. I can see you writing it—the history of the Warsaw Ghetto."

"What are you driving at?"

"How about writing such a book? Signed by you it would have the value of a document. I think we could arrange for it to be printed in many languages and distributed in many countries."

"I see. I who have written about thousands of years of great Jewish deeds am now to write about the greatest suffering ever inflicted upon Jews. It's a good example of your kind of sense of humor, or shall we say your sadism?"

Mende smiled again. 'Well, no. Look at it another way. You mustn't necessarily write about the sufferings. . . . Of course there is a war on and naturally there are hardships. . . . But on the other hand you could point out that we have tried to do our best . . . that we have gone to a great deal of trouble to solve the Jewish problem. The creation of the ghetto . . . the creation of reservations . . . You cannot deny that we have tried to do constructive work. If you could point this out in your book . . ."

Balaban had difficulty to keep himself in check. "You mean I should write an apology for National Socialism?"

"I am not trying to say anything of the sort." Mende's voice sounded slightly irritated. "I am just outlining your book as I see it. Do not forget that we are in a position to do you a favor, too. On the other hand, if you persist in refusing the offer . . ." He shrugged.

After a moment Balaban said, "You want me to write the history of the ghetto. Well, I will write such a history. Beyond this I cannot promise you anything. You will have to be patient till the book is ready."

Mende got up. "That's better. I knew that you were an intelligent man. Don't waste any time." He was seeing the professor to the door. "I tell you what I'll do. I am going to see that you have a room all to yourself. You can't possibly work where you live now . . . with all those people. I'll make the necessary arrangements at once. Is there anything else I can do?" He opened the door.

Balaban turned around. "I don't think so. Anyhow, you are furnishing me with the material for the book, I suppose."

That same afternoon he was notified that he was to move to the Jewish Community Building. He took his few belongings there and was given a spacious room—the room in which they had found Adam Czerniakow's body ten days before.

He had hardly installed himself in his new quarters when a man came to see him who in the past had been used by the Jewish Council as a courier between the Warsaw Ghetto and other Jewish communities.

"It is about the Medem Sanatorium," the man said, his lips trembling.

The Medem Sanatorium had been founded and maintained by the

Jewish Workers' Organization. It cared for sick children of the lower classes, rescuing them from the slums of Warsaw and Lodz. It was one of the finest and most modern institutions of its kind in Poland. At the outbreak of the war there were two hundred and fifty children there and, thanks to the noble efforts and sacrifices of the staff, the Medem Sanatorium had been able to continue its work even after the Nazi occupation. Balaban knew the Medem Sanatorium well. He had been there only a few weeks before the war broke out. He was happy to see the small children convalescing in pleasant surroundings where they could play on green grass and lie in the sun and get well again. He had sat in their classes and watched them give performances of a play they had written themselves. He had seen and heard them laugh happily—they were happier than they had ever been before. When he left he had promised himself to come back soon. After all, the Medem Sanatorium was only a few miles from Warsaw. But then came the war. . . .

Now Professor Balaban learned what had become of the Medem Sanatorium and the happy children who had been there only a few days ago. And while the courier told his story, his voice trembling, sometimes too overcome with emotion to continue his report, Balaban saw once more before his eyes these happy, laughing children. . . . They hadn't laughed so much since the Germans came in, because they often went hungry, in spite of the fact that the teachers deprived themselves of most of their food rations so that they could give them to the children.

Then, on the first day of August, the sanatorium was surrounded by Ukrainian and Latvian police, led by Gestapo men. The Germans went inside, called the teachers together, and told them, "We are under orders to shoot the children. Now don't get excited. It is not you we want to shoot; it is the children. You may leave the premises. You are free."

The teachers were horror-stricken. They refused to leave. They would not accept their freedom at that price. They said, "Let the children go. Take us instead. The children have not yet begun living. We have lived our lives."

The Germans looked at each other. They did not understand. Then they shrugged their shoulders. If that was what the teachers wanted . . .

The teachers were allowed to go to the children who had been pushed in front of the main house and were crowding there trembling, frightened to death. The teachers joined them. Then came the Germans with machine guns.

It did not take long for them to mow them all down. Then they set the houses on fire.

The next morning Jewish gravediggers from a small neighboring town arrived to bury the little corpses. . . .

Long after the courier had left him, Balaban remained in his room, unable to take his thoughts away from the children of the Medem Sanatorium. He stared at the white sheet on the desk. He took out from a drawer the manuscript of the history of the ghetto. He was going to write now. . . . No, he could not write. He could not forget the children. He saw them before him, swaying and falling under the German machine-gun fire. He saw it like a slow-motion film. He saw every face, the expression of surprise and pain on each of these faces.

"Why do I have to know all this?" he murmured. "Why must I see all this? It is too heavy a burden. I don't want to know, I don't want to see." His shoulders sagged, and he broke down, burying his face on the desk, crying for those whom he had seen suffer and die and for whom he was dying a thousand deaths every day.

Later he went out. In front of the building he passed the deputy police commissioner, little swarthy Jacob Lejkin, who seemed to be in a great hurry. "I am so terribly overworked, Professor Balaban," the former lawyer murmured. "Every day another action. I don't get any sleep any more with all these actions." The Jewish police called the daily deportations of their Jewish brethren "actions." Balaban thought grimly that it was just too bad that Lejkin did not get enough sleep. He did not like him any better than he ever had.

Balaban listened awhile to the Jewish policemen who were standing around in front of the building. Most of them had their loaves of bread under their arms. They were discussing in a calm, matter-of-fact way today's "action" and tomorrow's probable "action." One said, "Tomorrow the action starts at six in the morning. What an awful time!"

Balaban was revolted at such a display of callousness. But he corrected himself; it was not their fault. Human beings got used to everything. This was what they had to do every day, and they had become used to it.

The next day Dr. Ringelblum, Balaban's pupil and friend, called on the professor in his new home. They saw each other several times a week, since they worked together in the Cultural Department. Often Ringelblum would accompany Balaban on his long walks through the ghetto.

The old man told his friend about his interview with Mende. "It won't be long now. One day Mende will want to read what I have written. I may be able to hold out on him for a while, but he is nobody's fool. In the end he will find out that I have not precisely filled the assignment he gave me."

"But there must be something we can do."

"There is nothing. Of course I could have told him right away that I would not do it—and that would have been the end. Perhaps it would have been better. I don't know. It is not that I want to live. I do not want to live any more than poor Czerniakow wanted to live. But perhaps I should live for a while longer to see what is happening, to bear witness . . ."

It was shortly after noon when the professor and Dr. Ringelblum left the building. Children and old people were crowding the sidewalk trying to sell their few pitiful possessions—some secondhand garments, old, broken household goods—anything to get a little money for their daily needs. But their hearts were not in the selling. Even while they shouted their wares they seemed to listen for some faraway noise. At any moment a car with Nazis might turn around the corner and shooting begin. At any moment the streets now so crowded with people might be deserted.

The only time when the streets of the ghetto were halfway normal was around five o'clock in the morning. That was the time when the Jews could be certain that no Nazis would be around. The torturers did not like to get up that early.

Then the streets were crowded. Everybody was there. Most of the women were looking for food. Their husbands were trying to reach friends and relatives, to find out something about those of their family who had already been taken away.

Around six o'clock one could see Jews in groups of ten or twenty marching through the ghetto toward one of the gates, led by special German police called *Werkschutz* (Workers' Protectors). They were taken to German-owned factories, where they spent the whole day. If they did not march fast enough, some of the German policemen would hit them with the butts of their rifles. Wherever they passed, the Jews would look after them with envy in their eyes. The lucky ones! They had the documents! They were not going to be sent to Stawki Square, to the Transfer Point.

The Jews would continue to roam the streets till seven or sometimes eight o'clock. But by eight the streets were deserted. At that time the first annihilation squads were due. Sometimes they came earlier to launch surprise attacks, but they could hardly ever surprise the Jews any more. Even without any means of communication, such as telephones, the news that an annihilation squad had entered the ghetto would spread within a few minutes to all of its streets, and the Jews would rush into the nearest house to wait there until the storm had passed.

There was hardly any life on the streets till about six in the afternoon. During these hours the silence was interrupted only occasionally when the annihilation squads came through.

Occasionally, too, cars would pass through with two or three German officers in them. Sometimes these officers would take out their revolvers and shoot at windows or house entrances. Their faces were like iron masks as they engaged in this wanton pastime. They did not even enjoy it. They just felt that they had to shoot from time to time.

The "action" sometimes took place early in the morning, but most of the time shortly after noon, and by four or five o'clock the streets of the ghetto would be filled with long processions of men, women, and children—the Jews who had been rounded up and were being brought into the Transfer Point on Stawki Street. The daily average was about three thousand. They were herded to the Transfer Point in many groups of two or three hundred each, marching three in a row, Jewish policemen with clubs in hands marching on the outside of the columns, and German soldiers with guns and whips in the vanguard and rear guard of the processions. Most of the Jews carried bags on their shoulders. Some of them had cards or papers in their hands—their last hope that they might be released at the Transfer Point.

The columns had to walk pretty fast. If an old man stumbled or an old woman leaned against a wall for support, the Germans would beat them over the head. If they felt like it, they just shot at those who could not keep the pace. Then they hurried on. They did not even look back to see what had become of their victim.

The Jews marched on in silent despair, looking neither to the right nor to the left. . . . Transfer Point. That was all they thought of. Transfer Point. With every step nearer to Transfer Point they became more terrified. They could not think of anything else. They could not think beyond Transfer Point. There was nothing beyond Transfer Point—Stawki Square was the end of the world.

When they had passed, silence fell once more in the streets of the ghetto.

Professor Balaban was looking after the group of Jews being marched off to Transfer Point.

Dr. Ringelblum said, "You take things too hard, Professor. Why do you insist on exposing yourself to all this? You can't help. None of us can help. You know what is going on. Why must you see every day for yourself? Come. I'll see you home."

"You are right. I have asked myself the same question a hundred times. Why do I have to see all this? But I must. There is something in me which forces me—against my will, against my wish not to see, not to have to face all the dreadful things which are happening. I don't know. There is something that tells me that I must not make things easy for myself, that if I refuse to know what is going on I will be as guilty of what is done as if I were doing it myself."

"But if we could do something—anything at all. If we could fight them . . ."

"There isn't much fighting an old man like me can do. Or is there? I could fight in my way. By writing down what I am seeing. By arousing those who will read what I have written to protest against what they read there."

Ringelblum remained silent.

Balaban smiled. "I know what you are thinking. Nobody is ever going to read what I am writing now. I know it, but still I don't believe it. They will destroy my manuscript, of that I am sure. But I believe that they will not erase the thoughts I have thought and written down—if the thoughts and the words are strong enough. I believe that they will not be lost. I believe that they will somehow pervade the walls which the Nazis have built around us. I believe they will be taken up somewhere in the world by others, perhaps years after I have recorded them."

At six o'clock the worst would be over. Jews would come out of their houses and cellars again, and for a brief time they would rush around, more afraid, more frantic than ever, but somehow never quite losing hope that something might happen to help them escape.

It was during these hours that the never-ending search for the documents, for the lifesaving identity cards, was enacted all over again. It was then that the straw men of certain Gestapo officers did a thriving business selling fake papers to the Jews—papers which did not mean a thing, but for which the Jews often gave their last penny. The worthless paper which they acquired in this way at least gave them the illusion of safety for a day or two. A few of them even got by with these fake papers and were set free at the Transfer Point. But that was only at the beginning. Later the Germans hardly even looked at these certificates when they were presented to them. They just took them and tore them up.

The Jews learned this—but they did not change their pathetic conviction that the little paper, the document which said they were working for a German firm and that they must not be taken away, would save their lives, somehow. So they went on hunting for these papers, imploring the help of anyone who they thought might know some member of the Gestapo, or who might have some connection with some German authority, to help them get their precious certificates.

Dusk was falling. The streets were still crowded. Everybody seemed to speak at the same time. Slowly Balaban and his pupil moved among the Jews, looking here, looking there, taking everything in.

Then suddenly there was a hush. Everyone looked in one direction. They saw a strange procession coming down the street. It was led by a tall, elderly man with long hair and flowing beard and kindly eyes looking out from a grave, yet serenely calm, face. He carried a two-year-old child in his arms and was followed by several hundred other children, walking three in a row and holding each other by the hand.

The crowd was silent as the procession passed by. They all knew the tall man with the saintlike face. It was Dr. Janusz Korczak, the famous writer and educator, who was also the director of a Jewish orphan asylum in Krochmalna Street.

Balaban knew that the Germans had decided to evacuate the orphanage and to deport the children. But he was astonished to see Dr. Korczak, since he knew that a special order had come from Berlin not to touch the famous man. Evidently the Nazis were afraid of world reaction if anything should happen to Dr. Korczak.

But for once things did not go to their liking. Dr. Korczak refused to leave the little ones to whom he had devoted so many years of his life. Like the tutors in the Medem Sanatorium, he told the Nazis that he would share the fate of his children. When they were told to leave, he, too, left.

The children's procession moved slowly. From time to time Dr. Korczak turned around to nod and smile at the children, and for a second their frightened eyes smiled a reply. They walked quietly. None of them spoke, none of them cried. They did not look at the people standing on the sidewalk. Balaban had the feeling that they would never speak or look at anything again. Here and there a woman in the watching crowd gave a sob as the children passed by. Others stood still, their eyes on the pavement, till the children had gone. They could not endure the look of these children who seemed so completely reconciled to an unknown fate, so much feared by most of the grownups in the ghetto.

The children never reached the Transfer Point. Instead they were sent to the cemetery which lay in the northeast of the ghetto. There they were shot. Dr. Korczak, who steadfastly refused to leave the cemetery, was killed last.

After eight in the evening the Jews would again disappear from the streets. It was not so much on account of the curfew, but because then the Germans, having eaten and drunk their fill, would start their individual hunts in the ghetto. Now was the time when German officers would get into rickshas drawn by poor Jews and whip them through the streets, looking around as they passed by for some victim whom they could catch with a lasso around the neck and force him to come along.

This was the time, too, when the Lithuanians and the Latvians, in case they had not reached their quota of murders during the day, would appear again to better their record. And sometimes, when surprise "actions" were scheduled for early the next morning, a few houses would be blockaded during this relatively late hour. The Germans and their satellites would come in cars, direct their spotlights against the blockaded houses, and start their searches. This nightmare sometimes continued till midnight.

There was no more sleep for the ghetto. There was not an hour within the twenty-four hours of the day when any of them had a feeling of anything approaching security. Even during the early morning hours Balaban found some people rushing around from house to house. Then the Gestapo-protected trucks loaded with foodstuffs would drive through the gates of the ghetto. Then the Jews tried to obtain some of the food which had been smuggled into the ghetto, when those who could paid small fortunes for a pound of bread or a scrap of butter or for some fruit or vegetables.

Professor Balaban wandered around most of the night in spite of the darkness—the curfew did not apply to members of the Jewish Council. Sometimes he stopped a moment, took out his notebook, and scribbled something in it. Then he continued on his way, arriving in his room in the Jewish Community Building only an hour or two before dawn. He sat down at his desk. He began to write his history of the ghetto. After a few lines he stopped and put away the pen. He thought of Mende. Mende wanted him to write a book to prove to the world that the Nazis were not so bad as it might seem. The conquerors wanted the victims to bear witness for them, to write the history of their own defeat and annihilation.

The Nazis didn't even want a history, they wanted a falsification of history. They wanted praise where only curses could apply. They wanted lies which could have been written by anybody, signed by somebody whom the world might believe.

Balaban was not going to write them.

He walked over to the window and opened it. It was very quiet now. Balaban knew that nobody in the ghetto was asleep. He knew that they were waiting inside their houses and cellars, huddled together, trembling and fearful, not daring to think what the next morning might bring.

And then came dawn.

Slowly Professor Balaban returned to his desk. He began to write. He wrote the story of these frightened, shivering, helpless people.

Chapter XIII

The House

On the front door of the house at 6 Walicow Street, from which Professor Balaban had moved, a notice was now pasted, which read:

I hereby announce to the inhabitants who are subject to deportation that, in accordance with the orders of the authorities, all persons who report voluntarily for deportation on the days of July 29, 30, and 31 will be supplied with food—i.e., three kilograms of bread and one kilogram of marmalade.

The gathering point and the place for the food distribution is Stawki Square, at the corner of Dzika Street.

The Chief of the Militia

Warsaw, July 29, 1942

The people who lived in the house studied the order silently. Stawki Square. Transfer Point. They had no intention whatever of going there voluntarily. They refused even to go near the place. They felt that unknown and horrible dangers awaited them there. For who knew what had become of those people who had already left the Transfer Point?

Let us look a bit at this house at 6 Walicow Street.

It was a big house: five stories facing the street, a courtyard, and in the rear five more stories. At one time, before the war, about one hundred and twenty people had lived in this house, all of them prosperous members of the upper middle class, living comfortable, well-ordered lives in spacious five- or six-room apartments. Then, when the ghetto came into existence, every room was made into an apartment for a family of newcomers, and the number of tenants soon swelled to more than a thousand. Families of five and six persons were huddled together into one tiny room.

At eight o'clock came the curfew, and the gates to the house were closed, not to be opened again until six the next morning. The opening and closing of the gates was attended to by the janitor.

Before the war the janitor of such a house was usually a Pole of the working classes. Since the establishment of the ghetto, only Jews could be janitors in Jewish houses. The job of janitor was now regarded by the Jews as a very desirable one, and former lawyers and teachers regarded themselves as very fortunate if they could get such a job. In a way the janitor was the master of the house. He knew what was going on in every apartment and every room. He knew who had food and where he got it from, and if he opened the gates for anyone after curfew, he was certain to get a large tip.

The janitor of the house at 6 Walicow Street had formerly been a well-known lawyer in Cracow and a member of one of its most prominent families, until he was forced to flee from the Germans with his wife and two daughters, carrying the few possessions they were able to save in a few suitcases. Now this once well-known lawyer was very happy to be able to have a position as janitor.

On the first floor, in a small back room, lived Mr. and Mrs. Spielglass. Mr. Spielglass had once owned several factories in Warsaw, and he and his wife had lived in a beautiful modern villa there. When he had to move into the ghetto he could not, of course, take his furniture with him, but he managed, nevertheless, to take along quite a few suitcases and packages full of valuables—jewels, silver and gold objects, and Persian rugs. Mr. Spielglass, therefore, in spite of the small space in which he had to live, was considered one of the richer men in the ghetto and was generally an object of envy to all the other tenants of the house.

In the first place, he could still buy food at the black market, no matter what the price. He also could, and did, use his money or his jewels to continue participating in profitable business deals—business as usual, since life in Warsaw went on as usual. Spielglass did not see why he should not invest some of his money in transactions which were consummated outside of the ghetto, such as the buying or selling of large quantities of goods, the financing of a new store or restaurant, et cetera. The man who arranged for these deals was an old friend of Spielglass, a Pole. He was cut in, of course, as was also a Gestapo man who closed his eyes when the Pole got in touch with Spielglass once or twice a week.

But Mr. Spielglass was by no means left alone to enjoy his business deals in peace. The fact that he possessed valuable stones and objects of gold and silver was well known to a number of Gestapo men, and every three or four weeks some of them would come to pay him a visit, supposedly to look for anti-Nazi printed material. They did not search very hard for it, however, because they knew very well that he had nothing of the sort in his possession. That was only the excuse they gave for coming to see him. Their visits were always very brief, lasting only long enough for him to hand over a few large bank notes or a diamond or two, after which they said good-by and went away, leaving him unmolested until the next visit. But Mr. Spielglass always knew that there would be a next visit.

When the deportation of the Jews started, Mrs. Spielglass became very upset and wept for days and nights. Mr. Spielglass did not like this. He thought that times were bad enough as it was, and that his wife should know better than to make both him and herself miserable. Furthermore, he insisted, there was no reason for her to get nervous. In the first place, there were his excellent Gestapo contacts. Nothing would happen—not to him, at least. Things were not so bad as they looked, either, he maintained. Had not the Jewish Council declared that only a certain part of the population of the ghetto—only those who could be regarded as ballast, those who were unable to work in the ghetto and to support themselves—was to be evacuated? And even those had nothing to fear.

Mrs. Spielglass, however, was not reassured by her husband's arguments, but continued to mourn and lament until Mr. Spielglass, in desperation, would leave their tiny room and visit some of their neighbors, hoping to find reassurance and calm there. Sometimes he would go across the corridor and visit Mrs. Wilinska, who lived in another, even smaller, room than he and his wife occupied. They had known Mrs. Wilinska before the war. Her house, in the city of Lodz, had been famed as the meeting place of the Polish intelligentsia; her husband, Mr. Wilinski, the owner of a large factory, spent a great deal of money to encourage young writers and artists. And at her soirees one could meet well-known writers, musicians, and artists of the day.

Then came the war. Their two sons were drafted, and Mr. Wilinski put himself at the disposal of the Polish government. When the Nazis were about to enter Lodz, Mrs. Wilinska fled to Warsaw. On her way she was robbed of all her possessions. When she arrived she had nothing except what she wore. She tried in vain to get in touch with her husband and sons, but for a long time she could find no trace of them whatsoever. Later she learned that they had all been killed.

Mrs. Wilinska had to make a living. But she had never been trained to do any work. A friend of her husband's gave her a few pounds of sugar—black-market sugar, of course. And now she went from house to house selling a lump here and a lump there. Hardly anyone who had known the beauitful and elegant Mrs. Wilinska before could recognize her now. She always wore the same dress, the same wooden sandals. Her face had become a mask. Her eyes seemed to look through the people she met without seeing them. They were eyes which could no longer cry—but who cared? Everybody had worries and troubles enough of his own in the house at 6 Walicow Street.

Mr. Spielglass fled to Mrs. Wilinska because she at least did not cry like his wife. Here he could continue to indulge in his wishful thinking. No, there was no sense in getting excited and there was certainly no sense in getting angry at the Germans. There was nothing to do but to obey them. After all, they were not going to carry out all their threats. They just wanted to frighten the people in the ghetto, that was all. But Mr. Spielglass was not afraid. They would not touch him. He didn't like them, of course; but if he could have his way . . . But that was another story. It was not the time yet to talk about such things. One had to be patient.

Occasionally Mr. Spielglass would meet Dr. Levy, a physican who also lived across the corridor. Physicians had certain privileges. They could go and come whenever they needed to, regardless of the curfew. They, of course, took a certain chance on getting killed, because the Nazis had an ugly habit of shooting before they asked whom they were shooting at.

Mr. Spielglass did not like Dr. Levy, because the small doctor with the thick glasses did not share his views. He was of the opinion that there was no sense in playing along with the Nazis. He ridiculed the rumors, allegedly from "authoritative sources," which said that the General Government considered the Warsaw Ghetto a representative working center and that its inhabitants would not be deported. Dr. Levy declared that these rumors were spread by the Gestapo and by Jews who were in their pay or who collaborated with them for other reasons. These men—who, Dr. Levy declared, should be shot—tried very hard to counteract the effect of tales spread by Jews who had escaped from Lodz and Lublin, tales about the tens of thousands of Jews who were being killed there. The Gestapo and their friends said that there was nothing to these rumors and that they were fabricated by Communists.

Mr. Spielglass had never liked the Communists. Sometimes he suspected that Dr. Levy was a Communist himself—particularly after Dr. Levy brought home one night a leaflet in which the Jews were asked to defend themselves with every means at their disposal and to resist deportation in every way possible.

"I won't talk to you any more, Dr. Levy," Mr. Spielglass declared excitedly. "You are mad! If any such leaflet as that is found in our house, we'll all be taken away by the Gestapo."

This was on the evening of July 30.

That same night Mr. Spielglass was once more visited by Gestapo men. This time his old friends made a thorough search. They took all the jewels and gold they could find and then asked Spielglass and his wife to step into the courtyard for a little chat.

There were two shots. The inhabitants of the house at 6 Walicow Street never saw the Spielglasses again.

In the cellar of the house, once used to store the coal supply, lived more than a hundred refugees who had come from the smaller cities and towns around Warsaw, from which they had been expelled during the German march on the Polish capital or in the first part of the year 1940. They had brought almost nothing with them. Most of them did not even possess a pillow on which to rest their heads.

Among the poorest of these poor there were many formerly wealthy businessmen, mill and factory owners, well-to-do physicians and lawyers. Some of them were so old and broken that they could not do any work. They would go out into the street and stand there for hours on end, and then, finally, taking all their courage in their hands, would ask a passer-by for a "loan" of two or three zlotys. Later begging became a little easier for them. They did not mention the word "loan" any more. They were happy when they could get a piece of bread for their starving children.

There was a young girl living in the cellar of the house at 6 Walicow Street. Her whole family was dead. But she still had some good friends outside the ghetto, in Warsaw. Somehow these friends got in touch with her and devised a plan for her escape.

One day the girl said she felt sick. Dr. Levy came to the basement to see her and declared that she was very sick indeed. She was accordingly removed to an apartment where a bed was made available for her, and a few hours later Dr. Levy pronounced the girl dead. He himself supervised her transfer to the cemetery.

Strangely enough, the body never arrived at the cemetery. The girl —who, of course, had not died at all—was smuggled out of the ghetto by her Polish friends. Later she was able to escape from Poland.

Many other inhabitants of the house tried to escape from the ghetto, but it became increasingly difficult to do so. The Germans kept constant watch on the other side of the wall, and if they saw a Jew climbing the wall, they took out their guns and shot to kill.

Sometimes, though, they took their time before they disposed of the victim. One of the inhabitants of the house had somehow been able to smuggle himself out of the ghetto. A German officer saw him and followed him to the Vistula River. The Jew jumped into the river, in an attempt to reach the other side. The officer whistled to his dog, who immediately jumped in after the Jew, reached him, sank his teeth into him, and dragged him back to the officer. Only then did the German take out his revolver and shoot the Jew through the head, patting the bloodhound afterward, in praise of his deed.

In spite of all the odds against them, however, not a day passed that some Jews did not successfully negotiate the walls of the ghetto. The children, in particular, were very adept at climbing over them. There were many children in the house, children of eight and ten, who climbed over the wall every day. If they were small enough, they sometimes managed to slip through the barbed wire, which was still to be found in a few places and which their bigger comrades disentangled for them.

Then they went into the city, where they obtained food, which they brought back into the ghetto. In this way they were able to make a little money and support their families.

There was a widow with two children, a boy and girl of nine and ten, who lived in the back of the house. She did not know that her children climbed the wall of the ghetto every day. The children were hired by somebody else in the house who gave them money to buy food outside the ghetto, where it was five times cheaper than inside. The children brought the food back, and the man who gave them the money would get enough food for himself and his family to live on for a while. In payment he gave the children a few zlotys or some of the food, so that they could take care of their sick mother.

The mother never knew where the food came from. She often asked the neighbors whether they knew anything about it, but no one had the heart to tell the mother about the dangerous activities her children were engaged in, and the children maintained stoutly that they got the food from the community kitchen.

One evening the mother waited in vain for her children. They did not come back. They stayed all day in Warsaw and its suburbs, looking for food. Finally a Polish woman, filled with pity for the hungry-looking children, gave them a whole loaf of bread and a few potatoes.

Happy in their success, they started back to the ghetto and came to the place where their comrades were waiting to help them through the barbed wire. This was a relatively safe spot, because it was usually guarded by an elderly German soldier who had children himself and looked the other way when the Jewish children made their way back into the ghetto. But that evening there was another soldier on guard. He shot the running children in cold blood, hitting them both. They fell down, their blood mingling with the food they were carrying pressed to their tiny starved bodies. Jewish policemen had to carry them away.

Many children of the ghetto perished in this way.

The most envied people in the house were the baker and his family. Bakers in the ghetto were really the aristocracy. They got flour from the Jewish community to bake the bread which was divided among the population. But they always had some flour which they could dispose of as they wished. They gave most of it to help people who were starving, but sometimes they sold it. And so valuable and sought after was flour that every baker in the ghetto had become quite rich by the time the deportations started.

Most of the people became panicky as soon as the evacuation got under way. They were obsessed by only one desire: to stay in the ghetto. True, they led a horrible existence there, but at least they were alive. They feared to exchange the certainty of being alive, under no matter what horrible conditions, for the uncertainty of deportation.

But how could they avoid deportation? There was only one way: They had to work for a German-owned factory. They had to get a document certifying that they were working for German-owned factories. And so everyone began to hunt for a document—any kind of document, any kind of paper with which they could prove that they had a right to stay in the ghetto.

Of course very few of the people could get the highly cherished papers, and the rest began to be very afraid. Many of the inhabitants of the house at 6 Walicow Street no longer dared to come home in the evening because they were afraid the Jewish militia and the Gestapo might arrive any moment to take them away. They no longer dared to go to their places of business because the police might look for them there, too. Many of them hid out in the cellar at the back of the house, but most of them finally came out because they knew they would be found sooner or later anyway. Some of them stayed on in the cellar, but they must have been betrayed, because one evening toward the end of July a few members of the annihilation squad went down into the cellar with a machine gun. There was a lot of noise and a few cries. And then it was silent.

The most prominent—as well as the most hated—man in the house was a Mr. Cohn. He lived alone, but in spite of that he enjoyed the luxury of two rooms. Everybody was afraid of him. They called him "Moishe Gestapowietz" ("Moishe of the Gestapo"). This Cohn was a member of one of the two big gangs of smugglers that worked hand in glove with Gestapo men, smuggling food and other products into the ghetto in exchange for foreign currency, gold, and jewels. Mr. Cohn was, in point of fact, a criminal who had spent many years in prison and who had been liberated by the Gestapo only to serve them in their endeavors to make a great deal of money. He had a partner called Heller, and both of them were protected by some of the highest Gestapo officers in Warsaw.

Once Cohn was asked: "Is it true that there is not one honest Gestapo officer in the city of Warsaw?" He answered cynically, "Oh yes, there are a few honest ones. But they are very expensive."

There was also a second gang of smugglers in the ghetto, a rival to Cohn's gang, which operated under the protection of still another group of Gestapo officials. Its leader was a certain Mr. Ganzweich, who, like Cohn, had been brought into Warsaw by the Gestapo, and for precisely the same reason.

Mr. Ganzweich proceeded to organize a "scientific" diamond hunt. Which is to say that he and his agents set out systematically to discover who in the ghetto possessed any jewels, and to confiscate them. Whenever Ganzweich learned of any source of booty, Gestapo men would appear at the victim's house, take away the precious stones, kill their owner, and leave his body in the courtyard. Ganzweich, of course, got a small cut from every such transaction.

All went well till the Ganzweich clique began to "muscle in" on Cohn and Heller. This also involved the two rival setups within the Gestapo which protected the two gangsters. For a few weeks both gangs even reduced their food prices in an attempt to obtain a monopoly in food smuggling.

But then on the first of August the Ganzweich gang decided to strike hard. A few Gestapo men came to visit Mr. Cohn in his apartment. They took him to the courtyard of the house. Mr. Cohn knew that the game was up. He was not so much afraid as he was angry.

"You bloody Ganzweich dogs!" he cried. "You'll pay for this with your lives!" The Gestapo men laughed and shot him. At the same time a few others visited Cohn's partner, Heller, and liquidated him in the same way.

Ten minutes after Cohn's assassination a car full of Gestapo officers, the silent partners of Cohn and Heller, arrived in front of the house at 6 Walicow Street. They tore upstairs, taking two or three steps at a time. But they were too late to save Cohn.

Two nights later Mr. Ganzweich disappeared from his home. When the people in the house heard about it, they figured that Cohn's friends had kidnaped Ganzweich and shot him. They were right, in so far as the kidnaping went. But Ganzweich was not shot. He convinced his captors that he was worth more to them alive than dead. He was to make a reappearance in the ghetto many months later at a highly dramatic moment.

During the last days of July the Germans began introducing a new feature into the ghetto life. The number of volunteers who came to the Transfer Point had steadily declined. The most pessimistic predictions of Dr. Auerwald proved to be mere wishful thinking. No one in the ghetto was willing to go voluntarily to the Transfer Point. The very sound of the word frightened them. The forced evacuations undertaken by the Jewish militia were not proving any too successful, either. Now units of about twenty to thirty men, composed of Germans, Lithuanians, and Ukrainians, would enter the ghetto and take over certain sections of street blocks or houses. They would then cut those houses off from the rest of the ghetto and search them. Whoever they found was taken to the Transfer Point without any further ado. The technical term for this procedure was "blockading." From the moment the blockading started, the Jews in the ghetto were seized by unbelievable panic. They did not dare to stay in their houses. But then neither did they dare to go to any other house. For there was no knowing which houses would be blockaded next; and there was always the chance that in his flight a Jew would run into a blockade, whereas he might be safe if he stayed at home.

It was even dangerous to be found out of doors at such times, because the blockade units also took people off the street. And then, of course, there were always Captain Reinhard's annihilation squads.

But the Jews had become too much afraid to be capable of judging soberly and logically where their safest place would be. They just kept on running. They ran up and down the streets, in and out of houses, and kept running even inside the houses. They rushed upstairs and downstairs, always seeking new hide-outs, always discarding their plans even before they had rushed a few steps further. They were like rats in a trap.

Early in August a few houses just opposite the house at 6 Walicow Street were being blockaded. At the last moment a number of people who lived in those houses had been able to slip away and get into the house. They were frantic with fear. So were the inhabitants of the house. No one knew when the blockaders would come. There was only one thing to do: wait and be as quiet as possible, so as not to attract the attention of the Nazis.

So they were silent. Every room and corridor was packed. People did not dare to move, though they could scarcely have done so even if they had wanted to, there were so many of them. Only near the windows was there plenty of space. That was a dangerous spot to stand in, for the Germans took pot shots at whoever showed himself there.

A young woman was sitting on the stairs. There was madness in her eyes. In spite of the efforts of those around her to silence her, she cried constantly: "My children! Where are they? Where have they gone?"

The others knew where the children were. They had been taken by the Germans to the Transfer Point a day or two before. But how could they tell her? Suddenly the woman jumped up and, before anybody could restrain her, made her way to one of the windows. There was a shot. The woman dropped. Blood and brains splattered the wall.

The next morning the house at 6 Walicow Street itself was blockaded. "They are coming! They are coming!" the people cried. But none of them could get away. The Germans had surrounded the back and front of the building with Lithuanian and Ukrainian troops.

The people who had lived together with Professor Balaban heard the shouting. Slowly the sick rabbinical student got up from his bed and went to the door. "Where are you going?" the young woman with the little child asked.

"Downstairs. There is no use running away. They'll get me anyhow."

"He is crazy!" shouted the old man whose shop had been taken away by the Germans. He and his wife grabbed two suitcases which they had prepared. They, too, rushed out, but not downstairs. They joined the procession of others in the opposite direction.

The young woman, the child in her arms, remained alone. Her eyes were wide with terror. She could not utter a word. She could not make a step.

All over the house people grabbed the little bags and cartons which they always kept in readiness, not knowing when the moment of their evacuation would come, and all of them tried to get to the fourth and fifth floors. A mad scrambling for the stairs started. There was method in this apparent madness, however, for the Germans, they knew, looked for only a certain number of people, and when their quota was filled they went away until the next time. Those who waited on the upper floors hoped that enough victims would be found below to satisfy the Germans for that day, at least. As for tomorrow—well, tomorrow was another day. Nobody in the ghetto could be sure whether he would be still alive tomorrow.

It was impossible to breathe in the halls and corridors of the top floors. People just stood there, sweating, scarcely breathing, with horrified looks in their red-rimmed, sleepless eyes. They tried to listen, to find out what was going on in the floors below. They heard only occasional shots. But they did not even react to those sounds. They were beyond that. There had been too many shots.

Some of them had documents in their hands that were almost worn to shreds from being taken out so often, folded and refolded. Some of these documents were not worth anything—and the people who held them knew it. But perhaps they would do anyway, just to get by the Germans today.

So they waited. The minutes passed slowly. Then some of them broke under the strain. They could no longer stand the waiting. They elbowed their way through the others to the stairs and went down to meet their fate. They knew that they were lost anyhow. It was better to face the inevitable now than to live on another day or two in constant panic.

And then the Germans came higher. Slowly they moved upstairs, bringing with them a number of Jewish policemen to do the dirty work. The crowd receded, trying desperately to get as far as possible from the Germans, to postpone for another small space the moment when they would be taken away.

The first person they took from the fourth floor was an old deaf-and-dumb Jew who had been living in the cellar. When they grabbed him he tore himself away and ran to the others. He tried to make some sign, convey something to them. He even uttered a few strange sounds. It seemed terribly important to him that they should understand what he tried to convey. But nobody understood him, and anyhow, everybody was much too afraid to do anything about him.

Two storm troopers entered another room, where they found a paralyzed Jewish woman. The family, unable to take her along, must have left her there. The Germans ordered Jewish militiamen to take her down. When they brought her in her chair to the street, one of the storm troopers took out his gun and shot her. The woman did not die immediately. She kept on mumbling and muttering till her body fell from the chair. Perhaps she had been praying.

In the next room the Germans found two old men. They were too old and too weak to move. "Too much bother to carry them down," one of the Germans remarked. And he and one of his comrades pulled the old men from their chairs and threw them out of the window, while others emptied their revolvers at the bodies as they fell.

The blockade had been going on for more than forty minutes. The Germans became nervous and impatient. If people did not move fast enough they simply killed them where they stood.

They rounded up all the people on the fourth and fifth floors. Nobody was left in the house. They even looked in the attic and in the cellar to make certain that they had done a good day's work.

After the Jews had been taken away by the Jewish militia, the storm troopers went through the house again, this time in search of spoil. They ran through the rooms, each one intent on not being outdone by his comrades. They found an unfinished meal on a table or a corpse sprawled on the floor, an unmade bed here, a forgotten suitcase there. Cursing, they tore open drawers and wardrobes. They didn't find much —a few shirts, a few stockings, knives, forks, crumbs of food. But they took everything they could lay their hands on.

After a while they left. The house at 6 Walicow Street became very quiet. The entire blockade had taken less than ninety minutes.

That evening the annihilation squads came through Walicow Street. They took pot shots at the vacant windows of the house at No. 6 and laughed among themselves, thinking of the possible damage and terror they might have caused. They did not know that there was nobody left to get hurt, nobody to care whether or not the windows were broken. After a while they moved on. There were so many other houses on other streets where they could see the people they were aiming at.

Late in the night a few starving Jewish children came by, slipped into the house, and wandered through the rooms, looking for something to put into their hungry mouths. They looked in the most impossible places; they had become wise to where grownups hide their last food. But there was little they could find. They left before midnight.

Now it was quiet again. From time to time the wind would rattle the windows or slam the doors of the deserted house.

Early next morning a man from the Jewish Community Council stopped in front of the house and pasted a sign on the door. It read:

> It is hereby announced, by order of the Delegate for Resettlement Matters, that all Jews working in German enterprises or for the benefit of the Germans are commanded to continue their work during the resettlement. Anyone not complying with this order may expect the heaviest punishment.
>
> THE JEWISH COUNCIL IN WARSAW

Then, having finished pasting the sign on the door, the man took up his pot of paste and his bundle of papers and continued to the next house.

Chapter XIV

TRANSFER POINT

THE VERY WORDS "Transfer Point" made the Jews in the ghetto of Warsaw whimper with fear, made their hair stand on end and their hearts stop beating. If they could help it, they did not even come near "Transfer Point." Those who lived in the neighborhood made wide detours in order not to cross the square on Stawki Street. But none of them could think of anything else these days but the Transfer Point.

There wasn't much to this Transfer Point. It was a square of perhaps one acre, at the northern end of the ghetto, flanked on one side by the large building which had formerly been a hospital and had now become the Resettlement Office. A few rooms were reserved for the

Nazis, who sat there putting together long lists of those to be evacuated and of houses which had been made vacant by the departure of the évacués. Most of the rooms, bare of furniture now, were used as waiting rooms for the Jews who had been brought to Transfer Point and whose trains were not ready yet to depart. There were perhaps two thousand of them thronged into the former hospital. But that was by no means enough. There were thousands more waiting, pressed together on the square.

The Nazis had set up an improvised railway station with tracks which led right to the gates of the ghetto. There were a few wooden barracks for the Nazis who conducted the evacuation. That was all. Even before the Nazis had established the Transfer Point that neighborhood had been unfriendly and uninviting. It was a typical poor district of a factory city. But now the atmosphere reeked of death.

There was no definite schedule for the evacuation of the Jews who were herded into Transfer Point. There were days when no evacuation —or, as the Jewish police called it, "action"—took place. And there were days when many trains left the improvised station, crowded with their human freight. The average was two trains a day, most of them consisting of twenty to thirty freight cars.

The large square was divided in two by the wooden barracks where Nazi officers were stationed. Here the so-called "selection" took place. The Jews would walk slowly by the SS men, who stood on both sides of the barracks. Sometimes some of the Jews would be lucky enough to be sent back to the ghetto. Sometimes their documents were approved of, and sometimes a friendly shop manager intervened for a man whom he needed badly if he was to continue production. But once they had passed the barracks there was no longer any chance of their being sent back. They were herded together near the railroad tracks to wait for the train which was to take them away.

Officially they were still being evacuated for the purpose of resettlement somewhere in the East. Many of the Jews, perhaps most of them, still believed it, because they wanted to believe it. Why, then, did they try so frantically to escape this evacuation? Why did they hide out and scurry about like rats in a trap, to get away before their houses were blockaded? Perhaps they did not know themselves. But the very fact that the Nazis staged the evacuations with such utter brutality spelled nothing good. Even if they did not admit it to each other, the Jews were well aware that one does not shoot people for not running fast enough, if all one wants to do with those people is to resettle them in some other part of the country. There was a contradiction there, and the Jews, in spite of their frantic desire to believe that nothing much would happen, could not help seeing it.

And so they came. . . .

There they came to the Transfer Point: men, women, children.

The announcement had said: "Families who report together will not be separated." This, to many, was a ray of hope in the darkness of their despair. Nothing was too bad if one could suffer it together with those one loved.

But would the Nazis keep their word? Would they not separate families? Once a troop of three or four hundred people approached the Transfer Point. Among them was a father, who was leading his boy of six by the hand and clutching a few-months-old baby tightly against his breast. The mother was not with them. She had been taken away three or four days before. "Families will not be separated. . . ." The father showed his document to one of the storm troopers. The Nazi studied the paper, then nodded. "O.K., you may go back, but the children must leave."

The baby started to cry, as though it had understood. The father stopped for a moment. His son's eyes were on him in terror, but the child did not say a word. Then the man's shoulders straightened. No, he could not leave his children to go on alone. Slowly he tore up his document, grasped the boy's hand again, and passed with the others in the direction of the railroad tracks.

There was a young woman with a little girl. She had been working in a factory. The Polish shop manager came with her to plead with the German officers that she be allowed to stay. He simply had to have her back, he said, because she was one of the few specialized workers he had left. The German nodded. "But the girl has to go."

The young woman fainted. When she was brought to again, her little girl was gone. The woman cried like a wounded animal and called her little girl's name. But there was so much noise that none but those standing next to her could hear. The woman tried to rush past the barracks, searching for her little girl, but a storm trooper blocked her way. No, she must go back; she must work for the German war effort.

And there was an old man, a very old man, perhaps seventy-five or eighty. He could not stand straight. He must once have had a beautiful white beard, but some fun-loving German must have cut it off, for only a few straggling hairs of different lengths hung from his chin. The old man was leading his grandchild, a boy of perhaps ten, by the hand. When he came to the Nazi, the old man fell to his knees. He told the boy's story: His parents had been taken away a few days ago. Now it was the grandfather's turn to go. What was to become of the little boy? "Let me take him with me," he pleaded. "I am all he has. No matter what happens, it will be better for him if I am with him."

The Nazi looked down at the old man. There was a smirk on his face. Frantically the old man grabbed the Nazi's hand and kissed it. "Please . . . please . . . I beg you." The Nazi gave him a kick that threw the old man past him. Then he tore the boy away from him. He said, "Better go home, kid." The boy started to cry. The Nazi laughed. . . .

Contrary to what Governor Fischer may have planned originally, there was no definite system of evacuating the Jews. Since volunteers had almost completely ceased to appear at the Transfer Point, the Nazis came to depend more and more on blockading of houses or entire blocks to fill the necessary quota. The pretense they made at first of evacuating people so that they might be able to work for the Nazi war machine had been dropped long ago. The Nazis grabbed anybody they could grab.

During the month of August the Nazis liquidated all the children's homes, nurseries, and orphanages in the ghetto. Almost every day large groups of children could be seen walking to the Transfer Point. They went as fast as their little feet could carry them, driven steadily on by storm troopers. All the clothing they had with them was the little short pants or skirts and the shirt they were wearing. They were sent away without any luggage. They did not even have a package of food.

They tried to huddle together as they walked or almost ran. They were frightened beyond belief. Some of them cried. But most of them seemed too paralyzed by terror even to cry. From time to time a German would shoot into the air just to frighten them a little more.

At a street corner a few hundred feet from the Transfer Point a group of Jewish women was waiting. When the children approached, one of the women ran up to the German who accompanied them and spoke frantically to him, pointing as she did so to one child in the group. The German shouted at her, pushed her back, and then pulled out his gun and shot her. Now all the children began to cry out, "Mother! Mother!" The German hit several of them over the head with the butt of his revolver. One of the children looked up to a window of a near-by house where a woman could be seen and made an imploring gesture toward her. The German immediately fired a shot at the window. The glass shattered and fell to the street. The woman had disappeared.

The children were driven on. They were led right to the train and forced into one of the freight cars, crowded in so tightly that they could scarcely breathe. Many of them died before the train even started to move. Others went mad with fear.

And still more children came, children whose parents had been taken away days or weeks before, helpless little children against whom the Nazis were conducting a war of annihilation. They made their promise good. They sent the children after the parents.

"Families will not be separated."

Toward the end of August there was a lull in the deportations. For three days no "action" took place. For three days no annihilation squad entered the ghetto. The Jews immediately became optimistic again. Perhaps this was the end of the terror. Perhaps now the Nazis would leave them alone. Perhaps those who had escaped so far could now consider themselves safe.

And then a wonderful rumor spread through the ghetto. It was true. The Nazis were not going to deport any more Jews. They were distributing so-called "life numbers." These were yellow cards with a number written on them and stamped by the Jewish Council. Anyone who held such a card was exempt from deportation—for the time being. German soldiers stood on the street corners distributing the cards. Endless lines of Jews waited to obtain them. But it was by no means certain that all of them would get a card. Some of them were refused for no reason at all. Some of them were given one, but their wives or their children were refused. Many of those tore up their "life number." They did not want to be separated from their families.

The ghetto, only a few weeks ago so hopelessly overcrowded, had by now become much too large. Everywhere there were vacant houses. Sometimes whole street blocks were deserted.

That was what the Nazis had been waiting for. In August and September they began to cut large numbers of blocks out of the ghetto. Except for a few blocks in the southeastern end, the ghetto shrank more and more to the north. By the end of September 1942 the ghetto had become so small that it was hardly a fifth of what it had been when it was first opened in November 1940.

Whenever the Nazis decided to cut another few blocks from the ghetto, the Jews who lived there were ordered to move more to the north. They had only a few days to vacate their former homes. Also they had to report in order to be registered. This device enabled the Germans to locate those who were hiding out in order not to be deported. "Those who will not report," the announcement read, "will be shot."

Once more the mad rush began. Thousands of families hastily collected their few belongings in a frantic attempt to reach the new ghetto frontiers within the given time. Many people believed that that was the end of the evacuation and that they would be left alone in the new, perhaps final, ghetto. Of course twenty-four hours was not enough time to move to other quarters. The Jews who moved had to leave most of their possessions in their old homes, which were to be turned over to the Aryan population of Warsaw. And they were not allowed to lock these old apartments.

Later, after the dead line set by the Nazis, some of them came back to where they had lived before, in the hope of finding what they had left behind and taking it back with them. But there was nothing left. The Nazis, combining business with pleasure, had taken whatever they found. They made no explanations to the former owners. It was easier just to arrest the Jews who had returned to their old homes and take them to the Transfer Point.

For they had no intention of stopping the evacuations. They had only interrupted them for a few days. Once the Jews had settled in what they hoped would become their final domiciles, the wholesale arrests commenced again.

And so once more the sad processions started toward Transfer Point.

Sometimes the évacués had to wait for more than twenty hours before they were packed into a train. They were exposed to rain; they were soaked, cold, hungry, exhausted. There they stood, so many of them that they could not even move. They were not even able to get a drink of water or to wash. There was no place for them to go to attend to their physical needs. The Transfer Point became a vast human latrine. People stood in their own excrement.

Some of them succeeded occasionally in bribing a guard, with the last cent they had, to allow them to escape from the Transfer Point. But for how long? How soon before their time, too, would finally come?

The lull was definitely over. The old routine was on again in full force. Every afternoon between four and five o'clock five to six thousand deportees left the Transfer Point.

In one of the groups was a former Jewish policeman who had been helping with the evacuations. But one day finally he broke down. He could no longer endure seeing the misery of the poor wretches who were being deported or bear the thought that he, a Jew himself, should help the Nazis with their inhuman work, so he had resigned from the force. A few hours later the Nazis picked him up and took him away. Now he, too, was here at the Transfer Point, awaiting deportation.

He was in despair. Not that he was afraid—he was beyond that. He no longer cared what happened to him. But there was his old mother. He had hidden her in a cellar. He had locked her in and had taken the keys away so that nobody would discover her. But if they didn't find her she would starve.

At the Transfer Point, hemmed in so closely by the crowd that he could hardly move, he managed to sketch a diagram on a letter, showing how to get to the hidden cellar. Now he was frantically looking around for somebody to whom he could entrust the diagram and the key. But before he could find anybody he was taken away to the train.

On some days there were even some Jews who came voluntarily to the Transfer Point. They were starving. And the German authorities had let it be known that there were 180,000 kilograms of bread and 36,000 kilograms of marmalade waiting for those who would volunteer to be evacuated. Those who decided to come before they were caught hoped to eat at least once more before they were sent away. But once they were at Transfer Point there was no more talk about bread or marmalade.

Others came because they had convinced themselves—or thought they had convinced themselves—that there was no reason to be afraid of deportation. They had heard about so-called "authentic" letters written by those who had been deported a few weeks before. From the letters it seemed that these people were doing very well. They were living in decent barracks; they had nice work, farming and road work; they were fed three times a day. They even received a few zlotys a day for their work. True, no one had seen any of these letters, but they seemed to be around. A lot of Jews talked about them, anyhow.

The noise at the Transfer Point was incredible. Everybody was trying to talk, as though this was his last chance to say anything. Some of the people who had money tried to get something to eat. Did anybody around them have anything to eat? They would pay anything for a few slices of bread. After all, they did not know how long they would be on the train before they reached their destination. Their children might starve before they arrived. Just a slice of bread or two . . . If they had no money, perhaps somebody would give them a loaf of bread for a shirt or two. They still had a shirt or a watch. How about a loaf of bread for a gold watch?

Everybody talked at once. Those who, in spite of the documents or identification cards they held, had been pushed along near the railroad tracks still clung to the precious papers in the vain hope of still being able to save themselves. They talked to those standing around them about the cards. Surely they would have another opportunity to present the cards before they entered the train. Surely they would be allowed to go back to the ghetto. But then they were pushed still further toward the tracks, and before they could say anything they were inside the cars.

Sometimes a few of them, though, would be saved even at this last moment. Often there were Catholic priests standing near the train with the Gestapo man pointing at this or that Jew. They would talk to the Gestapo man and show him some kind of document, and finally take the man away with them. But they never succeeded in saving a whole family. Sometimes the liberated man would refuse to stay. Sometimes he would follow his rescuer, silent, defeated, apathetic, shoulders sagging. Then, after he had walked with the priest a few steps, he would turn around and look in the direction of the train into which his family had been pushed. He would stand there and just look, not saying anything.

It was unbearably hot at Transfer Point, and the smell was suffocating. Many of the people were too exhausted and weak to voice their despair. They could barely manage to stand on their feet. Others, however, shouted and cried all the time. They were too frightened to be quiet even for a moment. They were afraid they would cease to exist if they could no longer hear the sound of their own voices.

About a hundred people were pushed into each freight car. When the car was filled, it was locked from the outside. Sometimes it stood for hours in the beating sun. Then slowly the train would start to move.

In August more than three thousand of those Jews who were left in the ghetto had been shot, more than a thousand had committed suicide, and more than two thousand had met with "natural" deaths, including starvation.

In September the number of shootings was about the same, although the number of deaths from suicide and other causes had dropped. The reason for this was that the constant evacuation had reduced the number of Jews still living in the ghetto.

One day the Nazis announced that the Jewish hospital could move back into the building on Stawki Square which had been seized by the Nazi authorities at the beginning of the evacuation period. Everybody in the ghetto thought that that meant the deportations were over once and for all. But as soon as the hospital had moved back, all the patients, more than a thousand, together with the medical and technical personnel, were pushed into a waiting train and evacuated.

The trains carrying the deported Jews moved slowly. Outside of Warsaw they would often stop, sometimes for half an hour, sometimes for many hours. But the doors were not opened. Many of those inside died from thirst or exhaustion.

At length they moved slowly on again, making many stops on the way. Within ten or twelve hours all of them eventually arrived at their destination.

It was always the same destination. It was always the village of Treblinka.

Chapter XV

The Man Who Came Back

On one of the trains which left the Transfer Point for Treblinka there was a young Jewish worker who lived in one of the houses included in the blockade. He had been rounded up while he was visiting a friend, Michael Klepfisz. The Nazis had not even looked at his papers. He had had no opportunity to get in touch with either his factory or his family. He was just taken along to the Transfer Point and put on the next train.

He did not know any more about where he was going than did the rest of the passengers. The train stopped quite frequently. Twice the door of the car into which the young man had been pushed was opened. German soldiers beckoned to several elderly people who stood near by, motioning to them to get out, and they were taken away. Not far, though. After only a few minutes those who were left in the train heard some shots. Then the German soldiers returned, and after a while the train moved on again.

It was about twenty hours later that the train finally stopped in Treblinka. Some of the passengers seemed to be relieved when they saw the name of the station. "We are glad that we are going to Treblinka!" they exclaimed. "We have heard that things are quite nice here. There is plenty of food and work for everybody, and nice quarters, too."

But only a few spoke in this way. Most of the Jews were quiet and apprehensive. If they had heard the nice rumors about Treblinka, they evidently did not believe them. There was very little these Jews still believed. They had been disappointed so often.

After a little while the train was switched to a spur track which led on a few miles directly into Camp Treblinka B. And then the cars were opened and the Jews were told to get out.

They gathered on the platform, wondering what would come next. They were to be pleasantly surprised. An SS officer appeared and took his position behind a loud-speaker. He was young and blond and had an easy smile. He began to talk to the Jews.

"Welcome to Treblinka," he told them. "Take it easy. You'll have time; you may rest up; and then we'll see what we can do for you."

The Jews had not heard such words for a long time. They could scarcely believe their ears; and they could scarcely believe their eyes when they lighted on the huge posters pasted on the walls of the station building, which told them in Yiddish that they would soon be sent East to work, while their wives would take care of households. There were specific directions for workmen of different trades: the tailors should go here, the shoemakers one block further, the carpenters to the right, the mechanics to the left, et cetera.

The officer continued: "But before anything else, you'll have to be cleaned up and deloused. You'll have to take a bath and your clothes will have to be disinfected."

Now the men and women were separated. The young man and his companions were led away and told to stand in rows of ten, take off all their clothing, including their boots and underwear. Next they were each given a piece of soap; they were allowed to keep their personal documents. After a while the first hundred men were led away.

A German policeman beckoned to the young man and three others to come forward and take the clothes of the other men to trucks which stood some few hundred feet away. The four Jews began to carry off the bundles of shoes and clothes. By the time they had made the trip several times, the second hundred men had been taken away to the baths. But the first hundred had not yet reappeared. This seemed strange to the young worker.

Another two trips to the trucks and back. Still the first bathers had not come back. Nor had any of the second group reappeared. By that time a third group had been called to the baths.

Then the young worker understood. When he returned to the trucks he crawled into one of them and hid himself under the clothes, where he remained lying completely quiet for many hours—he himself did not know for how long. Finally, after what seemed an eternity, the doors of the trucks were shut and they were driven away.

The truck in which the young man had hidden stopped after about an hour's drive. By that time it had become dark. Outside a few lights were burning. The young worker heard voices. Men were talking in Polish. He decided to crawl out from his hiding place.

The Poles who were about to unload one of the trucks looked at the naked Jew. "Where did you come from?"

"Treblinka." The young man shivered. "Get me something to wear, will you? It's cold."

One of the Poles waved at the bundle of clothes which had been unloaded from the truck. "Help yourself. Take whatever you like. The people who wore them won't need them any more."

The Poles helped the young Jew, hiding him in their huts in a little village about twenty miles from Treblinka for more than ten days.

It was during these ten days that they told him the story of Treblinka. At first they did not want to speak—they thought it would be better if the young Jew never heard the whole horrible truth. But they would mention a fact here and there, and by and by he learned everything.

On the eleventh day he found an opportunity to make his getaway. Slowly, traveling only by night and hiding during the day in woods or in the houses of Polish underground workers, he finally made his way back to Warsaw. And one night he managed to climb one of the ghetto walls. He went from house to house, always watching for German, Lithuanian, or Ukrainian policemen, until he reached the house in which he and his young wife and children had lived.

He entered the house. Even before he stepped into his apartment he knew the worst. The door had been opened. The room plainly showed that the Germans had been there. Wardrobes had been torn open, chairs and tables kicked about. No one was there.

The young man looked for some of his old neighbors to see if he could discover what had become of his wife and children. But he could not find the neighbors. There was not a living soul left in the house, nor indeed in any of the neighboring houses.

The young worker finally made his way to Michael Klepfisz. Sitting in a dark room on Klepfisz's bed, he told the latter what he had seen in Treblinka and what the Polish workers who had hidden him had reported about what was going on there.

When he had finished there was a long silence. Then, in the darkness, Michael Klepfisz said, "You must tell this tale again. You must tell it to the Jews in Warsaw who still want to hope. You must tell it again and again, till everybody knows what is going on in Treblinka."

Michael Klepfisz had good reason for saying this, for, unbelievable as it seemed, a new wave of optimism had spread through the ghetto. Everyone spoke about the "authentic letters," supposedly written by people who had been deported weeks before, telling how much better off they were than they had been in the ghetto, and, considering the circumstances, quite happy. A few people had even seen letters of this type, although none who saw them knew the persons who had presumably written them.

Then there were the Jewish agents of the Gestapo, the men who in return for a loaf of bread and a few zlotys busied themselves spreading rumors everywhere that soon, very soon now, the Germans were going to stop the deportations.

But neither these rumors, nor the agents who spread them, nor the existent or nonexistent letters could have been effective had it not been for the strange psychological condition in which most of the Jews found themselves by this time. They no longer had any resistance left in them. They were no longer able to think logically or to use any judgment. They were all beyond that. They had suffered so much that they were willing to believe anything, so long as they did not have to suffer any longer.

It looked as though neither Michael Klepfisz, nor the members of the Jewish underground, nor even Dagani's agents would ever be able to arouse any spirit of resistance in those who were left in the ghetto.

It was at just that moment that the young worker who had escaped from Treblinka came back to the Warsaw Ghetto and told his story. Michael Klepfisz lost no time. He and his friends arranged a meeting for the next night with some of the more prominent Jews, among them many members of the Jewish Council, all of them old and cautious men who had shown themselves opposed to action or resistance of any kind. It was to these men that the young worker told the story of Camp Treblinka B, drawing not only on what little he had seen himself but on what he had been told by the Poles who had helped him escape, to picture the horrors of what had happened to the Jewish men and women who had been ordered to strip themselves and then go to the baths.

First, he said, came the women and children. After they had been led quite a way inside the camp, German and Ukrainian troops would leap out from near-by groves and drive the frenzied women on—under the constant lash of their whips, blows from their rifle butts, or thrusts with their bayonets—into the so-called bathhouses.

All this happened so quickly and came as such a surprise that the victims hardly realized what was happening. Only at the last moment, just before the doors of the bathhouse were closed, they would break out into terrible, bloodcurdling cries.

Soon each one of the chambers inside the bathhouse was crowded. The naked women would slip and fall, and before they could get up others would be on top of them, driven in by the merciless whips of the Germans. When the room was so full that not even a little child could enter any more, the doors would be locked and sealed.

Meanwhile the first men were taken to their bath. They, too, were herded in, in just the same way as the women.

And then after the doors had been sealed lethal gas would stream into the chambers through the pipes on the wall. For five or ten minutes there would be muffled cries, sounds of struggle, hammering on the door. But soon the cries became weaker, and in a short while everything was quiet. After half an hour the doors would be thrown open from the outside.

Then came the work of the gravediggers. The Nazis had rounded up hundreds of able-bodied Jews whom they forced to bury the victims. In return for this work the poor wretches were given a few more weeks' lease on their own miserable lives. They had to work fast, though. The storm troopers were constantly behind them, driving them on, cursing at them, whipping them.

It was not easy to bury the dead Jews. Their bodies were intertwined. They stuck to each other—the arms, legs, and heads of several people pressed together by the last convulsions. The gravediggers had to use buckets of water to disentangle the corpses and then drag them out of the gas chamber. The Nazis had told them that each of them had to carry two corpses. Each of them had to take hold of two heads or two pairs of legs and drag the bodies through the camp to the vacant spot which had been reserved as a cemetery. There the bodies were thrown, one on top of the other, into pits that had been prepared for them. These pits stretched for miles and miles around, and more were being prepared every day. Always one could hear the steady drone of the electric excavating machine as it busily dug graves for new victims.

There were many more details the young worker had learned from the Polish workers who had hidden him. It seems that at one time the Germans had even employed Jews as guards in Treblinka, but this had not worked out satisfactorily. After only a few days most of them had begged the German chief of Treblinka for mercy. They wanted to be shot—immediately. They could no longer stand it.

There was a special way in which these men at Treblinka were shot. They had to stand at the edge of their graves, and then they were shot in the back of the head. Then the next victim had to step forward, shove his predecessor into the pit, and wait for the shot which would eliminate him. The Nazis had shot more than five hundred Jewish guards between seven in the morning and three in the afternoon in a single day. For some time they recruited new guards from the next transports, but after a while they gave it up. Evidently they decided that the Jews were too weak-stomached for this sort of thing.

But even the Germans themselves became somewhat tired of working at Treblinka after a time. The chief, Major Sauer, who evidently never became tired, decided that it might be well to change his men occasionally, and so from time to time he would ask for new SS detachments from near-by towns to replace those who had become "soft."

The clothes and shoes of the victims were sent back to Germany, where they were disinfected and later divided among poor German people. But Major Sauer kept a few things for himself. There were the gold fillings of the teeth, which the guards extracted with special tools and which they had to deliver to him. And then there was the food which the victims had brought along—bread, marmalade, fat, sugar. He had it shipped back to Warsaw, and his agents sold it in the ghetto. They got high prices for these things. Often enough they were bought by those who were about to be evacuated. The same provisions may thus have been brought back to Treblinka a second time, confiscated again, and shipped back to the ghetto again. A vicious circle. According to the Polish workers, Major Sauer had made quite a fortune disposing of these last crumbs of food brought along by the thousands of Jews who were put to death every day.

When the young worker had finished his tale some of the listeners began to weep. Then they stopped. They realized that weeping would not help. Now was no time for tears. They had to do something.

But what could they do? Almost three hundred thousand Jews had been taken away from Warsaw and killed at Treblinka within a few months. How many were left? So many had died of starvation, and so many others had been shot by the annihilation squads or had perished in other ways. How many were left? Perhaps fifty or sixty thousand.

What could they do? What could fifty or sixty thousand poor, starved, unarmed Jews do against the German Army?

But they had to do something. Because the Germans would not be stopped in their plan of systematic annihilation of the Jews. They would continue till there was not a single Jew left in Poland and perhaps in all of Europe.

The young worker who had fled from Treblinka told the Jews in Warsaw that a new death house was under construction there, a much larger one, which could do away with many more Jews at a much faster rate. Should they wait until this new death house started operations?

The tale of the young Jewish worker spread like wildfire throughout the ghetto, without the help of newspaper, radio, or even telephone. Within twenty-four hours practically every last inhabitant of the ghetto had learned what was happening in Treblinka and what was in store for all of them. And now it suddenly seemed as if the dreadful tale had opened up the locked doors behind which the secret fate of the Polish Jews during the last few months under the Nazi regime had been so well kept thus far. Now a flood of reports spread about, and they were whispered from house to house, from block to block.

There were reports from other death camps: reports from Sobibor, Chelmo, Oswiecim, Majdanek, Lublin. There were accounts of hundreds of thousands of Jews who were dying the slow death of starvation because their rations were reduced from week to week; or funeral pyres and furnaces where they were burned by the dozens of hundreds; of murder vans where they were asphyxiated by "cyclon" gas; of people shot in ditches or killed by a blow from an iron rod which broke their necks; of others drowned in artificial ponds or hanged on the gallows;

of death factories constantly perfected according to new ingenious ideas of the Nazis, who forced their victims to build their own prisons, their own gas chambers, their own furnaces.

There were stories of the freight trains into which the Jews were packed when they left their starting point, each car with space for forty persons being stuffed with one hundred and fifty. The cars, they heard, were hermetically sealed, and even before the train began to move, hundreds of the occupants suffocated.

The packed mass of Jews had no recourse but to perform their normal physical needs on the floor where they stood. The floors of the cars had been covered with lime and chloride which reacted chemically, and soon fumes rose up and ultimately poisoned all the Jews in the car. This took more than eight hours, though, during which time the air was filled with the shrieks and cries of the victims. At last, when it finally became quiet within the cars, the train moved off, and after a journey of several days the cars were shuttled off somewhere into a field.

Later the Germans utilized the decayed bodies to manufacture fertilizer.

Another report said that there were more than three hundred thousand Jewish corpses lying around the neighborhood of Belzec, making the air unbreathable for many miles. Passengers on trains passing through that district had to close the train windows lest they suffocate. Many of these passengers fainted, nevertheless. The non-Jewish population of Belzec had to evacuate their farms because of the foul air.

Most of the victims had been murdered by injection of electric currents in specially constructed "bathhouses." Hundreds at a time were killed thus and then thrown into former anti-tank trenches, which the Jews had been forced to dig for the Germans while they were fighting against the Russians in this region.

According to other reports then spreading throughout the ghetto, the Nazis had murdered almost a million Jews in one way or another by the middle of September 1942.

Some of the Jews were not even dead when they were pushed into the mammoth ovens where in a few moments they were reduced to ashes. Relatives of those who were cremated were permitted to have the ashes sent to them in a small box on payment of thirty marks. This was an additional income for the German officers in charge. It showed the fine sense of humor the Nazis had, too. For frequently the relatives had scarcely time to bury the ashes before they, too, were taken away, sometimes by those who delivered the ashes, and in turn burned and made into fertilizer.

All these and many more equally horrible stories were soon known to everybody in the Warsaw Ghetto. What people had so long tried not to believe they now knew as a certainty. Now they realized that there was no hope for those who were still alive.

The Germans soon found out that the people in the ghetto knew. But they did not care. They figured that the Jews were completely broken anyhow and that the knowledge of their certain fate would only serve to render them more apathetic, easier victims, since it would deprive them of even the last breath of will power.

No, the Nazis were no longer interested in keeping what they were doing a secret from the Jews. They were only trying to keep it a secret from the rest of the world.

Chapter XVI

The Vision

She was fifteen years old. Her body was still that of a little girl, but her face was much older. Perhaps it was her eyes—large, light blue eyes which seemed very old, which looked at you—nay, through you—as if their owner were seeing things invisible to ordinary eyes, things that a girl of fifteen does not usually see.

She had indeed seen many things that a girl of fifteen does not usually see. She had lived through all those years of the ghetto tragedy. The Germans had taken her father and mother away, and her little brother whom she had loved more than anyone else in the world. She had lost all her friends. Now she was living with strangers. She almost never ate. She almost never slept. Often she wandered through the streets during the long night hours, though the people with whom she lived tried to keep her at home—after all, there were the German guards, who shot to kill whenever they found anybody who had no business on the streets after the curfew.

The girl never cried, but she was sad, sad beyond tears. Then again there would be moments when she was not sad at all, when she would even laugh, suddenly, without reason and without explanation. The people with whom she lived were certain that she was mad. But so many people had gone mad, and there was nothing one could do about them.

No one knew anything about the girl. Sometimes the people with whom she lived would see her sitting at the table with a few sheets of paper before her, scribbling something on it. Once they looked over her shoulder, and then they exchanged glances. She was madder than they had suspected. She was actually writing a poem.

Yes, the girl was writing a poem. She had been writing for many weeks and months poems which dealt with life in the Warsaw Ghetto, with the misery of the Jews and with the human tragedy that she had seen unrolled before her eyes. But now she was writing another kind of poem. It, too, dealt with the Warsaw Ghetto. But it pictured a ghetto that did not exist in reality: a fighting ghetto, a ghetto at war, a ghetto that hit back. She saw it all so clearly before her. She knew it would happen . . . sometime in the future.

These were the first lines:

Warsaw, Warsaw, town beloved,
Warsaw, native city,
Where the brutal foeman knows
Neither pause nor pity.
From Krasinski Place the guns
At the ghetto firing—
Where's the God of Israel,
Great and awe-inspiring?

Outside the deportations still continued. The annihilation squads still roamed the streets of the ghetto; Jews were still being killed or rushed away to the Transfer Point. The Jewish policemen were still doing their duty, and hating themselves for it more every day. They still clung to the promise of the Nazis not to touch their wives and children, but they saw their parents and their brothers depart, and they dropped their eyes in shame.

All over Warsaw the people dropped their eyes in shame. The Aryan Poles did not feel superior to the Jews any more, if they ever had felt so. They could still live in relative peace; they could still walk around without being shot at or hauled away; they could even eat. But they no longer felt like eating; they felt almost guilty that the Nazis treated them better than they did the Jews. They felt that the word "Aryan" had become a word of contempt. And they wondered how long it would be before these Nazis would treat them, the Polish Aryans, as they were treating the Jews now?

The girl saw other things. Before her eyes another picture crystallized itself, a picture not of suffering but of fighting.

Deborahs and Samsons fight
Where the battle rages:
Though we die today, we'll live
In the future ages!

Forward march with hand grenades!
Nazi tanks we're meeting,
German monsters blow to bits—
Thus the foe we're greeting!

Professor Balaban had aged considerably. His strength was leaving him day by day. He felt very tired. But he could not find any sleep. He worked almost every night until early morning, and then he would go out in the street and stroll along, watching the people come out of their houses and crawl along, almost incapable of holding themselves up. . . . An old man buying himself a piece of bread with his last money, wanting to take it home, but suddenly taking it out of the paper bag and devouring it in a few seconds, his face first happy and contented, then, after the last crumb was gone, disappointed, then desperate . . . A young girl, well dressed but very thin, looking into a garbage can, turning its contents over in the hope of finding something edible, her eyes glued to the scraps she stirred with her hands, then, when she did not find anything, crying with the despair of frustration . . .

Balaban went on. He felt alone. Except for Dr. Ringelblum, few of his friends were left. Since the ghetto knew what fate awaited them in Treblinka and other death camps, many of the Jewish intellectuals did not wait till they were led away but killed themselves and their families to spare them additional suffering.

But it was extremely difficult during these days to commit suicide. The Jews had no guns. Poison could no longer be bought for any price, for the pharmacies had all been closed. One could not hang oneself in a room which was occupied by several other people. There were some Jews who were willing to pay thousands of zlotys for a revolver so that they could shoot their families and themselves. Fabulous sums were paid for small packages of veronal. Those who were lucky enough to get it took it when they went to bed and fell happily asleep in the knowledge that they would not have to awaken in the Nazi hell any longer. But only those who had Christian friends in Warsaw who would smuggle veronal to them could liberate themselves thus. Others had to wait till they were arrested and then fake a getaway in order to be shot. But most of the Jews who wanted to make an end of themselves were forced to use the only way left open to them, a way which, fortunately, did not cost them anything. They jumped out of the window. Many took their lives in this way, whole families sometimes dying together, mothers leaping down with their children in their arms.

The Nazis made no differentiation between Jews and converted Jews. Those who prayed in the church were rounded up with just as much brutality as those who prayed in their secret and improvised synagogues. It did not help them that all their lives they had considered themselves different or perhaps better than the Jews.

The historian Balaban could not help drawing historical parallels in his mind. Hundreds of years ago a Jew who was confronted with certain death at the hands of his enemies had been able to save himself by accepting the religion of his captors. This had always been a way out. Many Jews had saved themselves thus during the time of the Crusades and during the Spanish Inquisition. True, most of them had refused to pay this price for their lives, but the point was that they could have done so if they had wanted to.

The realization that they were the victims of the most horrible persecution their people had ever had to endure made the Jews of Warsaw long for those times when the only problem they had to deal with was Polish anti-Semitism. It was not a very heroic attitude to take, and the Jews themselves were the first to realize this and to make fun of themselves in countless stories and jokes, such as the following:

An old Jewish couple wakes up in the Warsaw ghetto. The wife says: "I had such a nice dream. I dreamed I was walking on a Warsaw street. It was warm and the sun was shining. There were shops full of goods, and all over the shopwindows you could read, 'Don't buy at a Jewish store.' "

"Well, what is so nice about such a dream?" the husband wants to know.

"Don't you understand? I dreamed I was in good old Poland again!"

In 1942 the most solemn of all the Jewish holidays, the Day of Atonement, fell on September 21. The Nazis, anticipating that the Warsaw Jews would want to pray, sent twice as many guards into the ghetto on that day to prevent them from reaching their secret places of worship. But the Jews were able to get together in their cellars just the same. They posted women along the streets to lead those who wanted to pray to newly improvised synagogues, unknown to the Gestapo.

When the Nazi guards found the streets of the ghetto deserted, they decided to spend their time doing a little more killing. There was a mass slaughter on this Day of Atonement. Hundreds were killed. A great many Jewish policemen, together with their wives, were captured and taken to the Transfer Point. The Nazis no longer needed so many Jewish policemen now that the ghetto population had been so drastically reduced. Of the 3,000-man Jewish police force not more than five hundred were left by the end of the year.

The Jews in their little praying rooms called on their God. He had not been very good to them. He had seen them killed in the streets, starved, called away to horrible death camps. But they still believed in Him and had faith that in the end He would save them and punish their enemies.

So they prayed:

"May our God avenge the blood of his servants which hath been shed; as it is written in the Law of Moses, the man of God, Rejoice,

O ye nations, with His people, for He will avenge the blood of His servants, and will render vengeance to His adversaries, and will make atonement for His land and for His people . . . And in the Holy Writings it is said, Wherefore should the nations say, Where is their God? Let there be made known among the nations in our sight the revenging of the blood of Thy servants which hath been shed. And it is said, For He that maketh inquisition for blood remembereth them; he forgetteth not the cry of the humble. And it is further said, He judgeth among the nations; the land is full of corpses; He smiteth the head over a wide land . . ."

The Jews in the ghetto of Warsaw, and the Jews all over Hitler-occupied Europe, were defenseless. But the world, in general, was no longer defenseless.

The Jews who sat glued to their few hidden radio sets heard the broadcasts of the Polish underground and realized that a decisive change had taken place. The counteroffensive of the Allies had begun on a global scale.

In August 1942 the United States had started the attack on Guadalcanal. The English began their all-out air raids over Germany. They even staged a dress rehearsal for the invasion by landing in Dieppe. And at the beginning of September the Free French and the English invaded Madagascar.

Some of the Nazis may have guessed even then that they would not achieve ultimate victory. But even those Nazis did not doubt for one minute that they could annihilate all the Jews in the territories they held. They wanted to enslave all the people in these territories, but as for the Jews—they only wanted to kill them.

On October 4 Hermann Goering threatened that if Germany were ever defeated she would revenge herself on the Jews. On November 8 the Fuehrer himself confirmed that the Jews were to be wiped out. At that time he was still of the opinion that he would take Stalingrad and eventually crush Britain. But even if he had any doubt as to these achievements, there was no doubt that he could make true his threats about the Jews.

The Nazis were busily engaged in making it come true.

A German soldier saw a three-year-old Jewish child with a badge of the Star of David just outside the ghetto walls near the Vistula River. He motioned to a Pole who was passing by and, drawing his gun, ordered the Pole to pick the child up and throw it into the water. The Pole had to obey.

As he turned around to go, the German soldier saw a Jewish woman approaching. He did not know how either the child or the woman had managed to leave the ghetto. He instinctively knew that this was the mother of the child. He drew his gun again. The woman came nearer. She was mumbling to herself. She was about to pass the German when she stopped. "I am looking for my boy," she said. "He ran away. He must have passed here. Did you see him? Can you tell me where my boy is?"

The German soldier tried to sneer at the woman, but he could not open his mouth. He started to press the trigger of his gun, but he could not move his fingers. He could only shake his head.

The woman went on. She spoke to the Pole. "Can you tell me where my boy is? He is a little boy of three," she said. "He is blond. He must have come this way."

The German soldier still had his gun in his hand. Suddenly the woman turned around and looked at him. He could not stand it any longer. There was something in her eyes that made him shiver.

He ran away.

The ghetto was in its last stages of despair, but the young girl of fifteen saw a different ghetto with her inner eyes and put this vision into words:

Many are the victims brave
In the bleeding city—
Set the Nazis' plant afire,
Show the beasts no pity!

Do they think this is the end
They so fondly cherish?
Phoenix-like, we shall arise,
They—forever perish!

And perhaps for Poland's sake,
More than any other's,
All the world so bravely fights
Like so many brothers.

Then one day they blockaded the house in which the girl lived and took all the people away. The girl did not carry any bag or any carton. There was nothing she wanted to take along of the little she possessed. Nothing except a few sheets of paper on which she had scribbled.

The girl was weak. She had a hard time keeping up with the others. Once or twice she stopped to lean against a wall. But there was a Nazi who pushed her on with the butt of his rifle.

A little while afterward she broke down. The Jews who marched at her side helped her to get up. They almost carried her along. But when the procession had passed, the few sheets of white paper she had clung to were on the street. They were no longer white. Hundreds of Jews had marched over them on their way to their deaths. Somebody picked them up. He was about to run up to the girl and give them to her, then stopped. Perhaps the girl had wanted it that way. Perhaps the papers contained some information. He looked at them. A poem. Then he started to read.

That night the poem went from hand to hand, until it finally found its way to the office of the underground newspaper, where Michael Klepfisz read it. The paper was already on the presses, but he had them stopped. "We must print this," he said.

And so they set up and printed the poem written by an unknown Jewish girl who was about to die, but who had, before her death, seen a vision of something that was to come later, so much later.

Klepfisz and his friends read the poem again and again. Someone gave Balaban a copy of the paper containing the poem the very same night. The professor learned how the poem had come into the possession of the editors of the paper.

A little Jewish girl, he thought. A girl who knows she is going to die. But not a word of fear, not a single plea for mercy, not even a farewell. Does it not remind us of the words spoken by our great prophets? Does it not remind us of the words formed by our great martyrs?

Black and yellow, brown and white,
All like blood relations,
Weaving wreaths to place upon
Freedom-welded nations.

Warsaw mourning, Warsaw hushed,
Foe and death despising—
You will live to see once more
Rays of Freedom rising!

Though TODAY, a muted song,
Lies prostrate and gory,
Wait—TOMORROW will arise
In a burst of glory!

That night Professor Balaban knew that everything the girl had seen would come true. There would be a Tomorrow for the Jews. But he also knew that he would not live to see the dawn of this tomorrow. He felt like Moses looking from the mountaintop at the Promised Land which he was never to enter.

Part Three: The Fight

Chapter XVII

Organized Resistance

Toward the late fall of 1942 it had become quiet in the ghetto. The annihilation squads were still roaming the streets, but they did not do much shooting. There wasn't any prey around. Some of the streets looked as though snow had fallen on them, but the white covering was nothing but the down feathers from bedding which had been thrown on the street from the homes of the vanished Jewish occupants by the German policemen.

Sometimes the silence was interrupted by revolver shots fired into the air by the Germans who did not want to lose practice. Occasionally a Gestapo car would tear through the streets.

The Nazis no longer seemed to care whom they took away from the ghetto. They had apparently discarded their carefully worked out plans that workers who directly or indirectly were contributing to the German war production should be spared. The German owners of the factories in which the Jews worked became panicky. They needed their Jewish workers. They conceived the fantastic idea of branding them with a stamp on various parts of their bodies in order to make them more recognizable and protect them from deportation. The workers, incidentally, had to pay three zlotys for such stamping.

But even this arrangement did not help much. High Gestapo officials would enter the smaller factories and declare them liquidated, and the workers would be taken away to the Transfer Point.

In addition, working permits, which so far had guaranteed the lives of their possessors and the lives of their wives and children, were now declared void. Certificates issued by the Health Department and other departments of the Jewish Council were also invalidated.

It happened more and more often that groups of workers on their way to the shops were stopped by Gestapo men and some of them pulled out to be sent to the Transfer Point. There was no system in this madness. Sometimes the Gestapo took highly specialized workers who could not be replaced. They did it simply to show the workers that there was no use in opposing them.

Many of the workers no longer dared to leave their families at home when they went to work. The Germans had promised the men that their wives and children would not be touched, but time after time they had been taken along just the same when their houses were raided, and when the husbands came home in the evening they found their homes abandoned, their families vanished. As a result, many of the workers had been taking their wives along with them when they left in the morning. Of course the women could not leave the ghetto, but they tried to hide out somewhere in the neighborhood and postpone going home till their husbands came back from work. The children, too, would trot along. Sometimes the German policemen who were escorting the Jewish laborers would lash out with their whips at the wives or children, but they did not mind being hit so long as they could stick together.

Then one morning a group of workers, accompanied by their wives and children, was stopped again on Leszno Street. A woman carrying a baby in her arms was dragged away from the others. His comrades held the father back when he tried to pull them back. "You can't do anything now," they whispered.

A German policeman drew his revolver and shot the baby in the mother's arms. Then he said, "Fine. Everything is in order now. March on."

The group marched on. The mother with the dead baby stood there alone. She did not comprehend. Then, just before the group of workers turned around the next corner, she seemed to wake up. "Wait! Wait!" she cried. And then she began to run after them, her dead child still in her arms.

Again, a few days later, another group of laborers returning from work in the evening was stopped just after they entered the ghetto. All of them had to present their papers to a storm trooper who was sitting at a table in the middle of the street. The storm trooper picked out some of them for direct transport to the Transfer Point.

Next to Michael Klepfisz a young worker stood waiting impatiently.

He was not afraid. He, as well as Klepfisz, knew that the factory could not operate without him, but he did not want to waste so much time. He whispered to Klepfisz, "I'm in a hurry. There is a girl, you know." He smiled.

His papers were examined and he was allowed to go. As he hurried away, still smiling, he inadvertently pushed against a Lithuanian policeman who stood behind him. The Lithuanian immediately fired, and the young man fell. The smile was still on his face.

The *Storm* told the Jews to resist—in every way possible. It told them: "Deportation means death."

Many leaders of the workers declared that the time had come to strike. It was becoming difficult, they said, to hold their men back much longer. Many of them were so furious that they were willing to attack a Nazi, any Nazi, with their bare hands or throw something at his head. They believed that even if they lost their own lives as a result of their act—as they undoubtedly would—each of them would at least have the satisfaction of knowing that he had taken an equal number of Nazis with him.

Michael Klepfisz shook his head at this. There was no sense, he said, in sending the Jewish workers to certain death. "The enemy would just shoot the rest of us summarily. We must fight, and we will fight. But we must have a general plan. We must have an army, and we must have weapons."

There had already been many disconnected individual acts of sabotage. In the second half of August 1942 more than one hundred warehouses and storehouses, as well as a few smaller factories within the ghetto, were set afire by unknown persons. Also a bomb was thrown into the Resettlement Office.

The Jewish workers organized in the underground met often in the few luxurious cafés and restaurants frequented by the Jews working hand in glove with the Gestapo. Here they were relatively safe from detection. Here they also witnessed the traitors whom they considered even lower than the Germans, spending their money and getting drunk; sometimes they would follow one or the other of them and finish him off at a dark street corner.

They considered the Jewish police, too, as traitors for the role they played during the evacuations, though by the end of September most of the policemen had been deported themselves. One day the police commissioner of the ghetto, Szerinski, was shot as he was passing a house in the ghetto. The Gestapo immediately arrested everyone in the house and later shot all of them, but the man who fired the shot was never discovered. The police commissioner was laid up for some time. He never came back to his job.

The Nazis decided that it might be a good thing to isolate the workers somewhat from the rest of the population. On September 28 it was announced that they would have to live in separate districts within the ghetto from which other Jews had to move out. The order said that in certain districts and streets "only those Jews may stay . . . who go to their places of work in closed formations . . . Whoever transgresses these regulations will be deported."

But the time had passed when the Nazis could keep the Jewish workers in check. They no longer slaved away for the Germans just to save their lives. They now had another and more important motivation for their labor: they used their working hours and the material handed over to them by the Germans to make bombs, hand grenades, and other weapons and parts of weapons, which they smuggled out when they left in the evening; they were also able to smuggle out some material for the other Jews in the ghetto to work on during the night. All this they did under the very eyes of the Germans. And soon a stock of grenades and bombs and other weapons which would be useful in case of armed resistance was slowly assembled in the cellars of vacant houses. Women helped, and children too.

All these preparatory actions started almost spontaneously in many different factories at once. Working without any definite, over-all plan, many thousands of workers made weapons, entirely unaware that others were doing the same kind of thing. All they knew, all of them, was that something had to be done and done soon.

When they looked back over the past two years they wondered why they had not hit back any sooner. To be sure, there had been a few isolated cases of individual resistance; some people had erected barricades in their buildings to make it harder for the Germans to get at them; an old Jew had thrown a candelabrum at a Gestapo man and had crushed his skull; a Jewish woman had dropped a bottle filled with acid on members of an annihilation squad who had posted themselves on the street. But such incidents had been few and sporadic.

Now, however, there seemed to be a general will to resist. How was it born? Perhaps the man who had returned from Treblinka had something to do with it. Perhaps the Germans had just become too careless and too cynical in their persecution of the Jews, believing that the Jews would take anything. Perhaps it was the fruit of the untiring work of Mordecai and Klepfisz.

But had it not come too late? Were the Jews not too defeated to start any real action?

If the Jews in the ghetto had analyzed the situation soberly, they might have come to the conclusion that it was, indeed, too late, that they were, in truth, too defeated, too crushed, to make an effective resistance. But they were no longer analyzing the situation soberly. They were convinced now that it was not too late to fight. Perhaps they thought of the vision of the Prophet Ezekiel, to whom the Lord had spoken: "Son of man, can these bones live?" and Ezekiel had answered, "O Lord, thou knowest." And he went on, "And as I prophesied, there was a noise, and behold a shaking, and the bones came together, bone to his bone. And when I beheld, the sinews and the flesh came up upon them, and the skin covered them over . . . Breath came into them, and they lived, and stood up upon their feet, an exceedingly great army."

Yes, a great army . . . and could it not happen again, though little more was left of the Jews in the ghetto than bones?

The agents of Dagani believed it. They reported:

"We have regarded it as our first task to awaken the Jewish masses to the point where they would not accept their death without resistance. We were the first to point out the truth. We printed leaflets calling the Jews to revolt against going to the resettlement center. We gave them complete information about the horrors of the annihilation centers. We, of the youth movements, who have always loved life and preached the joy of life, were forced to tell the harsh truth to the Jews, to urge them not to be misled by false illusions inspired by Nazi propaganda."

Most of Dagani's agents had come into the ghetto of Warsaw by now. Beautiful young Tosia had no illusions about the end. Soon after she arrived in Warsaw she sent to Palestine and the rest of the world the message which has since become immortal: "Israel is perishing before my eyes."

Young Breslaw had made his way into the ghetto, to be there for the last stand, and Zivia, the Mother, came too. Dagani wanted her to go back to Palestine, and her friends had arranged for transportation for her. But she declined. Her message to Dagani read: "Opposed on principle." She would not save herself when all the others were to die.

Dagani's disciples worked hard to organize the Jews. They set up "groups of five" in different sections of the ghetto. They knew that there was little hope, but they wanted to arouse the Jews to a last fight, and they wanted the world to witness that they could put up such a fight.

Their difficulties were well-nigh overwhelming.

In the first place, the boundaries of the ghetto had been changed. The ghetto was now divided into two parts, a so-called large ghetto, comprising what was left of the northern part, and the small ghetto which still existed in the southern part, with no connections between. This sudden change in the ghetto limits made it difficult for the fifty thousand Jews who were left to meet freely together. It also made it almost impossible for them to transfer certain centers of the underground in time to keep them inside the ghetto. Hence a great deal of the work of organization had to be done all over again.

The fact that most of the workers could no longer be reached openly, and only at great danger to life, also complicated matters. Hundreds of couriers and messengers risked their lives daily to keep the lines of communication between the workers and the ghetto intact. German patrols watched the houses in which the workers lived and blocked the entrance of anybody who did not live in those houses. If anybody was found trying to slip in, he was sent to the Transfer Point at once. They even made it impossible for husbands and wives to communicate. If the wife worked in one factory and the husband in another, they might be ordered to live in different houses and different districts of the ghetto, with no means of finding out whether the other one was still alive.

Another handicap which those who were preparing organized resistance had to overcome was that many of the original leaders of underground organizations had been taken to Treblinka, or had been shot, or had died of starvation. They had to be replaced. But too frequently it happened that those who took their places had hardly built up the machinery all over again when they, too, were taken away. Under such circumstances it was a miracle that the organization was able to remain intact.

But actually the most difficult task that was encountered in building up the resistance movement was not the fight against the Germans but the fight against those Jews who still believed that resistance would avail them nothing and that the only chance the Jews had for survival was to "play along" with the Germans and try to survive—no matter how. The representatives of these views were, for the most part, the older Jews. They pointed out that there was no real chance of survival in any kind of resistance. And they were right, too. But they did not understand the ideas of the younger ones, particularly of the Chaluzim, who preferred to die fighting, if they had to die at all. In contrast to their elders, the Chaluzim and the men around Klepfisz were not interested in prolonging their own lives another few weeks if they had to suffer nothing but misery and humiliation as the price for their continued existence.

But the older ones were not merely cowards. There were many good reasons for voting against resistance. There was, in the first place, the Nazi policy of collective responsibility. If anyone resisted, he not only risked his own life but automatically forfeited the lives of his family and perhaps of all the people who lived in the same house. Many Jews felt that they had no right to do such a thing. The old ones even pointed out that to endanger the lives of others in such a manner was contrary to the laws of the Jewish religion.

Precisely the same split had taken place among the Jews about two thousand years ago when Jerusalem was being beleagured by Titus and his legions. Then, too, the older and presumably wiser men had wanted to hand over the city to the Romans, while the younger generation wanted to make a fight of it. The ones who wanted to fight won. The Romans had a hard struggle before they finally succeeded in destroying Jerusalem. They killed most of the Jews who were still alive and took the others back to Rome as prisoners. True, the fate of the survivors would scarcely have been different if they had appeased the enemy, for the Romans were determined to destroy the Jews. But by putting up a fight they at least gave the generations which came after them something to be proud of, something to remember—a rallying point which helped to keep Jewry alive for centuries afterward.

The men and women in the Warsaw Ghetto who wanted to fight it out belonged to many political parties: there were Socialists of the "Bund," Communists, liberals, and there were many conservatives who belonged politically to the right. Then there were the Chaluzim, the Jewish scouts, and other Zionists. Finally there was a large number of religious Jews—men and women—who did not belong to any party or to any group.

All these various groups now found in themselves the identical desire to fight it out. They fought for different ideas and reasons and goals, it is true: they fought as Poles or as Jews, or simply as individuals who had been humiliated and persecuted. But the fight which they wanted to fight was the same one.

In the late fall of 1942 they formed the United Resistance Committee, which was to prepare for the coming fight. From that time on, all the different organizations which had hitherto worked separately, either in the underground or within the Zionist movement or the Socialist or Communist movements, now worked together.

A new era had begun. The Jews in the Warsaw Ghetto no longer hoped to save themselves. They were no longer content to watch their own destruction. They no longer wanted to remain passive. They were determined to take part in the gigantic struggle which had developed throughout the world and which was going to decide the fate of the world for generations to come.

It was during those days that Michael Klepfisz met a secret courier of the Polish government-in-exile.

This man was a young Pole of thirty, who had been taken prisoner by the Russians when they started to occupy the eastern part of Poland in September 1939. Since he had been born in the western part of Poland, he was later exchanged for a Ukrainian officer, according to the stipulations of the Ribbentrop-Molotov pact. In November 1939 the Germans arrested him. He escaped from the train on which he was placed and somehow made his way to Paris, arriving there in January 1940. In Paris he was made a secret courier of the Polish government-in-exile, which sent him back to occupied Poland soon afterward. He spent most of the year of 1940 illegally in Poland and left by the end of the year for London with important documents from the Polish underground. For the next two years he was a liaison officer between the Polish government-in-exile and the Polish underground. In October 1942 he came to the ghetto in Warsaw disguised as an Estonian officer.

This man belonged to those Poles who, up to the outbreak of the war, had not been very fond of the Jews. But whatever his prejudices or the reasons which motivated them, his entire attitude changed when in the second half of 1942 he spent a few weeks, disguised as an Estonian officer, in the concentration camp at Belzec, where he watched the extermination of thousands of Jews.

Now he came to the ghetto through the Court Building with the two exits, as a contact man for the high command of the Polish underground army. He talked to several Jews about the situation and finally met with Michael Klepfisz and other representatives of the underground. He asked them if there was anything he could do to help the Jews.

Michael Klepfisz answered, "There is something you can do. You can get us weapons."

For some time Klepfisz had tried to get weapons from the Polish underground. He did receive some; they were sent into the ghetto with the trucks of bread and flour and potatoes. But Klepfisz needed much more. He told this to the leaders of the Polish underground as early as August 31. But these men talked to other Jews in the ghetto who were opposed to the idea of resistance and came to the conclusion that the majority of the Jews did not want an armed uprising at that time. They told this to Klepfisz, alleging this as their reason for refusing to send him any more weapons. Anyway, they said, even if the weapons were sent in, they would only fall into the hands of the Nazis in the end, so what good would it do?

"All that happened two months ago," Klepfisz declared. "The situation has changed completely since then." He made a slight pause. "Let us be realistic. The murders and deportations have mainly eliminated the older ones who did not want to fight or could not have fought. Of those who are still in the ghetto the workers and the young Zionists are in the majority."

He became passionate. "We ask for weapons. We know that we cannot win the war with these weapons. We are far too few. However, we can and will save the honor of our people and show the world that Jews are not willing to die like sheep, and we will also prove that the Germans are not such supermen as they would like to think themselves, when they are met by armed opposition. The world will see that Germans, too, can be afraid. And this may help arouse all the other nations who are still suffering under Nazi domination."

The courier thereupon had a talk with the chief of the secret military organization in Poland. This man told him, "We cannot give the Jews any weapons. We have only the arms which were left by the Polish Army, which have been hidden away, and those which are brought to us by parachute. Our needs are increasing every day. We need everything we have for a real fight. We can spare nothing for a demonstration of a political and moral character such as the Jews are preparing."

When the Jews in the ghetto heard that they were not to be given any arms to defend themselves, they were deeply grieved. One report said:

"I will not dwell any more on the details of our underground work. Even if I wished to do so, I could not bear it. There is one offense committed against us that we will never forgive: We asked for weapons that would enable us to die as human beings, in organized resistance against the murderer. We did not receive them; we were refused."

But still the Jews did not give up. Small quantities of weapons were steadily smuggled in; explosives were made by the workers in the German-owned factories; Dagani's agents and the men around Klepfisz got more weapons from German soldiers. When they could pay in American dollars, they could get considerable numbers of weapons. But it took a great deal of money. A gun now cost twenty-five dollars. Two thousand dollars was demanded by a Nazi soldier as the price for ten machine guns which he had stolen from a transport on its way to the Russian front. In order to secure the necessary funds, the men of the Resistance Committee forced those in the ghetto who had become rich by smuggling in food to hand their money over to be used in purchasing weapons.

There were children commandos who would peer into barbershops and steal rifles and revolvers from under the very noses of the German soldiers who were being shaved. Hundreds of guns thus found their way into the ghetto, until the German Command had to issue a decree that German soldiers were to keep an eye on their weapons even while they were in the barbershop.

The Resistance Committee worked day and night. There were not enough arms as yet, but there were enough people who were willing to use them. Most of them did not know how to use them, however.

The train on its way from Warsaw to Treblinka was halted in the middle of the night. A Gestapo motorcar was standing on the tracks, and its occupants, high Gestapo officials, judging from their uniforms, were standing on the embankment.

They ordered the German guards to approach them for some confidential announcement, and when the guards did so, the Gestapo men fired their revolvers at them, killing them instantly. Then they proceeded to open the doors of the train, set all the occupants free, take over the train and smash it to bits, thus interrupting the regular traffic between Warsaw and Treblinka for many a day.

The Gestapo men were, of course, Jews clad in Gestapo uniforms who thus saved a few thousand of their brethren. They also collected about one hundred rifles which they could use for the coming battle of Warsaw.

There were numerous other exploits, such as assaults on prisons in small towns or outlying concentration camps, damaging of railroad tracks, blowing up of ammunition trains, all performed by Jewish partisans hiding out in the woods.

They usually wore German uniforms, and they hardly ever slipped up. They had intelligence officers who provided them with the most detailed information regarding the whereabouts of the people they wanted to liberate. Before they opened a prison they had familiarized themselves with every inch within the prison, every password; they had seen photographs of the German guards—they were completely at home.

The Jewish partisan group had been formed soon after the Germans came into Poland. Among the first members were young Jewish boys and girls who had fled before the Nazis and then decided to stay in the woods and fight it out. They got valuable reinforcement from Jews who left their cities and towns before they were imprisoned in ghettos, or later escaped from the ghettos when they began to understand that they were doomed.

Mordecai and his Chaluzim played an important part in the development of the Jewish partisans. Mordecai sent hundreds of his Chaluzim into the woods when he found that the camp in which they trained was going to be dissolved by the Germans. He also arranged for large numbers of the young Jews of the Warsaw Ghetto and other ghettos to join the partisans. This was by no means an easy job. The Jewish partisans were very exclusive. They accepted only those who could bring along their own weapons, as well as their own clothes and shoes. Mordecai saw to it that they got the necessary equipment.

The Germans tried to keep the partisans from getting reinforcements. They kept a careful lookout for young men and women who tried to leave the ghettos in search of the partisans. Some of Mordecai's best men thus got killed. Some of them, when they realized that they were surrounded by the Germans and about to be taken prisoner, began to shoot in order not to be taken alive. They were afraid that torture might force them to tell the Germans the location of their secret meeting place.

Still, dangerous as their existence was, those who joined the partisans had at least a chance to survive. But those who remained in Warsaw had no chance at all. Therefore Mordecai believed it his duty to get as many of the young Jews out of Warsaw as possible. Other members of the Resistance Committee, however, among them Michael Klepfisz, were of the opinion that the ghetto should not be deprived of its best fighters.

And then a strange thing happened. Partisans who had been living in the woods about fifty miles away from Warsaw suddenly appeared in the ghetto. That was in the beginning of December. All during that month more partisans followed them. When asked why they had come back, they said that they had come back because they knew that the final battle would be fought in Warsaw and they wanted to have a part in the great struggle.

So they returned voluntarily to a prison from which so many before them had tried in vain to escape. They took their posts for the final showdown.

Chapter XVIII

Decision in London

A BERLIN THEATRICAL COMPANY came to Warsaw to give a series of performances. A famous German Wagnerian tenor flew over to give a song recital. A circus from southern Germany made its appearance for a week or so. The German-controlled papers ran big ads and lent themselves to all kinds of "ballyhoo." Berlin had decided to bring German culture to Poland in an attempt to distract the mind of the average Pole from war and operation.

But the theater stood vacant except for the German officers and soldiers who went there. The Wagnerian tenor had never before sung to such a selected audience—the selection going down almost to the zero point. Tickets for the circus were given away for nothing to passers-by and children in the streets, but it seemed that the Poles did not want to see wild animals trained in Germany, even for nothing.

The German authorities in Warsaw knew well enough what was going on. The Polish underground had sent out word that any entertainment arranged for by the Germans should be boycotted. These boycotts succeeded almost one hundred per cent. The few Poles who acted contrary to the orders of the underground soon had reason to repent it. They would not even get home in one piece from the circus or the theater. They were given a sound thrashing and told that sterner measures would be taken against them the next time. The victims of the thrashings understood. There was no next time—so far as they were concerned.

These activities of the underground were relatively innocent. The Germans didn't like them, of course, but they could not afford to get too excited about them. There were other activities, though, of a much less innocent and far more damaging and dangerous nature. There were, for instance, many assassinations of keymen within the German administration in Warsaw and other Polish cities.

The German Commissar or Gruppenfuehrer or Obergruppenfuehrer would receive a letter informing him that he had been sentenced to death by the Directorate of Civilian Resistance. The letter would not come to him by mail. He would receive it inside a German newspaper handed to him by a newspaper boy. The frenzied German would look around for the messenger—but the messenger had disappeared. The German would immediately ask the Gestapo for a bodyguard, which would never leave him, day or night.

But then suddenly, while the German official was entering or leaving the building in which his office was situated, there would be shots. He would fall, pierced by many bullets. The Germans would immediately cordon off the entire street to find the assassin. They would search for a man who had been seen with a gun, but miraculously the man had disappeared. So had the gun. None of the Germans had seen that the man had thrown his gun into a laundry basket carried by a young girl. Nobody could see that, because two elderly ladies had started a quarrel and attacked each other with umbrellas at the precise moment the gun was thrown. The laundress passed the police cordon without being molested, and so did the others. Five agents working in close collaboration had worked out every last detail in order to kill a German criminal in broad daylight, in spite of all the protection the Gestapo gave him.

The Nazis had become exceedingly nervous about these incidents. They did not like being killed. They thought it was unfair. After all, had Poland not been defeated? It was not right that the Poles should continue to fight the Germans.

The German *Krakauer Zeitung* commented:

This country is being designated with increased frequency as the advance line of the front. As we sorrowfully follow the biers of our comrades-in-arms who fell at their posts giving their lives for our beloved Germany, we become aware of the truth of that designation. The Poles know no other method of fighting but murder. To shoot, to kill, to commit murder right and left constitutes their favorite pastime, and murder is the means by which they manifest the hatred they have for us.

What constitutes the greatest danger, however, is that they conduct themselves as if Poland were still in existence. They go so far in their blind aversion to facing stark reality that, just as they did when Poland rode high and mighty, even now they gloat over the murders they have committed on the Fuehrer's soldiers in placards they clandestinely post on the walls of houses, on which they say with cold cynicism that the sentence was carried out in the name of the Republic . . .

What enraged the Germans more than anything was the fact that while they themselves did not stop at killing right and left without the slightest legal foundation for their actions, the Poles proceeded legally, even in their underground work. There were no random assassinations. All sentences were arrived at in secret underground courts in which the pros and cons were discussed at great lengths, and the absent accused German even had a defender who tried to convince the court that his client did not deserve capital punishment. In many cases, too, the defender actually succeeded in so convincing the court—though the man for whom he spoke never knew, and perhaps never will know, that he had been in mortal danger.

Too, it infuriated the Germans and made them excessively jittery to realize that the underground watched all of them constantly. They could never do anything without its being noted and discussed in the underground tribunals.

The courts did not always give the death sentence. In many cases they contented themselves with admonishing the accused to stop his activities—or else. In the case of Poles who collaborated with the Germans, it often sufficed to have the culprit beaten up or boycotted by the rest of the population. But there was no mercy in the underground courts against those Polish traitors who worked actively against the underground. Neither was there any mercy for Germans who were responsible for the death of Polish citizens. As a rule the condemned person was done away with within twenty-four hours after judgment had been passed, no matter how he tried to hide out or how well he was guarded. Whenever the judgment was carried out, small posters would appear on houses all over the city with a written summary of the sentence, ending with a terse statement: "The sentence was carried out at —— on ——"

The underground courts were but a part of the entire setup of the underground state—for Poland had, indeed, become an underground state. It was well organized, and it functioned just as though there were no Germans occupying the country. There was the exiled government in London, surrounded by a Parliament which had the right of counsel in each and every case. This government was in steady contact with the Home Political Representation in Poland, a kind of underground government in which the Socialists, the peasants, the Democratic Labor party, and a number of national movements were represented. This Home Political Representation supervised military, political, and propaganda activities. Under its direction a steadily growing underground army was being trained and armed and was active throughout the country. Countless acts of sabotage were planned and executed by them. Groups of partisans harassed the German lines of communication. Underground dailies and periodicals informed the population. Secret radio stations told the people of Poland about the latest developments in the war.

All these activities could be found in every single country which Hitler had occupied. But the Poles were the ones who started it. And the Poles were the ones who protected organizations to a point where nothing was left to chance or improvisation. There was never a slip-up.

But even this admirable underground structure could work only defensively. The underground army was much too small to fight the Germans in open battle. That is why it could do little or nothing to help the Jews. It had to look on while millions of Jews were led to their deaths.

But they did not look on silently. They protested. They informed the Polish population of what was happening to the Jews. And they demanded that the Jews should be aided whenever it was possible to do so.

Around the end of the year 1942 there were many appeals like the following:

Warning! The entire Polish community, being alone committed to terror and oppression, looks with the utmost horror at the Nazi murderers, and expresses the deepest compassion with the remnants of the Jewish population of Poland, who are now being slaughtered by the Germans. The Polish community has already raised its voice in protest against this crime, a voice that awoke the conscience of free people throughout the world. The Poles are also lending support to those Jews who have escaped from the ghettos and slaughter camps to such an extent that the occupation authorities have found it necessary to publish a special decree, which provides the death penalty for Poles who help Jews hide. However, there are some among us without honor and without a conscience, virtual criminals, who have now developed for themselves a new source of income through blackmailing those Poles who give shelter to escaped Jews, as well as the Jews themselves.

The Commander in Chief of Public Resistance warns that all cases of such blackmail are being registered, and all guilty parties will be severely punished, if possible, immediately, and if not, without fail after the war.

THE COMMANDER IN CHIEF OF PUBLIC RESISTANCE

In December 1942 a group of Polish women addressed itself to the Polish Prime Minister-in-exile, General Sikorski:

Mr. Prime Minister and General: The women of Poland address to you their greetings for the army fighting abroad. They wish to express the might of their suffering, their yearning for liberty, and their determination to persevere, which is stronger even than death. We are fighting together with you each day, by day and by night, breathlessly, without respite. We desire you to know and remember these things. Upon your return we wish you to find houses and not ruins, living men and not decomposed corpses. We therefore cry out while there is yet time.

Our only weapon in the struggle against the enemy is silence. We are silent when at night they tear away our sons and daughters; when they drown a Jewish child in the sewer and with a knuckle-duster smash the skull of a mother who is bringing food to her family; when they shoot at our husbands and hang them in railway stations; when they round us up with their rifle butts and force us to watch them die. But our silence of two years ago differs greatly from our silence of today.

During the past few weeks we have witnessed many mass executions. People are being murdered by entire families or groups—men, women, and children. Hundreds of towns and villages have been thus depopulated. This is labeled the "liquidation" of the Jewish element. Each day thousands of Jews are taken from Warsaw and thousands from other cities are poisoned by gas or lime vapors in closed railway trucks. Others are machine-gunned and buried half alive, and their corpses converted into chemicals in underground factories. Every day whole families commit suicide. Mothers with small children leap out of windows to the pavement.

Children go insane. In the streets of the ghetto the soldiery shoot them like game. In Lublin children were thrown out of windows. In some small towns whole groups of Jews are driven to death on foot or in cars by whips of the Gestapo. In Przeworsk the Jews awaiting capture thronged around the Cross before the Cathedral, invoking Christ for help. All of them perished. The number set for the extermination of Jews has by now been almost reached. The raving monster is seeking new victims. The hunt has already started in the central part of southern Poland.

Why this silence? Are there no Polish, British, and American bombs? We have no tears left, but we are alive. We are capable of dying for Poland, but we want to live for her sake. We demand the ruin of a German city for every bloody massacre, air raids on German civilian population, and tenfold executions for every murdered victim in Poland.

Do not forget, General, this appeal of ours.

Catholic groups, too, protested, and their cries reached London by underground channels:

What is happening in the Warsaw Ghetto has been happening for six months past in a hundred smaller and larger Polish towns. The total number of Jews killed already exceeds a million, and the figure is rising every day. Everybody is perishing. Rich and poor, old and young, men, women, children, infants . . . everyone guilty of having been born in the Jewish nation . . . are condemned by Hitler to extermination.

We do not wish to be like Pilate. We cannot actively oppose the German murders; we can do nothing, we can save no one. But from the bottom of our hearts, filled with compassion, loathing, and horror, we protest. That protest is demanded of us by God, the God who forbade killing. It is demanded by the Christian conscience. Every creature who calls himself a man has a right to the love of his neighbor. The blood of the helpless calls to heaven for vengeance. Anyone who does not support this protest is no Catholic.

At the same time we protest as Poles. We do not believe that the German atrocities will turn to Poland's benefit. By no means . . .

He who does not understand this, he who would dare to connect the proud and free future with a base rejoicing in the misfortunes of his fellows, is neither a Catholic nor a Pole.

None of these appeals, however, could help the Jews, except for a few isolated cases. But at least the Nazis had not succeeded in their endeavor to keep the murder of the Jews secret from the rest of the Poles. All of Poland knew what was going on, and all of Poland understood that the Germans were the common enemy and that the Jews were but the first victims of mass extermination.

All of Poland knew; the Polish government-in-exile knew; Jews all over the world knew—and protested. Still, the great majority of people in the world did not yet know. Many governments could not bring themselves to believe the incredible accounts of the slaughter of those millions of people.

There were rumors in London, Washington, and numerous other

capitals of still free countries. But there was no official statement yet. And many people said there was surely a limit, even to the atrocities the German could commit, and whispered about Allied "propaganda."

Then the Polish government-in-exile acted.

For days the government and the rump parliament, the Polish National Council, had held almost uninterrupted meetings at Stratton House to discuss the Jewish situation. There were some Poles in high places in London who did not think that it was the business of either the government-in-exile or the Polish National Council to take any stand in regard to the mass murders of the Jews. Some of these men were not even too displeased at the idea that what they termed the "Jewish problem" of Poland was being solved for them. But they were only a minority. The overwhelming majority of the Poles in London felt that it was not only the right but the duty of the government to take a stand about the Jews.

On November 27, 1942, the Deputy Prime Minister and Minister of the Interior, Mr. Stanislaw Mikolajczyk, made the following statement:

> The Polish Government, in the fullest understanding of their responsibilities, not neglecting their duty to inform the world of the mass murders and bestialities of the Germans in Poland, have done everything in their power to counteract this terror.
>
> We are fully aware of the fact that the fundamental condition of an effective counteraction against the German program, which, in relation to Poland is best expressed by one slogan—TO DESTROY THE POLISH NATION WIPING OUT THE TRACES OF ITS EXISTENCE—is to shorten the time of suffering and resistance for the Poles in Poland and to defeat the enemy quickly. . . .
>
> The persecutions of the Jewish minority now in progress in Poland constitute, however, a separate page of Polish martyrology.
>
> Himmler's order that 1942 must be the year of liquidation of at least 50 per cent of Polish Jewry is being carried out with utter ruthlessness and a barbarity never before seen in world history. Every one of us knows the details, so I will not go into them again.
>
> The figures themselves are most eloquent. Out of over 400,000 people living in the Warsaw Ghetto, over 260,000 have been liquidated from July 17, that is to say in the last three months. Mass murders are in progress in the whole country. Polish Jews are being exterminated together with Jews from other occupied countries, transported on Polish territory.
>
> From Poland there comes a protest against the murders and persecutions.

The protest is accompanied by cries of pity, sympathy, and utter helplessness of these who have to look on what is happening there.

The Poles in Poland fully realize that, as the reports say, the speeded-up pace of the murders today applies to Jews only, but tomorrow may be applied to the rest of the population.

Mr. Mikolajczyk then proceeded to read the protest which the Catholic groups united underground in the Catholic Front for the Restoration of Poland had sent to him:

In the name of the Polish Government I support this protest of Poles in Poland and that of the Polish National Council. The Polish Government defends the interests of all Polish citizens of whatever religion or nationality they may be, and does it both in the interests of the state and in the name of humanity and Christianity.

The Poles in Poland and abroad have joined in the protest. Thus, at the congress of American Poles in Buffalo, Reverend Szubinski has moved for a protest against the ghettos and the bestial persecution of the Jews in Poland.

All the Poles are sharing this attitude.

Before the day was over, the Polish National Council passed a resolution dealing with the mass murder of the Jews in Poland:

The Government of the Polish Republic has brought the last news about the massacres of the Jewish population in Poland, carried out systematically by the German occupying authorities, to the attention of the Allied governments and of public opinion in Allied countries. The number of Jews who have been murdered by the Germans in Poland so far, since September 1939, exceeds one million.

From the beginning of the conquest of the territories of the Republic, the bestial occupying power has subjected the Polish nation to an appalling policy of extermination, to such an extent that by now the Polish population has been reduced by several million. Now the occupying power has reached the summit of its murder lust and sadism by organizing mass murders of hundreds of thousands of Jews in Poland, not only the Polish Jews but also the Jews brought from other countries to Poland with the purpose of exterminating them. The German murderers have sent to their death hundreds of thousands of men, women, children, and old people. Their purpose is to enfeeble the Polish nation and completely to exterminate the Jews in Poland before the end of this year. In the execution of this plan Adolf Hitler and his henchmen are using the most appalling tortures. . . .

In the face of the latest German crimes, unparalleled in the history of mankind, which have been carried out against the Polish nation, and particularly against the Jewish population of Poland, the Polish National Council again raises a strong protest and pronounces an indictment before the whole civilized world. . . .

The Polish National Council appeals to all the Allied Nations, and to all the nations now suffering together with the Polish nation under the German yoke, that they should at once start a common action against this trampling and profanation of all principles of morality and humanity by the Germans, and against the extermination of the Polish nation and other nations, an extermination the most appalling expression of which is provided by the mass murders of the Jews in Poland and in the rest of Europe which Hitler has subjected.

To all those who are suffering and undergoing torture in Poland, both to Poles and to Jews, to all those who are taking part in the struggle for liberation and for the preparation of a just retribution on the German criminals, the Polish National Council sends words of hope and of unshakable faith in the recovery of freedom for all.

The day of victory and punishment is approaching.

Soon afterward twelve governments of the Allied Nations joined the Poles in the following condemnation of the atrocities committed against the Jews in Poland:

The attention of the Belgian, Czechoslovak, Greek, Luxembourg, Netherlands, Norwegian, Polish, Soviet, United Kingdom, United States, and Yugoslav governments, and also of the French National Committee, has been drawn to numerous reports from Europe that the German authorities, not content with denying to persons of Jewish race in all the territories over which their barbarous rule has been extended the most elementary human rights, are now carrying into effect Hitler's oft-repeated intention to exterminate the Jewish people in Europe.

From all the occupied countries Jews are being transported in conditions of appalling horror and brutality to eastern Europe. In Poland, which has been made the principal Nazi slaughterhouse, the ghettos established by the German invader are being systematically emptied of all Jews except a few highly skilled workers required for war industries. None of those taken away are ever heard of again. The able-bodied are slowly worked to death in labor camps. The infirm are left to die of exposure and starvation or are deliberately massacred in mass executions. The number of victims of these bloody cruelties is reckoned in many hundreds of thousands of entirely innocent men, women, and children.

The above-mentioned governments and the French National Committee condemn in the strongest possible terms this bestial policy of cold-blooded extermination. They declare that such events can only strengthen the resolve of all freedom-loving peoples to overthrow the barbarous Hitlerite tyranny. They reaffirm their solemn resolution to insure that those responsible for these crimes shall not escape retribution, and to press on with the necessary practical measures to this end.

Among those present at the meeting of the Polish National Committee was Arthur Zygielbojm, once an important leader in the Jewish union movement and the Social Democratic party of Poland, and also one of the members of the Jewish Council of Warsaw when it was first created in October 1939.

Only by a series of miracles had he escaped death in Warsaw. The Gestapo knew his prewar record well, knew that he had been foremost among the Jews who had tried to unite his brothers in boycotting German goods after Hitler came to power. They therefore arrested him as a hostage shortly after the Nazis occupied Warsaw. Not wanting trouble with the Jewish workers just then, they released him soon afterward, but kept him under strict surveillance, thus making it impossible for him to do any real anti-Nazi work among his followers, the Jewish workers. Therefore he decided to go underground. He left his wife and little child and disappeared. Only his closest friends knew that he was hiding out in the ghetto under an assumed name.

Around the middle of 1940 he received a tip that the Gestapo had found his hiding place and was about to rearrest him for "subversive activities." He immediately changed his address. Several attempts to slip out of the ghetto with forged papers proved unsuccessful, because the Gestapo was on the lookout for him. He was finally smuggled out by some of his Polish friends, and under the greatest difficulties and in constant danger of being caught he made his way through Poland and at last came to London.

In May 1942 he was made a member of the Polish National Council, where he, together with Dr. Ignacy Schwarzbart, represented the Jewish population of Poland.

It was to Zygielbojm that the Polish courier who had talked to Michael Klepfisz and other members of the ghetto underground came immediately upon his arrival in London in the last days of November. He reported to Zygielbojm what he had seen in the ghetto and the demands of the Jews in the ghetto for weapons.

There were other things, too, which had to be discussed between the two men. The courier had been told by the Jews in Poland that many of them, particularly the women and children, could be saved if there were enough money. The Germans could easily be bribed. With a few million dollars, many thousands might escape.

This is what the Jews in the Warsaw Ghetto had told him. "See that the Allied governments are told of this possibility, and then let our Jewish leaders know. Let them go to Downing Street and to the White House in Washington. Let them sit there and wait, and neither eat nor drink until they are heard. Let them ask the Allied governments to avenge at once the murders committed upon millions of innocent people, to bomb open German cities and to inform the German people why they are doing so. But above all ask them to send us weapons."

Zygielbojm listened to the courier, his eyes full of sadness. "If we could only do something for them," he murmured. "If we could only do something for them!"

In a special audience with Prime Minister General Sikorski the courier discussed the desire of the Warsaw Jews to obtain arms. The general listened carefully. He was a man of vast human understanding. He did not belong to those who had governed Poland before the war in the interests of a small clique. He had never entertained the slightest anti-Semitic feelings, and, unlike some of his colleagues in the army, he was by no means gratified at the anti-Semitic excesses of the Nazis in Poland. He was, on the contrary, profoundly shocked. Sometimes he talked to his close friends about it. He was afraid of the future. Would the Jews ever forgive what had happened to them in Poland? Would not the sea of Jewish blood which had been spilled create a gulf between the Jews and the Poles which would not be overcome for generations?

Sikorski immediately understood that here was a justified demand which must be answered. "I'll do my utmost to make the government send weapons," he promised his informant.

The same day Zygielbojm also went to see Sikorski.

He had not slept at all the night before. A thousand ideas kept rushing through his mind. What position was he to take? Should he support the Jewish demands for weapons? He knew that there was no chance for the survival of the Jews once open resistance began. Sending weapons to the Jews meant sending them to their deaths. Zygielbojm felt himself responsible for the Jews in the ghetto of Warsaw—and, beyond them, for all the Jews in Poland. Did he, sitting safely in London, have the right to send others to certain death? He was thinking of his family and his friends. He was thinking of Czerniakow, his old friend and co-worker in the Jewish Council. Czerniakow had been opposed to any resistance—till it was too late. The thought of Czerniakow's death was a sign to him. Everything was lost. At least, thought Zygielbojm, he could save the Jews in Warsaw from dying like cattle. He could help them to die if they had chosen to die. And perhaps—Zygielbojm hardly dared to think it, though—perhaps not all of them would have to die. Was it not possible that once the Jews struck, once the open fight against the Germans began, the Polish underground and all the other Poles would follow the lead of the Jews and rebel openly? Was it not possible that a large-scale war inside Poland could develop? If this could be achieved, then the German Army would have to fight the Russians with another enemy in the rear. It might change the entire complexion of the war. Anything would be possible then. . . .

But even after Zygielbojm had seen Sikorski and presented the demand of the Polish Jews for weapons, he was not quite certain whether he had done the right thing. In a letter that he wrote during those days of indecision he said, "I am worrying now about the problem of the next steps I have to take in the National Council. The most important question is this: at home there is a division of opinion as to whether the time is ripe for an armed revolt against the invader. All Polish organizations without exception are opposed to such a move because, they say, it will only drain the blood of the people and destroy them without any results. It is for this reason that they have refused the Jewish people the arms they have asked for to fight against German annihilation."

But at the meeting of the Polish National Council in which the question came up for discussion, Zygielbojm made a fierce and passionate plea to give the Jews weapons. It was a secret session, and nothing was ever published regarding it. The members were very excited and the discussion became extremely heated. Almost the entire government was behind Sikorski in its approval of the Jewish demands. So were the Socialists, and the members of the peasant party, whose head was Mr. Mikolajczyk. On the other hand, members of the Rightist parties and a few army spokesmen were completely opposed to giving weapons to the Jews. Their reasoning was identical. They did not think that the

Jews would make a fight of it. They did not think they had enough weapons themselves to be able to afford to give them away for purely demonstrative purposes. Nor did they think that it was the task of the Polish government-in-exile to go out of its way for the Jews. Above and beneath their opposition was their still strong anti-Semitism, which even the last years of Jewish suffering and castigation had not served to diminish.

After many hours of passionate discussion the Rightists were finally voted down, and that same night an order was flashed to the chief of the military organization in Poland saying that the Jews should be given arms.

That was in December.

Once more the Jewish holiday of Chanukah had come around, celebrated all over the world in memory of the victorious revolt of the Maccabees against their Syrian oppressors under King Antiochus in 168 B.C.

Throughout the world the Jews prayed at this feast of Chanukah in 1942. Many of them said only the prayers appointed for this holiday. But some of them prayed not only in memory of those who more than two thousand years ago had fought such a courageous fight but also for those in their own day who were going to repeat this fight. Zygielbojm in London prayed for them; the people in Palestine prayed for them; the agents of Dagani throughout Poland prayed for them:

"In the days of the Hasmonian, Mattathias son of Johana, the High Priest, and his sons, when the iniquitous power of Greece rose up against Thy people Israel to make them forgetful of Thy Law, and to force them to transgress the statutes of Thy will, then didst Thou in Thine abundant mercy rise up for them in the time of their trouble. Thou didst plead their cause, Thou didst judge their suit, Thou didst avenge their wrong. Thou didst deliver the strong into the hands of the weak, the many into the hands of the few, the impure into the hands of the pure, the wicked into the hands of the righteous, and the arrogant into the hands of them that occupied themselves with Thy Law; for Thyself Thou didst make a great and holy name in Thy world, and for Thy people Israel Thou didst work a great deliverance and redemption as at this day. And thereupon Thy children came into the oracle of Thy house, cleansed Thy temple, purified Thy sanctuary, kindled lights in Thy holy courts, and appointed these eight days of Chanukah in order to give thanks and praises unto Thy great name."

The Jews in the ghetto prayed too, and many of them may have hoped that they, too, would have an opportunity to prove themselves as worthy as the followers of Mattathias.

And then they learned that they would get arms.

The Polish government-in-exile informed the chief of the military organization in Poland that he should issue to the Jews "the necessary number of mechanized arms, automatic rifles, revolvers, and principally hand grenades."

Stores of arms and ammunition were buried in woods and fields through the country. The Germans had found only a few of them. Now a great deal of digging began at night to bring some of these weapons to light again. And through various channels they found their way into the ghetto.

At the same time thousands of Jews inside the ghetto of Warsaw, men and women between the ages of eighteen and forty, enlisted for active service. They were immediately taken in hand by instructors provided by Mordecai and military experts of the Chaluzim and the "Bund." In order to cover up and hide these activities from the German authorities, a number of "charity" and "cultural" organizations were founded, or those already existing were transformed into training centers. The actual training took place in soundproof cellars.

This speedily growing army was further reinforced by the Jewish partisans who were still streaming into the Warsaw Ghetto from all over the country.

All this happened in the first part of January 1943.

Chapter XIX

The Revolt

Old professor balaban sat at his desk in his room in the Jewish Community Building. For many weeks he had been furiously writing his history of the ghetto. There was something which made him hurry up with his work. He forced himself to go on with it, even late in the night, when he could hardly keep his eyes open. He scarcely ever slept any more, seldom took time to eat, and talked to almost no one, under the compulsion he felt to get the book finished while there was yet time. How much time was left? Very little, he felt. There was nothing left in his life now except the book, the history of the ghetto which was to contain the facts, all the facts; which was to show the world what the Nazis had done, what human beings were capable of doing and what human beings were capable of suffering, a book which would keep the fight alive in the memory of man in decades far beyond the life of any of those who were now carrying on the greatest mass extermination of all time.

How much more time was left? The Nazis killed fast. During the last few months of 1942 more than 90 per cent of all deaths in the ghetto had been due to shootings. The starvation rations,. the lack of hospitals and doctors, the mercilessly raging epidemics, the suicides alone could have accounted for an almost fantastic increase of the death rate. But as a matter of fact all these causes of death together did not account for even 10 per cent of the deaths in the ghetto.

The ghetto of Warsaw, which at the end of 1940 had numbered more than five hundred thousand inhabitants, had shrunk by the end of 1942 to less than forty thousand. And there was a persistent rumor that the Germans were going to wipe out what was left during January. January 31 was the dead line set by Heinrich Himmler himself.

Now the people in the ghetto knew that they were going to die. But there was no more despair. There was only the will to fight. By the middle of January practically everybody had volunteered to help in the resistance movement. Even children were being trained, and also the old men and women who were still alive. Nobody wanted any part in appeasement any more. None of those who were given an opportunity to leave the ghetto wanted to go. They had seen what their duty was, and they wanted to do it.

Theirs was a strange kind of fatalism. In a way the people in the ghetto considered themselves as already dead. The world beyond the walls of the ghetto was no longer their world. They could not understand that world beyond the walls any longer, nor did they think that those on the other side could understand them. Even the youngest among them, full of life and full of expectation, began to feel that way. Even young and beautiful Tosia did when she wrote a letter to the man with whom she had hoped to live for the rest of her life but who seemed now so very far away. It was her last letter to the world beyond the ghetto walls.

DEAREST FRIEND:

Don't be alarmed by what I am going to say in this letter. Many times I have begun to write to you, but a feeling of the utter uselessness of writing letters has kept me from completing them.

Of Israel's [the Jewish people] sickness and my own [our movement] you are surely aware. . . . We have been struggling against it for a long time . . . But now it is perfectly evident that the malady is absolutely incurable. So the doctors have decreed. And one must become accustomed to this fate.

The most horrible thing is that we have no more time to become accustomed. You probably would be interested to know how the rest of our relatives fare. Well then, Praotsky [pogroms] and Shehita [murder] live together with me and Israel. There was no other way out. It ruined Israel's health, and I now see how this will lead to his death. But what can I do? These are the conditions, and there is no way of changing them. I do all I can to save his life, but all forces are against me. Have you ever tried to pound the wall with your head and bare hands?

Hurban [destruction] followed me faithfully and tried to make my days pleasant. For you know that in regard to the satisfying of emotions . . . He [destruction] was also very kind. I saw Haiyah [the animal]. However, I found none besides her.

About our economic situation all I can say is that we manage to live somehow. We work as before, Yosef [Kaplan] and I in our trades [in the executive of Hashomer Hatzair in Poland], and somehow the work continues. Only one thing has changed the prospect for the future. I have only one thought to tell the world: that Israel is so sick. He is my very best friend, and even if he can't be helped very much materially, even the knowledge that someone is with us, if only in thought, in our suffering—this brings some comfort. But don't be distressed at all this, dear friend, for you know our theory of adaptation to conditions.

This has turned out to be a strange letter. At the outset I had intended to tell you only about myself and to inquire about you. How could I capture in my memory all the small details about you and how often I think what you would do on a certain occasion. But sometimes I can't picture you in my mind, for I haven't even a photograph. Who knows what will become of me before you receive this letter. . . .

TOSIA

On January 18 the Germans began what they believed to be an "action" for the final liquidation of the Warsaw Ghetto.

At six-thirty in the morning strong formations of SS and Lithuanian troops entered the ghetto and immediately began to blockade a number of houses. But they met with a big surprise.

The Jews had barricaded themselves inside the blockaded houses. The Germans were received by a hail of bullets and hand grenades. They retired and demanded that the Jewish police should storm the blockaded houses. But many of the members of the Jewish police immediately went over to the side of the Jews and helped them defend the houses.

More than twenty Gestapo men and German and Lithuanian soldiers were immediately killed. Thereupon the Germans decided to leave the ghetto in great haste. But they returned later in the afternoon. And this time the SS was reinforced by regular German troops. Several houses were stormed and the inhabitants taken away. As they were marched to the Transfer Point there was almost constant fire from Jewish houses, and many hand grenades were thrown wherever the Germans showed themselves in the streets.

A regular battle developed at the Transfer Point itself. Jewish fighters had managed to mingle with those who were awaiting their evacuation. Then a signal was given. The fighters began to throw hand grenades at the German policemen. Before the Germans could do anything their weapons were taken away from them. Most of them were killed where they stood, and only a few escaped. In the general confusion most of those who were to be deported made their getaway.

More than thirty German military policemen and SS men were killed. Scores were wounded. The Jewish casualties amounted to nine.

The news of what had happened spread like wildfire throughout the ghetto. Everywhere the Jews rejoiced. Some of them believed that the day of liberation had finally come. But most of them understood that this was but the beginning.

Among those who were exuberant with joy was Mr. Ganzweich, the well-known Jewish gangster who had made such an excellent living as a food smuggler and as head of the "diamond research" organization. As you remember, he had been taken away by the Gestapo, who wanted to avenge the death of Mr. Cohn, the protégé of a rival Gestapo gang. But he had convinced his would-be murderers that they might do better business with him if they allowed him to live. This they did, and for many months thereafter Ganzweich had prolonged his life by revealing to them the secret whereabouts of highly precious jewels inside the ghetto.

On the day of the uprising the Gestapo felt that Ganzweich might be an excellent agent for discovering the plans of the Jewish Resistance Committee. That is why they set him free and dispatched him into the ghetto.

He appeared scarcely the worse for wear. He still was better fed than the other Jews and he still wore his swanky clothes. People who recognized him when he walked down the street looked the other way. Ganzweich did not mind. Somehow he found his way to one of the offices of the Resistance Committee. It so happened that Michael Klepfisz was present when he came in.

"Here I am," Ganzweich simply said. "The Germans let me go."

"To spy on us, I suppose?"

Ganzweich nodded. "No use trying to fool you. But I assure you that I have no intention of doing what they asked me to do. I want to stay here and do my duty as a Jew. I have finally seen the light."

Klepfisz looked at him in silence.

"You don't believe it. But I tell you . . ." Ganzweich felt his forehead becoming moist. He who had never been afraid, even when dealing with the most feared Gestapo men, now became panicky. "I assure you . . ."

"Oh, I believe you," Klepfisz said. "But the question is whether my comrades will. And then I may be mistaken, and a lot of us would have to pay for this mistake."

"Give me a chance."

Ganzweich waited a moment, but when no answer came he turned around. He walked out of the building and down the street. His steps became faster. When he turned around the corner he began to run. Once or twice he looked around, but nobody was following him. Still he ran as fast as he could, sweat dripping from his face, his breath coming in gasps. He was only a hundred feet from the gate when the shot came. Ganzweich fell down on the pavement, a surprised look on his dead face.

The Germans did not come back that day or the next day. They had not believed that there would be any resistance at all or that it would be so strong. Governor Fischer held a hurried conference in his office with Gruppenfuehrer Mende, Dr. Auerwald, and several others.

Fischer explained. Of course he was not afraid of the Jews in the ghetto. What could they do, anyhow? As far as he could see, they could not possibly have many weapons. On the other hand, he wanted this thing finished without much to-do. He did not want to have to report to Berlin about it, nor did he want to have to ask the army for reinforcements. He wanted to avoid publicity at any price, for, unimportant as such little uproar as this was, it could give the other Poles and people in other occupied countries some strange ideas. That had to be prevented—at any cost. So something had to be done about the ghetto at once.

After some discussion it was decided that no official recognition should be made of the underground attempts of the Jews at resistance. The Germans were to treat the events of January 19 not as a revolt but rather as a misdemeanor which had to be punished. Dr. Fischer ordered the day of punishment set for January 21.

On that day six hundred German policemen entered the ghetto in full battle dress, with sub-machine guns, hand grenades, and two field guns. Ambulances followed them.

The blockade of houses started at once, with the Germans throwing hand grenades and petards through the windows. They had no great trouble storming the houses. They killed everybody they could find, though again a great many of their own men were either wounded or killed in the ensuing fight.

An hour later Governor Fischer was informed that the Jews had been punished. He felt gratified. He believed that this was the end of the so-called Jewish resistance. Two days later the final liquidation of the ghetto was to start. No chances were to be taken. All available men were to be sent into the ghetto fully armed. Even tanks were to be employed.

On Saturday, January 23, the Germans arrived in the ghetto soon after noon and again began to throw grenades and petards and to kill all the Jews they found in the first houses they came to. Then they blockaded other houses and brought the trapped Jews down into the street. To their great relief, they found that the Jews were completely unarmed and unable to defend themselves. It was evident that only a few of them had possessed weapons at all or had been trained to use them.

On this day and on the following day more than six thousand Jews were deported to Treblinka. But all during these days some fighting continued. Every once in a while shots would come from a few windows and kill a number of Germans. All in all, the fighting lasted seven days. Many houses inside the ghetto were completely burned down. The Germans had suffered more than a hundred deaths. There were now hardly more than thirty thousand Jews left in the ghetto.

And this seemed to be the end of the revolt in the ghetto of Warsaw.

Was it the end?

"It cannot be the end," Professor Balaban said to his pupil, Dr. Ringelblum, who was visiting him in the Community Building. "I know it cannot be the end—but what can follow?"

Dr. Ringelblum was concerned. He saw that the old man was steadily losing weight. How frail and feeble he had become these last weeks! Dr. Ringelblum wanted to say something to comfort his old teacher. "We still have a chance to die in a dignified way."

"Die in a dignified way!" The old man rose to his feet, holding onto the desk with trembling hands. "You know and I know that the Nazis can never win! They will be beaten. They must be beaten! History would lose all meaning if they were to win. . . . No. They will not win. But is it not senseless, too, that while they are being beaten we must die? I am a very old man. I do not speak for myself. How long would I have had to live even if the Nazis had never come into Poland? Perhaps a few more years. I do not care." He sank into his chair again.

"I know what you mean. You are thinking of the others. Of the young ones. Of all our people. Yes, they have to die. But they can die fighting. To give posterity an example of what Jews are capable of doing."

"You are a historian, Ringelblum." Balaban smiled sadly. "I have always thought of myself as a historian. But lately it has been very difficult for me to keep a detached view of things. You know, it is all very fine to think of posterity. But how many of us really care about posterity? Isn't all that most of the people want just the right to live, nothing else?" After a while he continued: "Speaking as a historian, strictly as a historian, Ringelblum, it seems to me that there is something very unjust about history. There are generations who can live more or less as they please. Nothing much happens to them except that they are born, they work, do a job, beget children, are loved and hated, and one day they die. No great crises come into their lives—they don't have to make important decisions. They just have to be reasonably decent. That is all that is demanded of them. And then there are other generations who have the bad luck to live in what is later on called a 'decisive period of history.' It is not enough for them to be decent and to try to be reasonably happy. The times in which they live force them to make real decisions. They must take a stand. They are either cowards and traitors or heroes. They cannot get away from these decisions."

"It seems to me," Dr. Ringelblum said, "as though we Jews have always had to live in such decisive periods. No matter how secure the rest of the world lived, no matter how settled everything else seemed, we always had to take a stand. We always had to fight for something because somebody was always fighting us. We always had to accept the fight, no matter how superior the other side was and how hopeless the fight seemed. And when we ran for our lives, which is, after all, a reasonable thing to do in certain circumstances, we were called cowards."

"Yes. And perhaps some of us were cowards and are still cowards. And there will probably always be cowards among the Jews just as there are and always will be cowards among other people. Only we

Jews are always judged according to the behavior of these cowards who after all did nothing much, except that they wanted to keep on living."

"But this time we don't want to keep on living. This time we will not run for our lives. We will fight."

"I wish I were younger and could fight too."

"You are fighting in your way. Your book . . ."

Balaban smiled again. "I know. I wanted it to be a fighting book. It is a fighting book. But is it enough to write in such a moment? I wish I were younger. I have been thinking a lot of my students these days, Ringelblum. I see them, their young faces turned to me, listening to what I had to say. It seems so long ago that I talked to them. I wish I could talk to them again. I could make them understand. I could make them fight . . ."

"Young people throughout the world will read your book and will fight."

"I wouldn't be too sure. One day Gruppenfuehrer Mende is going to take the manuscript and have it translated. And then he will be furious and will burn it—and me with it."

"That must never happen. Why don't you let me have the manuscript? You know we have buried a lot of manuscripts, important testimonials, and even photographs in safe places. We may not be around when they are dug up. But one day they'll come to light again. . . . A few people in London know where they are hidden. Let me take your manuscript there."

The old man shook his head. "Not yet. I want to think it over. Perhaps one of these days . . ."

When Ringelblum had left, the professor slowly got up. The book. No, he was not afraid of Mende. He was not afraid of being killed. He was afraid that the Nazis would simply publish another book, the book they had wanted him to write, an account which would whitewash them, and would put his name on it. What could he do to stop them? There was only one thing to do. He had to destroy the book. And he had to make sure they knew that he had destroyed it.

Slowly he walked over to the stove. There was no fire burning there. The Jews had long ago forgotten what coal was like. Holding his manuscript with trembling fingers, Professor Balaban struck a match. He was going to set the papers afire and throw them into the stove. But he did not do it. He could not do it. He came back to the desk and put the manuscript there. He could not destroy his own work. It was like taking his own life.

Suddenly he felt overcome by extreme fatigue. He began to tremble. It was so cold. He was afraid, too. What would the Nazis do to him? He did not fear death. But if they should take him away and torture him, and force him to put his name to some kind of a history of the ghetto . . . Yes, that is what they would do. That is what they had wanted to do all the time. That is why they had made him write his history—just for the record, so they could produce one day whatever they wanted the world to know.

He looked at his manuscript. He ought to destroy it, but he could not. It was like taking one's own life. Taking one's own life . . .

Balaban was an orthodox Jew. And the Jewish religion, like most every other religion, forbids suicide. Under certain circumstances, however, it actually commands a man to commit suicide. When a Jew is persecuted for his religion, when he is asked to do things which his religion forbids him to do, when he is ordered to commit crimes or to behave in any way which cannot be reconciled with Jewish ethics, then he is under compulsion to take his life. Then his suicide may become a holy act.

Balaban opened one of the drawers and, taking out his prayer shawl, covered himself with it. As he stood there his eyes kept glancing upward to the chandelier in the middle of the ceiling. He could not take his eyes away from it. At length he took hold of a chair, moved it under the chandelier, and slowly climbed up on it. He looked around once more. This was the room in which Czerniakow had died only six months before. Czerniakow had not wanted to fight, and therefore he had to die. Balaban could not fight either. And so he, too, had to die.

Slowly he pulled the prayer shawl over his head. "Hear, O Israel, God the Almighty is the only God," he cried.

They found him hanging there the next morning. He had used his prayer shawl for a rope.

Within an hour or so Gruppenfuehrer Mende arrived, guarded by twenty SS men. Mende searched the entire room. He was white with rage. "Why, this double-crossing Jew!" he shouted.

He searched all through the room for the manuscript, but in vain. It was nowhere to be found. The people who had found Balaban insisted that they had seen it lying on the desk when they came in. But it was no longer there.

It looked as though the revolt in the ghetto was ended. The streets looked deserted. People everywhere seemed to have given up hope. One could walk for miles without hearing a voice or seeing a human being. Epidemics raged. There was almost no food left. It was only a question of time until the Germans would strike to liquidate the last thirty thousand inhabitants.

Outside the ghetto, throughout Warsaw, though, the Poles did not believe that everything was over for the Jews. They had witnessed the fight the Jews put up. They had seen German soldiers fleeing from the ghetto in great haste. They admired the Jews, who against all odds had put up such a heroic struggle. They felt that this heroic struggle could not have been in vain.

The Poles in Warsaw, and people everywhere who heard the story of the short-lived revolt, felt new hope. The Germans had finally been met in open battle by those whom they had tried so hard to enslave and destroy.

Chapter XX

The General

The general walked up and down in his office in the building once occupied by members of the General Staff of the Polish Army but since taken over by the German General Staff. The general was a tall, spare man in his late fifties. He looked younger, though, and he felt younger, too. At least he had felt younger until a short while ago. Lately he had had quite a few headaches. The war was not going too well.

But the general was not thinking of the war just now. He was thinking of the Jews in the ghetto of Warsaw. This was a *verdammte Schweinerei*—a damned mess. The Gestapo and the SS should have taken care of it. This was no business for the German Army. The German Army was there to fight a war, not to do away with defenseless Jews.

Not that the general liked the Jews. God forbid! He certainly did not! But there was a difference between not liking people and killing them. And, anyhow, the general knew a few Jews who were quite all right. Of course they were not like these Polish Jews, with their long beards and kaftans. The Jews whom the general had met in Berlin looked practically like any other Germans. They had good manners, too. If one were not told that they were Jews one would not know it.

The general kept on pacing the floor.

Of course, if the Fuehrer felt that the Jews should be annihilated, then they should be. But, damn it all, it was not the business of the army to do it! If Herr Himmler could not take care of those few Jews in the ghetto he should not have started the whole business in the first place. Now this unspeakable Governor Fischer and the even worse Gruppenfuehrer Mende—creatures of Himmler, both of them—did not know what to do because a few Jews had actually fired on them. Well, wasn't that just too bad! The general smiled grimly. He didn't mind if a few Jews fired on the Gestapo heroes. Served them right. But that was no reason to come running to him now to ask for help. Hell! The army wasn't going to make war against the ghetto. The army had other worries.

Yes indeed, the army had other worries. The general was not too certain that he still liked the war. A lot of things had happened lately that made him wonder whether victory was still just around the corner, as the Fuehrer constantly promised.

Only a few weeks ago the Fuehrer had declared that Stalingrad was in German hands and that the war was as good as won. But the general knew very well that Stalingrad was by no means in the possession of the Germans.

Instead the Americans had invaded North Africa. The English were driving Rommel before them. Africa was lost to the Axis. Berlin was being constantly bombed. The French Fleet had been scuttled at Toulon. Stalingrad had been relieved. On January 31, 1943, Field Marshal General Friedrich Paulus had surrendered with an army of more than three hundred thousand men, all of them now prisoners in Russia. The

Germans had been forced to retire in Russia. On February 14 the Red Army had retaken Rostov, and two days later Kharkov. The Fuehrer had had a nervous breakdown. And the general was not at all certain when and where the German rout in Russia could be stopped.

There was one thing the general had learned when he went to the Military Academy. He had learned that once you defeated a country, the country was defeated. But in this strange war that axiom did not seem to hold true. Poland had been defeated, but somehow there was no calm in Poland.

Now as to these Jews. If something had to be done, it should have been done years ago. Instead now, when Germany really needed every man, there was trouble with the Jews. There was this mess in the Warsaw Ghetto. And in other parts of the country things were going wrong too. In February one hundred and thirty thousand textile workers in Lodz had gone on strike to prevent the deportation of more Jews to Treblinka and Lublin. And since the labor of these men was needed at that moment in the war effort, the authorities were forced to give in—for the time being.

None of these things did the general like.

In his office Governor Fischer was not in a much better humor than the general. He, too, did not like the present state of affairs. He, too, was angry, though he did not know precisely at whom. So many mistakes had been made, unnecessary mistakes.

There was a report lying before him on his desk, a report dealing with a new institution which was housed in what had formerly been a Jewish orphan asylum not far from Warsaw. It seems that a professor from Berlin had installed there laboratories for experiments in race improvement. They had brought Russians, Poles, Czechs, and Jews there whom they forced to have intercourse with gypsy girls and Mongolian women, so that they could study the practical results of these mixed unions. They also had a number of Jews there on whom they practiced vivisection. Furthermore, a number of newborn babies, mostly of Jewish descent, were brought there to be operated on like so many guinea pigs.

Dr. Fischer certainly did not like the Jews. As far as he was concerned they could all go to hell. But . . . well . . . there was a limit to everything. There were some things that were just not done. The governor had an odd feeling in the pit of his stomach.

But anyhow, if such things had to be done, the least one could expect was that they should be kept secret. But the professor from Berlin and his collaborators did not seem to be interested in secrecy. Now they had castrated two hundred Jewish prisoners in order to make experiments about changing a man's sex. Also, twenty-five Jewish girls had been given injections to cause artificial pregnancy.

Why, for God's sake, couldn't they keep those things secret? Why did they allow them to get out, so that the Polish underground could write about them in their filthy papers and pamphlets?

There were other things that worried Governor Fischer too. Many of his men were no longer satisfied with their stay in Poland. They wanted to be transferred to France or Italy. They were cynically open about the reason. They said that business was no longer good. They declared that it was too bad that most of the Jews were gone, because they at least had represented a steady source of income.

Now that was a nice state of affairs! When the governor had told some of his men that they should be grateful to the Fuehrer that he had done away with those Jews, they simply laughed at him. Even Captain Reinhard, who was in charge of the annihilation squads, had laughed. And, after all, Reinhard was a personal appointee of Heinrich Himmler.

Governor Fischer was conferring with the general in the latter's office. There were several papers on the general's desk—pamphlets from the Polish underground.

One of them, dated March 11, read:

> The Polish people, although itself a victim of frightful terror, looks with horror and deep sympathy on the murder of the remainder of the Jewish population in Poland by the Germans.
>
> It has voiced its protest against this crime, a protest which has reached the conscience of the whole free world, and it gave to the Jews who escaped from the ghetto or from annihilation camps help so extensive that the Germen occupiers published a decree threatening with death those Poles who help Jews who were in hiding.
>
> But there are some individuals devoid of honor and conscience recruited from the criminal world, who seek to create for themselves a new source of

income by blackmailing both the Poles who helped the Jews to hide and the Jews themselves.

The Leadership of the Civilian Struggle warns that these cases of blackmail are noted and will be punished with the fullest severity of the law, immediately if possible, but in any case in the future.

THE LEADERSHIP OF THE CIVILIAN STRUGGLE

"Just big words," the governor remarked dryly.

"I wonder if the Poles are going to stop at words," the general said. "How about the Polish police? What do you know about them?"

"We have investigated every man. They are working for us, all right. We can depend upon them."

"Indeed!" The general adjusted his monocle in his eye and looked hard at the governor. "Indeed!" There was another pause. "Would it surprise you, Governor, if I told you that the Polish police have been delivering weapons to the Jews?"

Governor Fischer started to say something, but the general cut him off with a sweep of his hand. "Our Intelligence . . . You know, our Intelligence is still pretty good. It says here"—he rummaged for a while among the papers on his desk—"it says here that a transport of arms destined for the Jews fell into the hands of Polish militia. Before the Poles could do anything about it, the Jews sent them an ultimatum that the arms would have to be returned within an hour—or else." The general looked at the governor again. "What do you suppose happened?"

"The arms were returned?"

"The arms were returned."

There was a long pause.

"And that is not all," the general continued. "Those men in the ghetto are doing quite a job, you know. I think they must have a lot of weapons by now. I have also been informed that they have been building secret fortifications and underground shelters inside the ghetto."

"Exaggerations, my dear general."

"Perhaps. But am I supposed to take your word for it, Herr Governor? Or do you have some . . . proofs?"

The governor cleared his throat. "What kind of proof do you want? Aren't the Jews proof enough in themselves? Look at them. They have not done anything for years. They have taken everything we have dealt out. All they could think of was to cry for help. If you come to my office I can show you a dossier in which we have collected all their cries for help which they sent abroad. That is, all we could intercept. Messages to the National Committee in Poland, to the Jewish World Congress in New York, to the authorities in Palestine, and so on and so on."

"I see what you mean." The general smiled. "But has it ever occurred to you, Herr Governor, that people sometimes change? That they are able to do certain things when they become desperate that they would not have dreamed of doing before? Take the Poles. It took the army three weeks to defeat them. As far as I can see here, you are still trying to keep them defeated after more than three years—and you are not having too much success."

Governor Fischer's face became red. "I am not sure that I like your insinuations, Herr General."

The general was unperturbed. "Naturally you don't like them. But I am stating facts, cold facts."

"All right, all right! So the Jews have weapons." The governor became quite incensed. Trying to convince the general was like banging one's head against a wall. "Well, we saw what they could do with weapons in January, and the next time we will not be taken by surprise. We will make short work of them."

"I wonder. Incidentally, why has nothing been done about the Jews during the whole of February and March? Now here it is almost April."

"Time is on our side, Herr General. There is practically nothing left to eat in the ghetto. But we would have struck before except that there was no place to send the Jews. Treblinka is full. I was told to wait for a while. Orders from Berlin."

"I see."

"But it won't be long now, you can be sure."

The general summoned Gruppenfuehrer Mende to his office. The general was pale.

"I have here a report that two of your men last night arrested a young man who was walking on Poznanska Street. They said he was a Jew. They told him that it was a crime to be out of the ghetto. He said he was not a Jew. Do you know anything about it?"

"Well, no."

"Then let me tell you. Your men asked the man's name. He said it was Berson."

Mende relaxed. "Well, so he was a Jew after all."

"Please do not interrupt me, Herr Gruppenfuehrer. Where was I? Oh yes. Berson, to be sure. Well, your men thought that he was a Jew. They struck him in the face, and they tore up his papers. When the man began to protest, they shot him dead. Any comment, Herr Gruppenfuehrer?"

"These things happen."

"So I am told," the general replied dryly. "Only listen to this! The victim was a certain Vladimir Berson. He comes from one of the best Polish families. They are Christians . . . and as Aryan as you are—if that is anything to be proud of. But that is not all. His mother is a German. She is a member of the party—has a high post in it, in fact. She has been sent here to do some educational work."

There was a moment's silence. "That's bad," Mende said.

"You bet it's bad," the general barked. "What are you going to do about it?"

"What . . . am I . . . going . . . ?"

"Yes, of course. Do you think I should do something about it? Shall I arrest you and have you shot?"

"Herr General!"

"Get out! Do something about it! Do something fast! The mother is beside herself with grief. She has already reported to Berlin. There will be a scandal. I hate scandals!"

The general collapsed into his chair. He felt almost exhausted.

By that time Governor Fischer and his collaborators had already made their plans for the final annihilation of the ghetto. The managers of the plants for which Jewish workers were slaving had notified their employees that the plants were to be transferred from Warsaw and that the Jews were expected to report voluntarily for transfer to the new locations. They assured the Jews that they had nothing to fear because their work was fully appreciated.

But none of the Jewish workers volunteered.

Next came a move of Colonel Walter Tebens, who held a key position in the Transportation Board of the Government General. The colonel had been extremely busy since the trains began running between the ghetto and Treblinka. He had not done a very good job. Many trains had failed to run on time, although the German administration in Poland had always prided itself that everything went precisely on schedule. But nobody blamed the colonel personally. Not even the most ardent Nazi was interested in whether a batch of a few thousand Jews died a few hours earlier or later. And however the passengers felt about the trains put at their disposal, they never could make a complaint afterward. That was a nice thing about Colonel Tebens' job. But now the job had suddenly become complicated. There seemed to be no more passengers for him and his trains. And the governor put it up to him to get them.

After considering the situation the colonel decided that what he needed was a bit of propaganda for his trains. He had posters put on the ghetto walls, in which he addressed himself to the "Jewish War Production in Warsaw." This poster attempted to refute the warnings of the Resistance Committee that the Jews who volunteered for transfer would be killed. It read:

> On the eve of March 15 the Command of the Fighter Organization posted a placard which I wish to refute.
>
> Jewish war-industry workers! Do not believe those people who are trying to confuse you. They wish to incite you to actions which will inevitably lead to regrettable consequences. There is no security at all in their shelters, and life there is impossible, just as it is impossible for Jews in the Aryan district. Insecurity and inactivity by themselves will morally break down those who are accustomed to working.
>
> Jewish workers! Go to Travniki, go to Poniatow, because there you will be able to live and survive the war. Take your wives and children with you, because they too will be taken care of.

The poster created some excitement in the ghetto. For once the people left their houses, gathered near the walls to read what the Germans had to tell them, and then went home discussing what they were going to do. There were still a few of them who wondered if it might not be a good idea to follow the Nazi advice. But the overwhelming majority said no, and there was in every group at least one person who passionately denounced the Nazis as liars and the new offer as a new trap.

Colonel Tebens waited for a few days. When nothing happened, he sent a detachment of men into the ghetto and took a dozen of the more prominent citizens away. Perhaps he believed that this was the best way to prove his good will to the Jews.

Colonel Tebens never got an answer to his generous offer to the Jews. The Resistance Committee soon pasted its own slogans on the walls of the ghetto above the posters of the Nazis. "No men and property" was the slogan issued by the Jewish Resistance Committee. It called upon the Jews to "die as soldiers rather than be transferred to the death camps."

Now all of the Jews were unified behind the Resistance Committee. Especially was the youth firm in its resolve to fight. Death no longer spelled terror for them.

When Colonel Tebens had the hostages murdered, and the bodies sent back into the ghetto, he did precisely what the Jews had expected of him.

Some of the older people still hoped against hope. Perhaps they would be liberated before it was too late. They, too, knew now that Germany was no longer winning the war. They heard with joy about the Allied air raids over Germany, about Rommel's flight from Africa. But if the liberators did not come in time—well, anything was better than being butchered like so many sheep.

Could they be liberated before it was too late? By now the world had become conscious of the Jewish plight throughout Poland and the Hitler-occupied countries. By now pressure was being brought upon the Allied governments to help the Jews of Europe—before it was too late. The State Department in Washington and the Foreign Office in London received thousands of appeals, many of them from personalities or organizations which could not be disregarded. Still the State Department and the Foreign Office hesitated. The men there felt that it was not their job to do anything about the Jews. It was their job to see to it that the Axis was defeated. The Jews formed only a small part of the people who were suffering under Hitler. True enough, the other people were only being enslaved and starved, while the Jews were being murdered. True enough, the defeat of the Axis, even though it might take another year or more, would liberate most of the people under Hitler, but it would come too late to liberate the Jews; the Nazis would have murdered all of them by that time.

Finally a compromise was found. It was decided to hold a semi-official conference to discuss the plight of the Jews. The State Department and the Foreign Office in London were not to be represented officially but would send observers. There should be delegates from England and from America, but since they were to have no official capacity, they could only discuss and advise, but not formulate any definite plans, let alone make any clear-cut decisions.

It was finally decided that the conference should take place at Hamilton, Bermuda. It was to be called The Anglo-American Conference on Refugees. Even the word "Jews" was studiously avoided. As far as the State Department and the Foreign Office were concerned, there was no such thing as a plight of those whom Hitler had decided to annihilate. There was only "the plight of refugees." The conference was to start on April 19.

On April 19 Governor Fischer decided that the time had come to liquidate the Warsaw Ghetto.

Chapter XXI

They Hit Back

The Anglo-American Conference on Refugees opened at Hamilton, Bermuda, on April 19, 1943, for a ten-day session. The American delegation of four, headed by Dr. Harold Willis Dodds, president of Princeton University, included Representative Sol Bloom, Senator Scott Lucas of Illinois, and R. Borden Reams of the State Department. The four British delegates were all Parliamentary Under-Secretaries, with Richard K. Law as their leader.

All these men were intelligent, progressive men; all of them had an excellent record of opposition against Fascism and everything Fascism stood for. All of them were horror-stricken about what had happened to the Jews, but none of them saw or wanted to see that Hitler had made a special case of the Jews; that he wanted to exterminate them while he was content to enslave the other nations. None of them saw or wanted to see that the Jews could not, like the other peoples, wait for the liberation that would come with an Allied victory. They did not see, or they did not want to see, that because Hitler had proclaimed his intention of murdering this particular part of humanity it was the duty of those who fought Hitler to prevent him from carrying out his intention.

Perhaps it could not be done. But it could at least be attempted. That is what might have been expected from the Bermuda Conference: some kind of statement, some kind of decision taking up the challenge which Hitler had thrown in the face of the civilized world, some kind of proclamation that the Allied governments were not going to allow the wholesale murder to continue. . . .

Was it too much to expect? Was there any reason why the world which was fighting Hitler should not try to protect those whom Hitler had declared to be his foremost enemies?

It was on this day of April 19, 1943, that the Jewish holiday of the Passover began, the Jewish holiday that has been celebrated for more than three thousand years in memory of the liberation of the Jewish people from slavery to the Egyptians by Moses. It is a celebration not only of their liberation, but of their unification and emergence as a nation among nations.

On this first evening of the holiday the Jews throughout the world stay home, singing and praying, and opening the doors for the entrance of the Prophet Elijahuh, who for them is the symbol of a Saviour, whose memory gives assurance to the Jews that they will always be saved from their enemies, even though a miracle should be necessary to accomplish it. They open the door for the Prophet, and they rise and pray:

"Pour out Thy wrath upon the peoples that have not known Thee, and upon the kingdoms that have not called upon Thy name. For they have devoured Jacob and laid waste his dwelling place.

"Pour out upon them Thy indignation and let Thy fiercest anger overtake them. Pursue them in wrath and destroy them from under the heavens of the Lord."

This is not so much a prayer as a protest. An outcry. A demand that their oppressors be smitten. There has always been ample reason for Jews of every generation, ever since they left the slavery of Egypt to make such an outcry, to make such a demand on their God. Never was there more reason, though, than on this April 19 for the Jews of Warsaw. But on that night they did not assemble in their houses. They did not celebrate Passover. They did not open their doors for the Prophet to enter. They did not demand of their God to smite their enemy. They had learned that their God would not help them if they would not help themselves.

On that evening of April 19, while a number of English and American gentlemen began to deliberate about their fate in lovely Hamilton, Bermuda, the Jews in the Warsaw Ghetto were mounting the barricades.

On that evening armed German detachments surrounded the ghetto. They closed all gates. Then they entered, a few thousand of them, heavily armed SS units. They drove in on cars mounted with machine guns and stop tanks. Ukrainian, Latvian, and Lithuanian detachments followed.

The streets of the ghetto lay deserted. For a while the Germans moved on without any interference. No one tried to stop them. They advanced to streets where stood buildings that had been evacuated some time ago. Suddenly they realized that the buildings were no longer vacant. From a balcony a bomb fell down, hitting the first car and destroying it. The bomb had been thrown by a fifteen-year-old girl. Next to the girl stood Tosia, directing other women in the throwing of bombs and grenades. Within a few seconds the Germans were being bombed from all sides. Rifles appeared at hundreds of windows in the neighborhood. The German cars could not continue on their way because the first completely destroyed car blocked the street. They tried to turn, but the street was too narrow. They tried to get out of their cars, only to be hit by a rain of bullets coming from all sides.

Then a terrific explosion shook the whole street. One of the tanks was in flames. The next moment the other tanks, too, were a sea of fire. Jewish fighters had approached the tanks, crawled underneath them, thrown their hand grenades and bombs, and destroyed themselves together with the tanks.

None of the Germans or their satellites who had penetrated into the ghetto returned. Those who had stayed near the gates turned and sought the safety of Warsaw.

The first battle lasted less than an hour.

But the Jews did not sleep that night. Their leaders went out on the street to give their last commands. Weapons which had been hidden were distributed. Boys and girls were posted as guards on street corners. The larger houses were converted into fortresses. Arsenals were established in every street so that if certain districts should be cut off by the Germans, the fighters would not be left without ammunition. Trenches were dug and cellars converted into shelters; community kitchens were established where the older women were to prepare food for the fighters, food which the children had to take to them wherever they were posted.

Early in the morning a few fighter units led by Mordecai sallied forth from the ghetto and surrounded a number of German workshops where Jewish workers had been on the night shift. Among these shops were some tailor shops where German uniforms were made or repaired. The Jews took the workers along with them and also a number of German uniforms. They also invaded a number of German stores, seized large quantities of foodstuffs, and hauled them back to the ghetto.

When dawn came, banners of revolt hung out of countless windows in the ghetto. There were Polish flags, and flying next to them, the blue and white flags of Palestine. There were also the red flags of revolution. No one was in the streets. Everybody was waiting for the battle to commence.

On the walls of the ghetto new posters appeared. They carried only a few words: "The Jews will fight to the last drop of blood."

The fight had already begun. It was the first organized resistance, the first real battle, that had confronted the Germans in any occupied country. And the Germans had lost the first battle.

That was the morning of April 20, the birthday of Adolf Hitler.

The Germans were taken by surprise. Looking back now, it seems strange that they had no inkling of what was coming. But at the time the Jews of Warsaw revolted there had been no open resistance to the Nazi regime anywhere as yet. There had been countless acts committed by the agents of the underground: in Poland, France, Belgium, Norway—in every occupied country. Bridges had been blasted; factories had been destroyed; Nazis had been killed in revenge for crimes which they had committed. But in no country, in no city or town, had there been an open fight against massed military units of the Nazis. It was the one thing the Nazis were not prepared for—not yet. They did not believe that anybody would be so mad—or so courageous—as to wage such a hopeless fight.

But how was it possible for the Jews to be able to conduct so brilliant a fight as on this first night of Passover? They had obtained weapons. They had a certain number of men and women willing to fight and die. But, after all, they were no soldiers. They had had no previous training. Moreover, they had been systematically starved for years, and were certainly not in fit physical condition to put up a long fight. How was it possible, then?

It was possible because once the Jews had decided to fight they did not wait for the Germans to come in to do away with them. They made use of the few weeks of relative calm which the Germans let them have. In January, when they had their first resistance, they did not yet have enough arms. They were not yet trained. They were just people who wanted to fight. But they saw that that was not enough. So in the meantime they had learned how to fight.

It was the Resistance Committee that made the people of the ghetto into an organized army. Michael Klepfisz divided the city into defense sections and had his men dig tunnels to provide means of communication with the city outside the ghetto walls. All this had to be done in complete secrecy, mostly at night, so that the Germans could not discover them too soon.

The man who had been in charge of all preparatory work and who was elected by the Resistance Committee to the post of commander in chief was Mordecai. He was indefatigable in organizing and training his new army. He divided the Jews into squads. Many of these squads were composed entirely of girls and women. He drilled them in cellars or in outlying places where he was reasonably sure that the Germans would not intrude. He held constant conferences with the military leaders of the Polish underground. He arranged for some former high Polish officers to meet him outside the ghetto to prepare plans for the coming struggle.

Mordecai was not thinking of the fight which was to come as the sum of small localized skirmishes. He was thinking of it in terms of war. "The Jews are declaring war on Germany," he once told a number of Polish officers, and in a letter which was to reach Palestine through underground channels one year later he wrote: "I am not organizing sporadic outbursts. I am organizing revenge. We will give our death a historic meaning and full significance for future generations. . . ." The end of the letter showed that he had no doubt as to his own fate. "I am working hard trying to do my job. But soon, very soon, I shall go to a country where no one wants to go, and from which no traveler returns."

Mordecai decided also that the women and children who could not possibly help in the fight should leave the ghetto before the hostilities began, and so, with the help of the Polish underground, they were smuggled out. Their husbands and fathers knew that they would never see them again.

Some of these women and children found a hide-out with Polish peasants in the neighborhood of Warsaw.

The morning after the first Passover night the Germans returned in full force, with their tanks and armored cars. They were prepared for the worst. They wanted to make an end of it.

At the same time there were quite a number of arrests in Warsaw of Poles who were suspected of having helped the Jews prepare for their last stand. Posters informed the Polish population that it was strictly forbidden to go near the ghetto.

This time the Germans came shooting. All Warsaw reverberated from the tremendous fusillade. Thick flames broke out everywhere in the ghetto, and smoke began to fill the sky.

The battle was on. And it was a real battle, lasting the whole day until dusk. The Jews fired from every house in the ghetto that the Germans tried to approach. Countless German machine guns and tanks were destroyed or put out of commission.

Around five in the afternoon most of the German units retired. But before they left the ghetto they blew up some of the houses that were situated near the ghetto walls and destroyed the gates. Evidently they were afraid that the Jews might stop them from entering the ghetto on the following day.

But not all the Germans had been able to retire. Many of them were surrounded by Jews and taken prisoner later in the evening. They were disarmed and put into cellars to be guarded by units of girls.

The ghetto was quiet then, but many houses were still burning, and whole districts were so filled with smoke that it was hardly possible to get near them.

Mordecai sent an order that no Jew was permitted to leave his post. All guards were reinforced.

But the Germans did not come back that night.

They did not come back the next day, either. Evidently they wanted to take no more chances. They wanted to finish with their Jewish enemies in the shortest possible time with the least possible sacrifice.

The Jews waited the whole day. When nothing happened, Mordecai and Klepfisz decided to counterattack. They sent units out of the ghetto to the poorly guarded SS and Gestapo arsensals and killed the guards at once. German-speaking Jews in these units took over the telephone, and for many hours others labored to fill German trucks with ammunition and arms which they finally dispatched into the ghetto. Whatever was left of the arsenals was blown up. Only when Warsaw resounded from the explosions did the authorities in the center of the town realize what was going on. But the reinforcements they sent came much too late. The Jews had disappeared into the ghetto.

The next morning the whole of Warsaw knew that some of the arsenals had been seized and blown up and that more than a hundred Gestapo agents had fallen into the hands of the Jews.

Then the Germans made another attempt. They were greeted by stronger fire than ever before. When the first wave of attackers, compounded of Lithuanians and Ukrainians, tried to run away, they were driven back by special SS units who confronted them with machine guns.

By afternoon the Germans had taken a few outlying blocks and bombed the rest of the ghetto from the occupied houses. But they did not seem able to get any farther, and finally retired to their armored trucks.

Late during the third day, when the rebellion was about to go into the fourth night, the Jewish army received a valuable addition. Six thousand young workers who had been living in the closed-off part of the ghetto killed their guards and joined the revolt. They also set fire to the district to which they had been confined. Their action was spontaneous and entirely voluntary. The six thousand highly qualified workers were in no danger of deportation or annihilation. They were too necessary to the German factories in which they worked.

The next morning the Germans tried it once more. But not being able to achieve anything except to burn more houses and shatter practically all the windowpanes, they retired again about noon.

The Jews were puzzled to know why they did not continue to fight and suspected a ruse. But there was no plan behind the withdrawal. The SS and Gestapo troops had been recalled by the German military authorities of Warsaw, in obedience to a furious complaint from the German civil authorities, who declared that it would not do to start a regular war within a city like Warsaw. The Poles might get strange ideas and begin to revolt themselves. Also there was the problem of the German inhabitants of the city, the men and women who had been sent from the Fatherland to Warsaw to take over businesses or to attempt cultural missions. They did not like at all to stay in a city in which so much shooting was going on. They liked the shooting even less than they did the Russian air raids.

During the next days, therefore, relative calm reigned. There were only minor clashes with German units which drove into the ghetto, did a little wild shooting and retreated again immediately.

The Jews staged a new coup during the eighth night.

Mordecai had received a strange plea the night before from the Pawiak Jail, which now lay outside of the ghetto. The jail was full of several thousands of prisoners, the majority of them Jewish or Polish, but there were also some deserters from the German Army among them.

These prisoners asked to be saved, promising in turn that they would fight with the revolting Jews.

That same night more than five hundred Jews dressed in German uniforms left the ghetto. When they arrived near the Pawiak Jail they began to fire. Indescribable confusion prevailed. The guards could not tell which of the men in German uniforms were Jews and which were Germans. Evidently they had not studied closely enough the writings of the Nazi leaders which made so clear the differences between the German race and the Jewish race. They did not dare to shoot at Jews in German uniforms, although they probably would have shot without thinking twice at pure "Aryans" wearing the Star of David.

Thus the Jews had no difficulty in entering the jail and taking out groups of prisoners, some of them even dressed in German uniforms provided by their liberators. Long before dawn the jail was emptied.

All of the liberated prisoners, including even the German deserters, made good their promise to fight for the ghetto. But Klepfisz took care to scatter the Germans about in different units so that there would be no danger of betrayal at their hands.

This coup made an enormous impression throughout Warsaw. Polish youth openly rejoiced. The Germans, who had been feared and despised in Warsaw for so many years now, became the laughingstock of the city.

They were still not quite sure what they were going to do about the ghetto. There were constant conferences in the Gestapo headquarters and the Commandantur.

For once the general was furious. "You will admit, Herr Governor, that it was not the army that started this mess. It was the Gestapo and the SS."

Governor Fischer had not slept well lately. "I don't understand."

"As I see it, this revolt is a protest against the brutal treatment you have accorded the Jews."

"So you refuse to lend us troops to clean out the ghetto?" Again the governor had the same baffled feeling he had before in dealing with the general.

The general shrugged.

"With a few pieces of heavy artillery, the whole affair could be finished within a few hours," the governor insisted, and knew at the same time that he would be refused.

"Heavy guns!" The general became more angry. "Artillery in the middle of a big city! The civilian authorities will not stand for it. You should know that. After all, you are the head of the civilian authorities yourself, aren't you?"

Governor Fischer hardly knew any more where his first loyalty lay. Naturally he was the head of the civilian authorities, but the SS had demanded heavy guns, and he certainly did not like to refuse anything to Heinrich Himmler's units.

The general finally said that he would have to consult Berlin. He wanted it to be understood that there would be no artillery used inside of Warsaw till Berlin had made the decision.

Governor Fischer nodded. That might be a good idea. Why should he stick his neck out further? He, too, put in a call to Berlin.

That night the Jews made another thrust beyond the ghetto. They burned a large factory which made mattresses for German hospitals and set fire to houses inside the ghetto which had served the Germans at strategic points.

The sky north of Warsaw was covered with a cloud of black smoke.

The Germans certainly did not want to take any unnecessary risks. They would drive into the ghetto and start shooting, but as soon as the battle began to get too hot they would run away. They always left burning motorcars and great heaps of weapons behind them.

These skirmishes took place mostly during the following nights. Since the Jews had no light artillery even, and no facilities for lighting the scene of battle, they had to wait for the Germans to attack before they returned the fire. The Germans did not feel like entering the ghetto in broad daylight. That had proved much too risky.

Still, they made progress. More houses went up in flames. Many were destroyed by incendiary bombs dropped by German airplanes. Whole blocks were reduced to ashes. The smoke all but suffocated the Jews and made it more difficult for them to fight back. In several places the Germans blew up the waterworks.

The Jews had to withdraw farther and farther to the north of the ghetto. Already over three thousand Jews had been killed. Those who were taken prisoner were shot immediately. This was all the more reason for the Jews not to be taken prisoner and to fight to the end.

The smoke became denser. The sky was now almost black.

In a tiny room in the back of a former store Michael Klepfisz was sitting in front of a typewriter. He had been charged by the Resistance Committee to compose a manifesto. It was like in the old days when he had written so many protests and manifests, published in Socialist newspapers or distributed as pamphlets. Klepfisz remembered well those days and nights when as a young student he had discussed "the situation" and the steps which had to be taken with his comrades. They had all felt so full of fire then. They wanted to fight, though they knew very well that it would not be a real fight they could put up. They could only shout, demonstrate, strike. And all that could happen to them was to be thrown out of their jobs or expelled from the university or perhaps get a short prison term.

This time it was different. This time it was a real fight and one without any chance of survival. Yes, it was the real thing. And strangely enough, it was more difficult to find big words now than it had ever been before. It was more difficult to express what was in his heart and mind now than in those times when words were almost never followed by action.

An elderly man entered the room. "Are you ready, Michael? We are all set to print."

"No. I am not ready yet." The old man remained behind him, waiting. Michael Klepfisz ran his fingers through his hair in desperation. The words would not come.

"You better hurry, Michael. We haven't got much time left."

And under this pressure, with the printer waiting to take away every sheet as it came out of the typewriter, Klepfisz began to hammer away. No big words. Just the situation as it was; just the facts. . . .

Poles, citizens, soldiers of Freedom! Through the din of German cannons, destroying the homes of our mothers, wives, and children; through the noise of their machine guns, seized by us in the fight against the cowardly German police and SS men; through the smoke of the ghetto, that was set on fire, and the blood of its mercilessly killed defenders, we, the slaves of the ghetto, convey heartfelt greetings to you. We are well aware that you have been witnessing breathlessly, with broken hearts, with tears of compassion, with horror and enthusiasm, the war that we have been waging against the brutal occupant these past few days.

Every doorstep in the ghetto has become a stronghold and shall remain a fortress until the end! All of us will probably perish in the fight, but we shall never surrender! We, as well as you, are burning with the desire to punish the enemy for all his crimes, with a desire for vengeance. It is a fight for our freedom, as well as yours; for our human dignity and national honor, as well as yours! We shall avenge the gory deeds of Oswiecim, Treblinka, Belzec, and Majdanek!

Long live the fraternity of blood and weapons in a fighting Poland!

Long live Freedom!

Death to the hangmen and the killer!

We must continue our mutual struggle against the occupant until the very end!

JEWISH ARMED RESISTANCE ORGANIZATION

The manifesto was set and printed within the hour, sent out of the ghetto by couriers and distributed throughout Warsaw and Poland by the underground.

The response of the Polish masses was spontaneous. The Jews received literally thousands of messages filled with expressions of solidarity and admiration from the entire underground press and via the secret radio broadcasting stations. Warsaw seized eagerly on the daily communiqués issued by the Jewish Resistance Committee—veritable military communiqués regarding what was happening in the ghetto, which were published in the underground press.

Then all the Polish underground labor papers published an appeal dealing with the situation in the ghetto.

COMRADES AND CITIZENS!

Since April 18, when the occupant launched his drive to exterminate finally and completely the remaining Polish Jews, the Warsaw Ghetto has been in arms against the brutal enemy. Condemned by Hitler to death, the Jews in the ghetto have refused to submit passively to the Nazi hangmen. They are resisting furiously the bloody ruffians in defense of their rights as citizens and their honor as human beings.

Once more the glare of flames reddens the sky over Warsaw; once more the firing of rifles and guns, the explosions of grenades, resound in the streets of the city. Workers and professionals are the heart and soul of the groups of fighting Jews who have risen in armed protest against Nazi violence. The Polish national flag floats over their heads as they give battle to the enemy. Their action is not an isolated one; it is a link in the uninterrupted chain of resistance that for four years has been carried on throughout Poland.

It is most important, at the present historic moment, that all Poland and the entire world fully understand the significance of each episode in our struggle for liberation. The battle of Krasnobrod, the series of clashes between detachments of the Underground Armed Forces in Poland and the invader, the present armed fight of the Polish citizens confined behind the walls of the Warsaw Ghetto—all these testify to Poland's irreconcilable hatred of the occupant, to our unshakable determination to win complete independence. No drop of blood spilled in these battles for freedom will be lost. Every new victim will cement more firmly the future edifice of liberty and social justice for all the citizens of the New Poland.

We send our fraternal greetings to the Jewish workers and professionals who, in the face of certain and inevitable death, have chosen to perish with arms in hand rather than submit passively to the executioner.

We pledge solemnly to them that their deed will not be lost without an echo. It will join the heroic legends of Fighting Poland; it will become the common heritage of the Polish people, a heritage that will provide a firm foundation for the structure of the future reconstructed Polish Republic.

We appeal to the peoples of the world! In the face of the Nazis' brutal pattern of destruction, which they have consistently imposed upon our land for the past four years, since its defeat and occupation, in the face of unprecedented terror, our people, murdered, oppressed, and maltreated, have risen constantly in flaming protest. But we need help. This help must come soon. The enemy must be defeated before he crushes the vital forces of the land and finally destroys its people.

We call upon the fighting world for the earliest possible offensive against German power, but in the meantime we shall not remain passive. We shall redouble our efforts in order to prepare for the general uprising in Poland that, together with the Allied offensive, will strike the death blow at totalitarianism of all shades.

Freedom—Equality—Independence!

THE UNDERGROUND MOVEMENT OF THE WORKING MASSES IN POLAND

Warsaw, April 1943.

The Germans were still waiting for word from Berlin. In the meantime they sent an ultimatum to the Jews. They made it known that unless the fight were stopped immediately, and the German prisoners given up, the whole ghetto would be destroyed.

The Jews replied at once. They let it be known that the fight would not be discontinued. They were willing to give up the German prisoners —but on condition that for each German prisoner ten Jews should be freed by the Germans. They announced that they figured that each Jew was worth ten Germans.

The Germans made no answer to this. By April 28 they had thrown into the battle six thousand heavily armed troops and had sustained more than a thousand casualties. The Jews had lost between three and five thousand during the same period.

On this same April 28 the conference in Hamilton, Bermuda, was drawing to a close.

The decisions arrived at by the members of the delegations were declared confidential. It was made known, however, that an agreement had been signed "making joint recommendations assigned to relieve a substantial number of all races and nationalities."

It also became known that the delegates had agreed on "the impossibility of large-scale evacuation of Jews and other oppressed persons from occupied Europe because of the transportation problem, and the difficulty of negotiating with the enemy."

The Bermuda conference was a failure, as had been expected from the very beginning by those in the know. The delegates had not even tried to help those unhappy people in Poland and in other occupied countries whose main crime was that they were Jews. They had carefully avoided any direct reference to the Jews as such. Why? Had not Hitler's propaganda blamed the Jews for the war? Had not the Jewish issue formed the main weapon in Hitler's psychological warfare on democratic nations? Had not his offensive against countless people been prepared by years of anti-Semitic propaganda preceding the actual war?

Here was an opportunity to contradict Hitler, to show him up. Here was an opportunity to launch a psychological counterattack, to shatter prejudices. But the delegates in Bermuda avoided the issue just as the Allied governments had. They all felt sorry for the Jews, but it was thought wiser to ignore the existence of a Jewish tragedy.

The delegates at Bermuda discussed and deliberated for ten days. They were not disturbed by representatives of Jewish organizations. They could not be reached by the cries for help uttered by Jews fighting and dying in the ghetto of Warsaw. The delegates "examined the refugee problem in all its aspects." They "felt bound to reject certain proposals." They "were able to agree on a number of concrete recommendations." They were glad to assure the world "that in the course of the discussion the refugee problem was broken down into its main elements."

All this was said in the one and only communiqué which they composed at the end of their pleasant stay at Bermuda. The word "Jew" did not figure once in this communiqué.

And the Jews in the ghetto of Warsaw continued to fight and die.

Chapter XXII

Inferno

On April 30, after more than ten days of fighting, Heinrich Himmler himself made the final decision about the ghetto of Warsaw. He sent SS General Sommers as his personal representative to conduct the war against the Jews. Before the general left for Warsaw he had a personal interview with Himmler.

"You understand what you have to do, I trust," Himmler told him. "The ghetto must be destroyed, and quickly. Throw all your Elite Troops and police troops against the Jews. If you do not have enough men, the army will supply sufficient units so that you can make short work of the business. Use heavy artillery against them, except where it might seriously endanger the lives of the people in the rest of the city. Shoot all Jews at sight. Under no condition are you to offer a compromise or a truce of any kind."

When the general was already at the door, Himmler called after him, "I expect final results within a week."

The very next day the Germans started their all-out assault. Large detachments of storm troopers had arrived from Galicia and other points in the East. More than one hundred tanks were ready to invade the ghetto. More than fifty planes were to fly over, partly for purposes of reconnaissance, partly to bomb the strongholds of the Jews. Heavy artillery was ready to lay waste the houses in the ghetto. There was, as Himmler had ordered, to be no letup until all resistance had been broken.

And so the great battle began.

For an hour or so it looked as though the whole ghetto could be cleaned up on the first day. No resistance seemed possible. Everywhere in the ghetto the buildings collapsed like houses of cards under the heavy shelling of the German artillery. The tanks had the right of way, racing through the narrow ghetto streets as though the Jews were non-existent. Planes dropped incendiary bombs and also flashed the news to headquarters in Warsaw that the streets everywhere were deserted and that no resistance seemed likely.

But after the first hour or so, strange things began to happen. Tanks exploded, seemingly without any reason at all. German soldiers fell dead in the streets. The second and third waves of German invaders found to their amazement that those of their comrades who had gone into the ghetto before them were wiped out—apparently without a struggle. All these things seemed weird and made them shiver with fear. They looked about. There were no Jews to be seen. They entered the houses: no Jews. They raced to the roofs, to the cellars: still no Jews. They came back to the streets and found their comrades, whom they had left only a few minutes before, now lying sprawled on the pavement. They entered their cars and tanks again, and the next minute these cars and tanks were in flames.

It took SS General Sommers till evening to solve the mystery of what had gone on that day in the ghetto. It was simple enough. The great losses suffered by the Germans were caused by Jewish suicide squads, who roamed the streets clad in German uniforms, apparently looking for and fighting Jews, biding their time till there was a moment when they could strike at genuine German units with the greatest possible effectiveness. Their basic method, as conceived by the Resistance Committee, was to wipe out everyone on the scene of the action, so that no witnesses would be left alive to tell the story of what the Jews were doing on this day. And that is why they had been able to continue the whole day with their very efficient work against the Nazis.

But even after the general found out what it was all about, there was little he could do about it. The Germans could not very well change their uniforms overnight. Nor could they rely upon identifying their enemies by means of language. This would have worked in the case of regular Polish troops, or regular troops of any other nationality; but many Polish Jews spoke faultless German, and Mordecai and Michael Klepfisz had seen to it that a great many German-speaking troops were among the suicide squads.

SS General Sommers was enraged. "Typically Jewish, these tricks. It's against all international rules of warfare."

His officers asked what they were supposed to do about it.

"Fight them! Kill them!" the general stormed. "Kill the Jews wherever you find them!" Then, in a calmer tone, "After all, there aren't so many Jews left. Sooner or later all of them will be dead."

In the meantime they tried to annihilate as many of them as possible by long-range warfare, by heavy artillery and bombs dropped from planes. The Jews had, of course, no way of fighting heavy artillery, nor any anti-aircraft guns with which they could chase the planes from the sky.

That night was a night of inferno. Incendiary bombs rained down on the ghetto. The entire district was a sea of flame. There was hardly a street in which houses were not burning, hardly a minute in which one did not hear the noise of an explosion or the crash of houses tumbling down. The air was filled with the cries of wounded men, women, and children perishing in the ruins.

Mordecai sent out special fire fighters to try to localize the fires. The Warsaw Fire Department, of course, made no attempt to stop the fires. The Germans had given strict orders that the Poles should intervene only in case the fire threatened to spread to the other parts of the city. They even tried to cut off the water supply of the ghetto, but they had to abandon this idea since the main source of water for the ghetto also supplied water for the rest of Warsaw.

For many days and nights the ghetto was transformed into an inferno. Mordecai, Klepfisz, and a number of other leaders saw clearly that things could not go on as they were much longer. One of the Polish officers who was advising the Resistance Committee let it be known that he saw no chance whatever of continuing the battle.

"Of course we haven't a chance," Michael Klepfisz snapped. "We knew this before we started."

"We must not lose our tempers," Mordecai said. He was as calm as ever. "This is simply a problem of tactics. It is true we cannot continue our battle much longer the way we have fought thus far. We must devise new methods of warfare. There must be some way . . ."

The Jewish leaders tried to reach an understanding with the Polish underground. Their idea was that the Poles in Warsaw should stage an uprising, in the hope that the Germans would then have to turn part of their strength away from the ghetto to subdue the Polish rebels. All the Jews needed at that moment was a breathing spell to extinguish the fires and to re-form their lines. Then they would be able to renew the fight.

A meeting took place outside the ghetto walls between leaders of the Polish underground and two delegates of the Jewish Resistance Committee. Also present were two Polish officers who had helped to map out the strategy of the ghetto battle. The meeting lasted through the whole night. A number of the members of the Polish underground were all for supporting the Jews. But the majority was against it. "The time for a general uprising has not yet come," they said.

Mordecai wanted to know why.

"We could kill many of the Germans," was the answer. "We could even destroy their matériel. But in the end they would defeat us and kill many more of our men than we could kill of theirs."

"What is wrong with that?" Michael Klepfisz asked. "That is precisely what we are doing."

The Poles said that they could not make any decisions themselves. "We have to act according to orders from our government in London. We have been ordered not to start any uprising as yet. We have only a limited quantity of arms, and we have to preserve our forces."

The Jewish leaders had not really counted on active help from the Poles. But it would have prolonged the fight if any active help at all—no matter on what scale—had been forthcoming. It would also have aided the morale of the average Jewish fighter in the ghetto. Many of the Jews still had some hope left. They no longer believed that the Germans would spare them. But they felt that if all of Poland and all of Europe would rise in armed revolt against the Germans, perhaps not all of them would have to die. They realized now, however, that the Polish underground would not join the revolt. They were irrevocably committed to a policy of watchful waiting.

The underground papers were full of expressions of sympathy and respect for the Jewish cause. These days they spoke of almost nothing but the fight in the ghetto, urging the population constantly to help the Jews in every way possible, not by active revolt, but by hiding those who could escape, by smuggling food into the ghetto, and by hampering the German efforts to exterminate the Jews whenever there was a chance.

The Polish people, however, did not need such advice or admonitions. They were already doing everything in their power to help the Jews, short of participating actively in the revolt. In many cases Polish public opinion was much further advanced and more radical than the organized underground. The Poles in Warsaw and in many other cities, who had wondered so long why the Jews took everything that was meted out to them without hitting back, now wondered why the Poles did not join the Jews in hitting back. They felt closer to the Jews than ever before. They felt like their brothers.

The members of the Resistance Committee realized the attitude of the Poles throughout the country. But they also realized that their sympathy was not going to be of much help to the Jews, since the organized underground was not allowed to strike. Nothing was left for the Jews, then, but to fight and die. Perhaps their example would incite the Poles to rise later and join the United Nations to help defeat the Germans. Later, long after the battle of the ghetto of Warsaw was over . . .

In this spirit Michael Klepfisz composed another appeal, this time not to the organized underground, but to the people of Poland and to all those in the world who might be reached by his words:

People of Warsaw!

We realize that the Polish underground movement pays homage to the fighters of the ghetto. But only the United Nations can give immediate and concrete aid.

In the name of the millions of murdered Jews; in the name of all those who were burned, tortured, and slaughtered; in the name of those who are still fighting heroically though condemned to certain death in an unequal struggle, we call to the world to listen to us today.

The Allies must avenge our death and our suffering, so that even the bestial enemy may understand why he is being punished. Our Allies must finally realize that a tremendous historic responsibility will fall upon those who remained passive in face of the unbelievable Nazi crime against a whole people whose tragic epilogue we witness today. The desperate heroism of the people of the ghetto must stir the world to an action equal to the greatness of the moment!

The Jews once more stood alone. But in their last fight they had become a united group, fighting for one and the same goal. Some called this goal religion; some national independence; while others called it the right to live. But in the last analysis they all fought for the idea of freedom.

And since they had to die, they wanted at least to die in such a way as to arouse the conscience of the world.

It was impossible to fight the Germans in regular battles because of their overwhelming superiority, not only in manpower but in fighting equipment. Hence Klepfisz and Mordecai reorganized their defenses. They shortened their lines. Houses on the outskirts that had suffered the ravages of fire were vacated, and the arms stored in them were taken to the center of the ghetto. Foodstuffs, which had been deposited near strategic points on the outskirts, were also saved. Houses were transformed into fortresses and filled with fighters who were told to stay there and hold the enemy as long as possible. They were not to leave the buildings, and they were to kill as many of the enemy as they could.

From that morning on a new kind of fight developed. The Jews no longer defended the whole ghetto at once. They defended each house separately. They did not retire when a house was shelled by heavy artillery or hit by bombs from the sky. They waited in the cellars till the shelling and bombing were over and the Germans arrived in their armored cars. Then they began to shoot. They defended the ruins as they had defended the houses, fighting from the cellars and retreating to the last available room or hole, cave or corridor, until the last one of them fell. It took the Germans hours to clear a single house. And when they thought they had quashed all resistance, when there was not a single Jew left alive among the ruins, a time bomb would blow up the Germans in the neighborhood. Thus the Jews were avenged even in their death.

It was during this phase of house-to-house fighting that the girl

Tosia died. She was one of the last defenders of the house to which she had been assigned. She had retreated to one of the rooms in the basement after the house had collapsed and was waiting for the Nazis to come. She knew this was her last moment. Young, beautiful Tosia . . . Was she not born to live a full life, to be happy and to make those around her happy? How different her life could have been if only she had been lucky enough to be born a few decades later or in another country.

When the Nazis entered the room Tosia threw a bomb, killing herself along with the intruders.

SS General Sommers was beside himself. This was no longer regular warfare. This was guerrilla warfare! And though he never admitted it, he knew quite well that the partisans who had come into the ghetto for a last-ditch stand were proving themselves excellent specialists in this type of warfare.

General Sommers was losing his nerve. He knew Heinrich Himmler. Himmler had given him one week to clear up the ghetto. The week had long since passed, and still the resistance had by no means been quashed.

The Jewish partisans had built veritable subterranean fortresses and bunkers beneath the ground, which could be reached only through sewers or secret tunnels from the cellars of the houses. The Germans now began blowing up the sewers to isolate the men in these bunkers. Every day hundreds of Germans were killed and wounded. Red Cross ambulances became a common sight inside the ghetto. They picked up the German dead and wounded but of course did nothing for the wounded Jews.

General Sommers could not sleep. He sat in his office in Warsaw, waiting for news from the ghetto, making countless telephone calls, giving orders, rescinding them, shouting at everybody: "Why don't you kill them? There must be a way to kill all of them. There can't be that many left!" He was thinking of Himmler. "Get out! Do something!" he ordered his staff officers. "Don't sit around and wait! Get into the ghetto and kill those damned Jews!"

After the Germans had destroyed the houses they began to flood the cellars beneath them, in the hope of drowning the Jewish fighters who were hiding there. They no longer wished to fight the Jews. They preferred to kill them without any risk to themselves. The unexpectedly long siege—the fight was now going into its sixth week—was beginning to make them jittery.

Every house had become a fortress. But the number of those fortresses, and the force of fighters who could defend them, became smaller every day and every hour. There was little food left and almost no water, since it had to be brought to the houses and it was next to impossible for the Jews to get out on the street. Occasionally some Jews who did venture forth were caught alive by the Nazis. Most of them were immediately strung up on the nearest lamppost in plain view of those who were still defending the neighboring houses.

During these days Zivia died after a long fight with the German detachments. She was caught in a burning cellar and died with a gun still in her hand. It was a strange death for the girl whom they had all called "Mother." She had done so much for the people in the Polish ghettos: giving them comfort, bringing them medicine, helping them in a thousand ways. They had called her "Mother," and she really had been like a mother to them—this girl whom the fates did not permit to become a mother herself or to bring up children of her own, this girl who, so full of love, so ready to show kindness to others, had to die hating others, killing others.

Most of the streets in the ghetto were now completely destroyed. Many houses in the immediate neighborhood of the ghetto had also been hit by artillery shells and bombs. The Germans did not mind. They no longer thought about anything except destroying the ghetto. They did not care that non-Jewish Poles perished, if only the Jews perished.

They blew up a synagogue without bothering to warn the hospital of the Maltese Order which was situated next to the synagogue, just outside the ghetto walls. The hospital, too, was partly destroyed, and many of the patients were either killed or suffered severe wounds.

The Germans now also resorted to poison gas to destroy any fighters who they thought might be hiding in shelters.

Young Samuel Breslaw died soon after Zivia. He had been a squad leader assigned to the defense of Dzilna Street. Strangely enough, it was in this street that he had been born, and it was in this street that he fell, torn to pieces by a Nazi grenade.

In some cases the Jews had to retreat so quickly that they could not evacuate a house or a block before the Nazis were there. It was thus that the temporary Jewish Hospital on Franciskanska Street fell into the hands of the Nazis. The Germans shot most of the sick people in their beds and then set the building aflame. They did not allow any of those who could still walk to leave the burning building. Those who tried to escape were shot or pushed back into the flames. Polish firemen were not permitted to do anything to help them. One Polish fireman who tried to drench a Jewish woman with water as she rushed from the house with her clothes afire was shot on the spot.

When the house was in flames a Jewish mother with her two children appeared on the roof. The Germans looked up and called to her, "Come on, come on! Hurry up! Jump!" There were German nurses in the street, too, looking up, clapping their hands, and joining in the laughter. The mother threw one of her children down. This was an easier death than being burned. The second child resisted and clung desperately to the mother. There were more shouts from below and more laughter. Then mother and child jumped together.

There was a sudden burst of gunfire, and the SS men and the nurses who had so enjoyed the suicide of the Jews were lying dead on the street.

That night German newspapers reported with deep indignation that Jewish snipers were shooting at German nurses.

SS General Sommers was opposed to all publicity, as far as the battle of the ghetto was concerned. He resented the very idea that newspapers should speak about the fight of the Jews. He had thrown out of his office personally the representative of the Deutsches Nachrichtenbureau, the official German news agency, who wanted to interview him.

"If you write as much as one line about this mess, I'll see to it that you are sent to a concentration camp!" he screamed. And the German newspapers did indeed not mention the battle of the ghetto of Warsaw. But it was not possible to deny for any length of time that fighting was going on inside the Polish capital. After all, the whole city of Warsaw was witness to it. The Polish underground reported on the fight to the country at large and to the government in London. The Allied and neutral presses had already mentioned that there was some shooting inside the ghetto, though no detailed description of the fighting had been received anywhere, and the world did not yet know the scope of the revolt.

Dr. Goebbels had always gone on the theory that there was no sense in denying a thing when there were too many witnesses to it. He therefore finally allowed the German newspapers to mention the fact that the ghetto had put up a fight. Of course they said that the fight had been started by the treacherous and deceitful Jews who had attacked German troops without any warning and obviously on orders from Moscow and London.

In the fifth week of the fight in the ghetto Dr. Goebbels sent a number of newspapermen to Warsaw to see conditions for themselves and to write stories saying that everything was now in order. Most of the correspondents who came were Germans, but there were two Italians, one Hungarian, one Finn, and one correspondent for a Swedish newspaper.

Gruppenfuehrer Mende was charged with the job of arranging a sight-seeing tour through the ghetto for their benefit.

The tour was, of course, to lead only through those parts of the ghetto that had already been evacuated. The procession started early in the morning, at its head half a platoon of soldiers with guns ready to fire, followed by several armored cars filled with photographers and newspapermen, accompanied by General Sommers. There was still a great deal of smoke in the air, and the visitors could plainly hear the reports of machine guns and rifles not too far away.

Here were the German journalists in the ghetto again. But this second visit was strangely different from the first one. No longer could they, the representatives of a super-race, look down upon the Jews as inferior people. No longer could they laugh at them. The scenes they gazed upon spoke for themselves. They saw that there had been a fight here—a real battle. No longer could they laugh at the poor people who tried to sell their goods; no longer could they sneer in their superiority at the poor conditions under which these Jews had to live. Once they had written that it was all right with them, the Germans, if the Jews choked in their own filth. But the Jews had not choked in their own filth. They had preferred to go down fighting.

The representatives of the German press looked at the corpses lying in the streets and at the ruins of houses and did not feel any too good. Finally one of the Italians asked, "Why don't you bury the dead?"

"We don't know which ones are Jews and which are Germans," General Sommers declared bluntly.

There was a pause. The Italian looked at him but made no comment. Sommers cleared his throat and went on, "You see here, gentlemen—it was quite a fight. We had many difficulties to overcome. The Jews have been preparing this uprising for a long time—for years. They converted their cellars into reinforced concrete strongholds, which they connected by means of underground passages. The whole ghetto is literally honeycombed with these passages. When we captured one house, its defenders escaped to another. Some even managed to escape through tunnels to beyond the ghetto walls."

Some of the journalists looked very impressed.

General Sommers shouted, "The only effective means is to destroy the Jews. Destroy all the Jews, all their houses, all their food, all their ammunition."

The cars continued on the tour of the ghetto, past the ruins of houses which had been transformed into forts. The Jews had demolished the stairs so that the Germans could not easily invade the upper floors.

"You see what difficulities our men had to overcome," Sommers complained. "We had to conquer each house individually."

The German journalists nodded. They made notes. They were going to report precisely what they were told. They were not giving their own opinions or their own interpretations. They had long ago ceased to think for themselves. It was too dangerous. Furthermore, it was much easier to write what one was told to write.

So they nodded and took notes. But unconsciously, perhaps without knowing it themselves, they were a little impressed. They had always been told that the Jews were cowards, unable and unwilling to fight. But here was visible proof that they had fought, and fought bravely and well.

And perhaps they thought of something else, too. These ruins reminded them of something: they reminded them of home. Many German cities and towns now had districts which were just as badly damaged as this one. Not a day or night passed when Allied bombers did not come over Germany and drop their bombs. Would this go on for long? And if it did, would the whole of Germany look like the ghetto of Warsaw looked now?

These were just thoughts, of course. The German newspapermen would not put them into words to be printed. That would be too dangerous.

And what were the other journalists—the Italians, the Hungarian, the Finn, and the Swede—thinking? They looked at the dead bodies, at the destroyed houses, and they listened to the not-too-distant shots, and perhaps they thought: This is the New Order. This is how it will look all over Europe before the Germans are through. This is what will come in Italy, in Hungary, in Finland, and in Sweden.

If they had any such ideas, they certainly did not put them into words. No newspaper in Italy, Hungary, or Finland would have printed anything like that.

In the sixth week, toward the end of May, Michael Klepfisz fell. The report of the Jewish Resistance Committee did not give any details or the exact date. A few days later Mordecai Anilewicz, too, was killed in street fighting. Again nothing definite was reported on the circumstances of his death. And for a long time afterward the leader of the Chaluzim and his role in the fight of the ghetto remained almost unknown to the outside world. When some of the reports smuggled out of the ghetto finally began to mention Mordecai, he was referred to as the mystery man of the ghetto. But there was nothing mysterious about this young Jew. He was simply a quiet young man who had always tried to do his duty without desiring any fame for himself. He went out of life just as he had lived; calmly, quietly, almost without others noticing it. . . .

New leaders sprang up. The fight went on. There were few houses left now. The struggle was continued from cellars, sewers, and underground bunkers.

One morning the Germans took hundreds of Jewish prisoners in different parts of the ghetto almost simultaneously. They surrendered in groups of five and ten. When they were surrounded by German soldiers they dropped the hand grenades which they had hidden in their clothes and thus perished together with their captors.

Most of the fighting now went on underground. General Sommers had not exaggerated. The Jewish partisans had created what amounted to subterranean fortresses. The Germans addressed the fighters through loud-speakers, asking them to come out, promising them food and work. They received no answer except shots. When an underground bunker was surrounded and no escape seemed possible, a group of volunteers would sacrifice themselves to cover the escape of the rest, shooting it out with the Germans while the others made their getaway.

Sometimes groups which had remained underground were cut off from the rest of the fighters, with no chance of making their way back to them. They tried to escape to some place outside the ghetto and then make for the woods. The Polish underground helped to bring about sixty of these fighters to comparative safety. The Germans learned of this and many times lay in ambush, waiting for the retreating Jews.

Jewish children, too, escaped through underground tunnels and wandered through the streets of Warsaw. Sometimes Polish women would pick them up, take them home, and hide them. Sometimes the children would wander far out beyond the city limits, through fields and villages, for days and nights, through fields and forests, aimless, tired, hungry, their feet bleeding, wandering still, wandering.

Chapter XXIII

The Last Report

In far-off London Zygielbojm had hardly closed his eyes since the fight in the ghetto had begun. He would sit in his office till the early morning hours in order not to miss any report of the fighting which might come through. Only then would he go to the modest boarding-house where he occupied a little back room and throw himself on his bed.

The government officials and the Polish National Council were kept informed by the Polish underground. They had received immediate news flashes when the first shot was fired. And later there had been constant radio communiqués from the Jewish leaders in Warsaw themselves. But Zygielbojm wanted more. He could not be satisfied with mere figures on the losses of the Jews and the Germans. It was not enough for him to know which streets had been evacuated or destroyed —though he knew every stone in the ghetto. Things looked so hopeless from London. Every day he expected the end of the fight. He could not believe—which almost no one of the members of the Polish Parliament or government could believe—that the Jews could hold out for more than two or three days. When the first week of fighting was over and the communiqués still kept coming in, Zygielbojm was torn between despair and hopes which he knew could never be fulfilled. It was impossible for him, realist that he was and schooled in the rigorous discipline of a Socialist education, to believe in miracles. But now, during those sleepless nights when he thought of his wife and child in the ghetto of Warsaw and of his friends involved in this hopeless fight, he wanted to believe in them. He longed desperately to believe in them.

There were countless rumors spreading through the Polish circles in London. Men and women who had made their way out of occupied Poland were telling horrible stories of the ghetto in flames, of women and children perishing, of Jewish leaders hanging from lampposts, of unspeakable German atrocities. Zygielbojm listened to all of the rumors and reports with a heavy heart. If he could only be there to fight and suffer with those so near and dear to him! But he had to sit in the comparative safety of his office in London and content himself with helping to carry on the business of the Polish Parliament. There was nothing he could do to help the friends with whom he had spent his whole life. Weeks passed by, and still all he could do was wait.

On the afternoon of May 10—the fight in the ghetto was now in its fourth week—an old friend of Zygielbojm's, a Catholic Pole and a fellow member of the Polish National Council, came to visit him. For a while they discussed the latest news from the ghetto.

"There is no hope, I suppose," Zygielbojm said, almost imploring the other to contradict him.

His friend shook his head. "Not much hope." After a moment he resumed: "If the Allies would do something about it . . . if they would let Hitler know that he cannot go on exterminating the Jews . . . if they would bomb German cities every time Hitler has another contingent of Jews killed . . . if they would drop leaflets telling the German population that this is the reason why they are being bombed . . ."

"Nothing of the sort is being done. Nothing of the sort will be done." Zygielbojm's voice was sad.

"I have talked to some English and American officials," the Pole continued. "They are sympathetic, but they feel that the general plan of strategy cannot be changed, even to save a million people. They simply don't understand."

"No, they don't understand. Will they ever? How many Jews must die to make them understand?"

The visitor got up to leave. Zygielbojm saw him to the door, shaking his hand in farewell with more than his wonted warmth and determination. The friend was to recall this later. He looked at him. How tired and overworked Zygielbojm was! He needed sleep, that was plain to be seen. But who could sleep these days?

"You better take care of yourself," the friend said.

There was a strange light in Zygielbojm's eyes. "I will," he answered. "I will take care of myself."

He left the office earlier than usual that night, walked back to his boardinghouse, and locked himself in his room. There he sat down at his desk and looked at the picture of his wife and their small child. He thought of his friends in Warsaw, of the men, women, and little children who were being annihilated by the Germans, of the burning houses and the ruins. He heard the explosions; he felt the heat of the flames; he smelled the burning flesh. And his heart was heavy within him. He knew now that he would never be able to banish these pictures from his mind. He would never be able to think of anything else—never as long as he lived.

Zygielbojm felt let down. He had never dared admit it to himself, but he had always hoped that something would develop from this fight in the ghetto. He had hoped for some time that the Poles throughout the country would take the cue and rise in revolt against the Germans. The murders in the ghetto would have seemed less pointless if that had happened. Or if the world had only raised its voice in a cry of furious protest! But the echo that followed the battle of the ghetto was much too dim. Why? Would the world never understand? Had not enough Jews died? Did it not suffice that the Jews had suffered for thousands of years? Would their persecution and suffering go on forever and ever?

Zygielbojm had not conceived the idea of the fight. In fact, when he had been asked to help the Jews find weapons, he had been reluctant. But once he had cast his lot with those who wanted to fight, once he had decided to help them obtain weapons, he felt that the fight as such was his responsibility, too. He could not help the people in the ghetto kill the Germans. But if their suffering and their death were not enough to arouse the world, perhaps he could help them arouse the world.

He took a few sheets of paper out of his drawer and began to write:

To Premier Wladyslaw Sikorski:

I take the liberty of addressing to you my last words, and through you, to the Polish Government and the Polish people, to the governments and the peoples of the Allied states—to the conscience of the world.

From the latest information received from Poland, it is evident that the Germans, with the most ruthless cruelty, are now murdering the few remaining Jews in Poland. Behind the ghetto's walls the last act of a tragedy unprecedented in history is being performed. The responsibility for this crime of murdering the entire Jewish population of Poland falls in the first instance on the perpetrators, but indirectly it is also a burden on the whole of humanity, the people and the governments of the Allied states which thus far have made no effort toward concrete action for the purpose of curtailing this crime.

By the passive observation of the murder of defenseless millions, and of the maltreatment of children, women, and old men, these countries have become the criminals' accomplices. I must also state that although the Polish Government has in a high degree contributed to the enlistment of world opinion, it has yet done so insufficiently. It has not done anything that could correspond to the magnitude of the drama being enacted now in Poland. From some 3,500,000 Polish Jews and about 700,000 other Jews deported to Poland from other countries—according to official statistics provided by the underground "Bund" organization—there remained in April of this year only about 300,000, and this continuing murder still goes on. . . .

Zygielbojm paused for a moment. All his strength had left him. He did not feel capable of going on. The terrible toll of those millions of deaths all but broke him down.

And then he saw the ghetto at Warsaw again. It was the ghetto as he had never seen it before. He saw a vast scene of ruins. There was only one house left. And from the roof of this house the blue-and-white

Jewish flag was still flying. And now he saw it quite distinctly. A man was standing on the roof holding the flag aloft. And then suddenly the man was no longer there and the flag was gone too. Zygielbojm wanted to cry, "Wait! Don't go! Don't!" And then he was staring at the walls of his little room again. But he was still seeing the young Jew on the roof, holding the flag, jumping down. It was something more than just suicide. It was like a procession of workers marching through the street, demonstrating for their cause, showing the world that they were willing to fight or die for it. It was not just suicide. It was not the last act of despair. It was a last tremendous demonstration not to be overlooked, not to be forgotten. A demonstration, thought Zygielbojm. And now he knew what he was going to do.

His eyes wandered to his desk and the letter he had commenced. I must finish it, he thought.

I cannot be silent—I cannot live—while remnants of the Jewish people of Poland, of whom I am a representative, are perishing. My comrades in the Warsaw Ghetto took weapons in their hands on that last heroic impulse. It was not my destiny to die there together with them, but I belong to them, and in their mass graves. By my death I wish to express my strongest protest against the inactivity with which the world is looking on and permitting the extermination of my people.

I know how little human life is worth today, but as I was unable to do anything during my life perhaps by my death I shall contribute to breaking down the indifference of those who may now—at the last moment—rescue the few Polish Jews still alive from certain annihilation. My life belongs to the Jewish people of Poland and I therefore give it to them. I wish that this remaining handful of the original several millions of Polish Jews would live to see the liberation of a new world of freedom, and the justice of true Socialism. I believe that such a Poland will arise and that such a world will come.

I trust that the President and the Prime Minister will direct my words to all those for whom they are destined, and that the Polish Government will immediately take appropriate action in the fields of diplomacy. I bid my farewell herewith to everybody and everything dear to me and loved by me.

S. Zygielbojm

When he had finished the letter and sealed the envelope he got up. He felt tired. Slowly he undressed himself and went to bed. He took out of the night table the little box of veronal tablets which he had kept there for so long. He took the entire contents of the box and gulped it down with a glass of water. Then he put out the light. He saw his wife and his little child. He saw the apartment in Warsaw in which they had lived and been so happy together. He saw himself speaking to the workers, admonishing them to keep discipline. He saw himself marching down a street with the workers, a worker himself, marching, following a flag, demonstrating for his and their right to live and be happy; marching . . . marching . . . the road seemed so incredibly long . . . marching . . . there was no end.

They knocked at his door the next morning when he did not appear for breakfast. They had to break the door down. A doctor was called immediately. He took Zygielbojm to a hospital. Zygielbojm died there without regaining consciousness.

His death created some excitement in all Polish circles and in London. Many newspapers commented upon his tragic suicide. At least one German newspaper also decided to mention his demise. The *12 Uhr Blatt* of Berlin wrote:

> The ghetto Jews are now concerning themselves with a Hebrew from Warsaw who, after a run around the world, finally landed in England and committed suicide in London, allegedly because of a broken heart. The reports of the fate of his racial brethren are supposed to have broken him. However, we think it more reasonable to assume that S. Zygielbojm's difficulties were caused by business troubles.

Zygielbojm's wife and child were killed at about the same time that he decided to make the supreme sacrifice in the hope of thus drawing the attention of the world to the plight of the Jews. His last letter was made public soon after by General Sikorski. On July 1, 1943, it was read into the *Congressional Record* of the United States, where it will be preserved as a historical document for generations to come.

The Jewish holiday Lag b'Omer fell on May 23 that year. Lag b'Omer is celebrated in memory of the revolt of Bar Kokba and Rabbi Ben Akiba against the Romans in the year 135 A.D. The Romans had defeated the Jews only sixty-five years before, had destroyed Jerusalem, had taken many Jews away into slavery, and fondly believed that this was the end of Jewish resistance once and for all. But they were mistaken. Bar Kokba rose up and smashed the Roman oppression, and though the Romans succeeded in re-establishing their mastery over

Palestine later on, his revolt was not in vain. It proved to the world and to the Jews, wherever they wandered, that no tyrant was strong enough, no empire had sufficient power, to keep them down forever.

Now in 1943 the Jews were again celebrating Lag b'Omer, under conditions surprisingly similar to those of Bar Kokba's time. Once again they were engaged in a desperate, well-nigh hopeless struggle for freedom from the oppressor.

At the end of the sixth week of the battle, on the morning of May 31, the Polish underground flashed the news that the fight of the ghetto was over. On the same day the Germans triumphantly reported that there was not a single Jew in Warsaw left alive.

It was true. All the Jews in the ghetto had been killed by bullets or bombs, or burned alive, or hung on lampposts, or suffocated by poison gas. The Warsaw Ghetto was one enormous cemetery. More than a hundred thousand homes had been destroyed. The German bombing of Warsaw in 1939 had destroyed only seventy-five thousand homes.

The Germans had lost between five and seven thousand men, not counting the wounded. They had also lost tremendous amounts of matériel.

According to experts, the fire in the ghetto had been the largest fire in the history of the world.

The end of the Warsaw Ghetto brought the number of Jews killed in Poland to about two and a half million. At that time between one hundred and two hundred thousand were still living in German camps. Another half million had been saved by the Russians. Nobody could tell how many Jews were hiding out in the forests and continuing the fight.

In the first days of June a young man appeared in London. He was a Jewish Pole who had fought in the ghetto until the end, when he had managed to fight his way out of the ghetto together with a few companions and had hidden in a Polish house adjoining the ghetto.

He was almost unable to speak coherently for some time. He acted like a man who had been running away from something for many hours and now was in a state of utter exhaustion. Indeed, that was actually the case, for he had been traveling day and night, making his way across the Polish border and then, armed with a passport from a neutral country, had finally reached Stockholm, whence a plane had taken him directly to London.

Now he was sitting in the office of one of the members of the Polish National Council. There were four or five men around him. They knew already that the fight in the ghetto was over. But they had not yet seen an eyewitness or heard any details of the struggle. They waited impatiently till the young man was able to speak again.

"The ghetto is no more," the young man said. "Almost all the buildings have been destroyed. They say that the damage is greater than the damage caused by the German bombardment of Warsaw in September 1939.

"We fought for forty-two days. On the last day only two or three houses in the northernmost part of the ghetto were still standing. And then finally only one house, a four-story building, was left. The blue-and-white flag still waved from the top of the house. It took the Germans eight hours to get that one house. They had to fight for each floor, for each step. The defenders slowly moved up until only a few of them were left on the fourth floor. Then they, too, were gone. But one of the Chaluzim was still left, up on the roof. He stood there, holding aloft the blue-and-white flag. Now it was midnight. The Germans directed their floodlights up to the roof. You could see the young man from far off, him and the flag. Then you could not see him any more. He had wrapped himself in the flag which he had guarded for forty-two days and forty-two nights and hurled himself down to the earth. That was the end. It was just midnight."

Chapter XXIV

The Fight Goes On

German guards in pairs patrolled the streets of what had been the Warsaw Ghetto. There was a standing order that no guard should ever be on duty there alone. But then no Nazi would have dreamed of being alone in the ghetto, particularly at night. Strange tales were whispered about the place. It was said that some of the Jews were still alive, hiding out in the subterranean tunnels and sewers and coming up during the night to kill Nazis wherever they found them. . . .

Shortly after the end of the battle of the ghetto, Heinrich Himmler made another visit to Warsaw, flying in without any advance publicity and taking up his headquarters in the governor's palace. Immediately after his arrival he sent for SS General Sommers.

"I do not mind telling you, General, that the situation has been very badly handled," Himmler began. His manner was calm and he spoke softly as usual, but Sommers knew that his chief was really furious. "I gave you one week—that was plenty. You have made a mess of things. The Fuehrer is extremely displeased."

Fifteen minutes later General Sommers left the Commandantur. One hour later he was arrested. Six hours later he was tried, and early next morning he was shot. No reason was made public.

After SS General Sommers, Himmler received Gruppenfuehrer Mende, Colonel Tebens, and finally Governor Fischer himself. The first two disappeared immediately afterward from Warsaw. Whether they, too, had been arrested and punished for their inefficiency in doing away with the Jews has not yet been revealed.

The conference which Himmler had with Governor Fischer was somewhat longer. "I would like you to tell me, Governor, exactly what happened on May 3 in the streets of Warsaw."

May 3 is the most important of all Polish holidays—the anniversary of the day on which, in 1791, the Polish nation adopted a democratic constitution, the first to be established in Europe. When the Germans occupied Poland in 1939 they forbade the Poles to celebrate that day. The decree was violently resented by the Poles, and every year since then there had been street fights and massacres in Warsaw on May 3.

Governor Fischer said: "We had taken all necessary precautions. If there had been any attempt at violence we would have clamped down on them. . . . The Poles didn't seem to be out for any trouble that day. They walked the streets in complete silence; their way of paying tribute to their heroes."

"And?"

When Governor Fischer hesitated, Himmler went on. "You had posted loud-speakers on every street corner; they played waltzes and other dance music. You did everything to provoke the Poles."

"We did it to show them that they weren't the masters. If we felt like playing music—well, what was to stop us?" Governor Fischer interjected defiantly.

"Yes, that is what I thought," Himmler said quietly. And he continued without raising his voice, "You fools. You damned fools. As though we did not have trouble enough. Provoking the Poles at a moment when we have our hands full everywhere . . ."

"How could we know——"

"How could you know that the Poles would find a way to disconnect your precious loud-speakers? That they would play their national anthem and a record with an appeal spoken by a delegate of the Polish government? Imagine! On every street corner in Warsaw, right under our noses, with thousands of our soldiers and policemen around, the Poles could listen to an appeal from their government calling for resistance and promising liberation soon!"

There was nothing the governor could say.

"Your men could have at least watched the wires leading to the loud-speakers, couldn't they? If you start such a thing, the least you can do is to carry it through." Himmler still did not raise his voice. "And why didn't you have the loud-speakers disconnected?"

"My men did. But before they could get to them the demonstration was all over."

"And that is all you did? You haven't found out how they did it, or who the ringleaders were?"

"We easily found out where it was done, and how. But by the time we got there, the conspirators had left."

"You might have thought that something like that would happen and have taken precautions!"

"How could I have imagined——"

"The trouble with you is that you have no imagination. But the people we are fighting have a lot of it. And we must have it, too." He made a slight pause. "Well, the harm is done now. We have made ourselves ridiculous. You have made yourself the laughingstock of Warsaw. That means that you are washed up here."

Governor Fischer was soon afterward removed to a minor post in Lublin. He was not too unhappy to leave Warsaw. He no longer felt safe there. Several assaults had already been made on his life, and he was certain that sooner or later the Warsaw underground would get him. As he sat in the train which was taking him to Lublin he wondered if the climate there would be healthier for him than Warsaw had been. Perhaps he was thinking, too, of Captain Batz, the first chief of the Gestapo in Warsaw, who had first had the splendid idea of creating a ghetto there, and whom Himmler had relieved of his post and sent to the Russian front. In December 1942, Captain Batz was severely wounded before Stalingrad. He spent two nights and two days lying alone in the fields where the hastily retreating Germans had left him. He lost blood steadily and was half mad with thirst. When the Russians picked him up he was delirious. He died without regaining full consciousness.

The man Dagani had been kept well informed of the developments in the fight in the Warsaw Ghetto. He received hundreds of coded reports from his agents everywhere in Europe. He knew about all the subsequent uprisings of Jews throughout Poland and of the activities of the Jewish partisans. He knew that only a handful of the suicide squad which he had sent into Poland was still alive. One report read:

"There is not one of our partisan groups that fought in Warsaw left. Five of us escaped here, but when you receive this letter we doubt whether any of us will still be among the living. We will fight to the last. We did what we could under the circumstances. We feel sad that our hope of seeing Palestine again will not be fulfilled."

Jewish guerrillas and partisans seemed to be everywhere. They stopped trains, killed German soldiers, and stole ammunition. They opened prison cells. They made attacks in broad daylight on towns and villages manned by small German garrisons. They constantly threatened the German lines of communication. They blew up bridges and burned down factories. They dug deep holes in highways along which military supplies were transported. They found many ways to prevent the Germans from accumulating food stores. No matter where the Germans tried to hide their food supplies, the improvised storehouses and granaries would soon go up in smoke.

The Nazis liked the Jewish guerrillas even less than they did the Russian ones, as reports which fell into Polish hands bear witness. Particularly interesting is a confidential memorandum sent to the Nazi commander of Brest-Litovsk from Pinsk. The report, twenty-four pages long, goes into considerable detail about "gangs" of Byelo-Russians and Poles which were attacking the Germans in towns and villages. "But," it continues, "our comrades who fall into the hands of Jewish bandits fare worst. The Jewish guerrillas are organized in well-armed divisions and roam the forests around Pinsk, Janow, Lachwa, and Dawid-Grudek. These Jews are refugees from the ghettos and concentration camps. They are bloodthirsty and possessed of beastly instincts. They often cut off the ears, noses, hands, or feet of our soldiers and release them without killing them. . . ."

The Nazi newspaper *Danziger Vorposten* complained bitterly that Jewish partisans had created special brigades to take revenge on German officials and policemen. The newspaper said that in June 1943 alone fifty-eight Germans had been killed by Jews in the districts of Warsaw, Cracow, and Lodz and that these reprisal killings were still continuing.

Another German report about Jewish guerrilla activities read:

> The population in the region of the dense forests of Rudnicka, Bersztansak and Galibocka, in the Vilna District, complain bitterly of the depredations they suffer from bands of peasant and Jewish robber-partisans, who lord over and terrorize the entire neighborhood. These bandits number about one hundred groups, each consisting of from twenty to thirty men, who attack towns and villages, set fire to administration buildings, kill guards and officials, and indulge in lynchings. About three fifths of each band are Jews who have escaped from Lithuanian or Polish ghettos, and the other two fifths are villagers whom criminal activities or want compelled to flee their native towns. These partisans are considered the most dangerous.

It was, of course, entirely untrue that the Polish population complained about the activity of the Jewish partisans. Quite to the contrary, the Poles rejoiced whenever the Jews killed any of their Nazi oppressors. They fed them and covered their escape or hid them in their houses, in spite of the threat of death that hung over their own heads for such activities.

Only a few, a very few, Poles continued to be rabid anti-Semites. These were the members of the National Radical party, Nara. They were, of course, opposed to the German occupation of Poland, but they were equally opposed to the exiled government in London, and most of all they were opposed to the Jews. They still edited three underground papers in which they continued to mock the memory of the Jews who had fallen as victims of the Nazis. In one of these papers, *Dobroni* (*To Arms*), they wrote, during the summer of 1943—weeks after the ghetto of Warsaw had been destroyed: "The Bolsheviks, the Jews, and the Germans will always be our mortal enemies. They should be destroyed wherever we meet them. No mercy, no pardon, for them. No honest Pole will adopt one of the trades in which the Jews excelled so famously, such as white slavery, and the keeping of public houses."

About the Jewish partisans the same paper wrote as follows:

"The guerrillas on the left bank of the Vistula are Polish in name only. In reality 80 per cent of the partisans are Jews, and that is enough for us not to recognize them as brothers in our fight."

The Jewish partisans could hardly have asked for a greater compliment than such words as those.

It was not only in the Polish woods that Jews fought. Everywhere throughout the Hitler-occupied countries, in the Balkans, in Carpathia, Ruthenia, and in France, Jewish guerrillas had sprung up. The Vichy radio even charged that the Maquis had invited Jewish guerrilla specialists from Poland to instruct and train French underground workers. Polish Jews were sentenced to death in the first months of 1944 in Paris, Lyons, and Marseilles. More than thirty Jews were court-martialed in Bucharest for aiding Tito's partisans and British paratroopers. A large number among those who fought with Tito were Jews. The Russians created one-hundred-per-cent-Jewish guerrilla units. To the very end Jews played important parts in all the French resistance movements.

Dagani received more reports. They told him of the destruction of the last ghettos in Poland: of the end of the Jews of Grodno, of Bialystok, of Luck, of Tarnow, and many others. But still other reports showed plainly that the Jews throughout Poland no longer could be driven to their deaths like so many cattle. They attacked their guards and killed them with their bare hands or with whatever weapons were at their disposal.

There were revolts in all the Jewish camps during the summer and fall of 1943. An uprising occurred in Bialystok when in mid-August the Nazis tried to liquidate the Jewish inhabitants of that camp. The rebellion lasted for a month, and the Nazi losses were high. Most of the thirty thousand Jews in the Bialystok Ghetto were killed, and only a small number were finally shipped off to the Trawniki Labor Camp.

Shortly afterward a few thousand Jews who had been sent to the death camp of Treblinka attacked their guards and succeeded in disarming and killing all of them. Major Sauer and a few German officers barricaded themselves in Sauer's house and telephoned frantically for help. But soon the Jews broke down the door and killed Major Sauer and the other officers in charge of the camp.

All this happened in less than an hour. Then the Jews got hold of all the weapons and ammunition that were stored in Treblinka and took them away, setting fire to all the buildings before they left, and destroying all lines of communication. By the time relief arrived for the Germans, the Jews were gone.

There were other rebellions on a smaller scale in Tarnov, Bendin, Czenstchow, Borislaw, and Sobibor, all of them successful. Later the Jewish camps of Poniatow and Trawniki, too, staged armed uprisings in which the condemned Jews killed many Germans and then fled into the woods.

In many of these revolts the help of Christian Poles played an important part. The underground no longer held that "it was not the time yet." Now they not only sent weapons and food, but fought actively side by side with the Jews.

According to numerous reports, many of the Polish Jews had made their way across the Russian lines. One of this number was Isaac Zawada, the rabbi of the city of Sandomierz. In December 1941 the Jews of Sandomierz had been notified by the German authorities that they would have to leave the town immediately. They went on foot, without any baggage, thousands of them, men, women, children. Among them was the rabbi, a man of amazingly youthful appearance for all his fifty-odd years. He kept their spirits up. They did not know where they were going, but the rabbi had an idea. He had heard about what happened in the concentration camp about ten miles away from Sandomierz. While they were on their way the rabbi spoke to this or that Jew among the crowd. They waited until they had reached a forest which cut them off from the view of those in the town. Then, at a sign given by the rabbi, they attacked the soldiers who were guarding them, took their arms away, and scattered in all directions. Many of them were later caught by the Germans; others hid out in Polish villages; still others joined the partisans. But a few, led by the rabbi, found their way into Russia.

The rabbi enlisted in the Polish Division of the Red Army as soon as it was created. The other recruits in the division looked with astonishment at the orthodox Jew with the long beard. The Polish colonel in charge of the training saw that the rabbi was not partaking in the common meal. He had a talk with him and heard that the rabbi would not touch anything but kosher food. He was willing to live on bread and raw vegetables, he said. The colonel wanted to know why the rabbi had joined the army.

"I was a corporal in the Tsarist Russian Army in the first World War," the rabbi remarked. "I can fight again. There is more reason for me to fight now than ever before." He was soon afterward made a sergeant.

He fell on the second day after his unit had reached the front, killed by a mine splinter as he was leading an attack. They buried him with full military honors. On his gravestone there were three inscriptions, in Polish, Russian, and Hebrew. Each of them read: "Here lies Rabbi Zawada of Sandomierz, fifty-three years old, who fell in battle near Lenina. He was awarded the Polish Cross for Heroes and the Medal of the Red Star in recognition of his exceptional bravery."

Thus the Polish Jews fighting on the Russian front met—finally in equal battle—those who had tortured and persecuted them back in Poland. They fought against the Germans wherever they were allowed to fight. They fought in the woods and mountains and at the fronts far from home; they did not know what had become of their families or whether they would ever see them again. But they fought, wherever they were, for they realized there was only one world, that it was a small one, and that everybody in this world is responsible for everything that goes on in it.

Months after the end of the Warsaw Ghetto one of Dagani's agents, a girl named Chaya, appeared in Palestine. She made a full report to

Dagani and then to the Central Committee of the Workers' Organization of Palestine. "I confess that I have a sense of guilt that I, and not those who really led the movement and the rebellion, have lived to tell the tale," Chaya ended.

One of those present when Chaya made her report was the leader of the Palestine youth organization, Meir Yaari, who had played a large part in organizing Dagani's army of agents. After the girl had gone he said to Dagani, "If a girl as young as that is capable of such heroic actions in our desperate struggle, we have reason to believe that we will win this fight in the end. There must be many young Jews capable of equally heroic deeds everywhere—in Syria, Iraq, North Africa, in France, England, and America."

There were and there are and there will be many young Jews everywhere capable of such heroism. Of those young Jews who started the fight, of the Polish young Jews, of the Chaluzim, few are left. Perhaps none will be left when the war is over. And then . . . ? Who will grow up to take their place?

In October 1943 a member of the Polish National Council in London, questioned about the fate of the Jewish children in Poland, said:

"There are no more Jewish children; they have all been murdered."

There were no more Jewish children in Poland. . . . But no, there were a handful of them, a few hundred or perhaps a few thousand who had escaped from cities and towns where Jews were being slaughtered and who continued to wander through Poland, hiding out during the day, continuing their travels during the night, living on what they found in the fields and in the woods or what sympathetic Polish peasants would give them. They wandered on—they did not know themselves where.

One of these children, a boy of six, was finally found in Rumania. He did not speak to the other children because he could not speak. He had been barely three when he had fled into the woods with his father and mother from a Galician village. His parents were found and killed by the Germans. The boy was overlooked. For two years he stayed on in the forests, slowly continuing his way across the Rumanian border. He lived with the animals of the forest, with wild pigs and wolves. He forgot the language of human beings. He no longer wore clothes. Once a Rumanian guard captured him, but he scratched him and bit him and ran away again. When he was finally found again and taken to the orphan asylum in Bucharest, it was discovered that he could not sleep in a bed. He was lonesome for the animals of the forest, and during the night he would scream like an animal, throwing fear into the other children. When they wanted to wash him, he scratched and bit. Only slowly did he learn human ways and words again. He was finally taken to Palestine.

This is an incident that happened in Europe between the years of 1940 and 1943, in the world which we so fondly call civilized. The people of this civilized world allowed such things as this to occur in this little world of ours, which can be circled by a plane in less than three days and three nights.

The Warsaw Ghetto continued to be a problem to the Germans long after the fight was over. The southern part, which had been evacuated by the Jews between July and September 1942, was still intact because it had not been the theater of actual fighting. And the houses there had been handed over to the Aryan Poles. As to the rest of the ghetto, a few blocks were only partly demolished; but where the fight of the last few weeks had taken place, nothing but ruins were left. Even those houses which were more or less intact stood vacant.

On dark nights Polish women and children, the poorest of the poor, would make their way into the deserted houses and would look for anything left there which they might be able to use or sell. Whenever the German guard caught any such visitors, they seized them and immediately dispatched them to the gas chambers of Treblinka. There was little work these days in Treblinka. . . .

The underground warned the Poles not to go near the ghetto. "We are warning all Poles to refrain from the despicable business of robbing the dead," one pamphlet said. "Any Pole caught in the act will be branded as a traitor to this country. Leave this filthy, degrading pursuit to the Germans. They have always been expert in looting and pillaging."

The German authorities—the military authority as well as the Gestapo—had to send quite a few of their men back to Germany to be interned in asylums. It seemed that they were no longer able to endure what they had been forced to witness during the past few years. Some of the soldiers, too, had to be taken away from Treblinka and Lublin in strait jackets, while many of the others, who stood guard at the ghetto, committed suicide.

But the German authorities had much more important matters to worry about than the suicide of a few German soldiers. They were beginning to find that their wholesale slaughter of the Jews was proving to be something of a boomerang to them, from a practical standpoint, at least. Yes, ironically enough, they found themselves actually missing the Jews. In a report on the economic situation of Poland under Nazi occupation, submitted by the head of the Economics Department of the Government General to his chief, Hans Frank, the highest authority in Poland, we find the following highly interesting paragraph:

> We cannot as yet foresee all the economic results coming from the liquidation of the Warsaw Ghetto. We are devoting considerable time to the solution of this problem. The indisputable fact that the number of consumers of food in Warsaw has decreased by 400,000 owing to the liquidation greatly facilitates the provisioning of the city. Our real difficulty, however, lies in the loss of a revenue amounting to about 200,000,000 zlotys from the rents paid by the Jews in the former ghetto. Their houses stand vacant now. All the furniture, articles of apparel and other personal property left behind have been transferred to the Reichsfuehrer-Sturmabteilung (storm troopers). We must immediately get busy repairing and renovating the houses, so as to adapt them to the needs of new tenants.

Thereupon it was decided to rebuild part of the ghetto and make the houses available to Poles and to Germans who might want to move to Warsaw. Immediately large groups of foreign laborers were shipped to Warsaw to aid in the rebuilding of what had once been the ghetto, and in addition several thousand Poles were ordered to help with the task.

Early in October 1943 the slave labor of the Germans had rebuilt a great part of the demolished section of the Warsaw Ghetto. On October 5 it was announced:

"October 10 is the final day for the occupation of apartments that have not been listed in previous orders." This announcement referred to the houses in what the Germans called the "Former Jewish Quarters."

At the same time there was another announcement signed by the higher SS and police fuehrer of the Governor General:

> To protect the life and property of the population against the actions of criminal elements, the Governor General has issued a decree concerning punishment for attacks against the German work of rebuilding. According to this decree, every misdemeanor committed with the intention of interfering with the German rebuilding in Poland will be punished by death. Instigators as well as helpers will be punished like the actual perpetrators. An attempted deed will be punished in the same way as an accomplished deed.

Not many Poles applied for apartments in the former ghetto of Warsaw. But a great many German refugees whose homes had been bombed by the Allies eagerly occupied the vacant accommodations and moved in with all the household goods they had been able to save. According to the *Krakauer Zeitung,* though, the Germans were not very happy there. They felt depressed. There was no particular reason. It was just the atmosphere. They did not seem able to establish any neighborly contact with the Poles who lived near by. Their greetings were not returned. If they asked their way about the city they were not answered. Nobody had time to explain to them where they could get the bread due them on their ration cards. On all sides they were snubbed and slighted. No, decidedly they were not made to feel welcome.

And then in November and December typhoid fever broke out among the new inhabitants of the former Warsaw Ghetto. Soon all the available hospitals were filled. There were not enough doctors or enough drugs.

Every night shooting was going on in the ghetto. German authorities took members of the Polish underground whom they had arrested to the most devastated parts of the ghetto, where they were executed. Perhaps they considered the surroundings "symbolic"; perhaps they hoped thus to warn the Polish underground that they would annihilate the Poles just as they had the Jews, if the underground activities did not stop.

All this made life intolerable for the German refugees who had settled in the neighborhood. They were quite desperate. And finally they appointed a delegation to go to the Commandantur to demand that something be done.

But the delegation was not received by the governor or by any of the higher-ranking officials. It seemed that all these officials were extremely overworked these days. Small wonder, what with the constant retreats of the German Army in Russia and the extensive troop movements necessary to bolster the all-but-broken German front. Incessantly, day and night, troop and ammunition trains moved through Warsaw. The war came nearer and nearer. Nor did the constant bombing help to calm the nerves of the German officials in the Polish capital.

The delegation from the former ghetto finally found a short, stocky subaltern with nose glasses to listen to their complaints. "We are living under completely unsanitary conditions," the leader of the delegation declared. "Something has to be done. These houses are not fit for a German to live in."

The man with the nose glasses listened. "I will inform the secretary of the governor about your complaints. I can't promise you anything. Try to make the best of it. You know there is a war going on."

"But there is shooting going on every night!" the members of the delegation protested. "It's horrible! It's inhuman!"

"What is the idea? What do you want?" the man with the nose glasses shouted.

"We want to go back to Germany."

"Don't you know that German cities are bombed every night? Where do you think we could find houses for you?"

"But these houses are dreadful," the delegation cried in despair.

The man with the nose glasses opened the door. "The people who used to live there were quite happy."

The members of the delegation left, their heads bowed, discouraged and miserable. They went back to the ghetto. They went through the streets of ruins, which had something weird and mysterious about them. They passed as quickly as they could the vacant houses with the windows without panes and the doors opened and shut by the wind. They hurried along to be home before it became dark. They did not speak to each other. They were thinking of the strange tales about Jews still being alive, hiding in tunnels and sewers and coming up during the night to kill Nazis wherever they found them. They were afraid.

Epilogue

Thus ends the story of the fighting ghetto, which Dr. Shoskes told during many hot days and nights in New York in August and September 1944; a story woven together from countless episodes reported by eyewitnesses, one of whom was himself; of accounts smuggled out of Poland; of events described in newspapers; of men and women and Nazis who acted this weird and bloody drama, some of whom Dr. Shoskes knew so well that he could describe their very thoughts and words, thought and spoken at times when no witness was present; or of others whom he knew only by the deeds they had done, by the decrees they had signed, by the common struggle in which they were involved, but whose profiles could be drawn according to what he knew they had decreed and commanded and executed and suffered, whose faces and brains and hearts thus became unveiled, as though dissected and presented under a magnifying glass.

And while Dr. Shoskes was talking and recreating the sufferings and the fights in Warsaw between 1939 and 1943, we could hear the cries of the newsboys through the open window. Some of the latest headlines they announced dealt again with the sufferings and fights in Warsaw. Even as Dr. Shoskes was speaking of the revolt which had taken place in Warsaw more than a year before, the papers were carrying the story of a new uprising there. The present made a strange counterpoint to the past. Everything that had happened before seemed to be happening again. The melody had not been broken off. It was continuing right along into the very hour in which Dr. Shoskes tried to recreate the melody of those times past. It went on and on like an eternal fugue.

Warsaw had risen again, only this time, in August 1944, it was not the forty thousand Jews in the ghetto but the hundreds of thousands of Poles throughout the capital that had revolted against the Germans. They made a good fight of it. They entrenched themselves in many districts, defying German attacks with tanks, artillery, fighters, and bombers. For a while they held almost 40 per cent of the city. Everyone fought: women, old men, and even boys as young as twelve years of age, who ran out on the street to destroy enemy tanks with crude fire grenades of gasoline in bottles.

The fight continued throughout August and the better part of September, and for some time it looked as though the Poles might actually force the Nazis to retire from the capital. But it was a fight against too heavy odds. The food and water supplies ran low, and there were no longer any medical supplies available for the thousands of wounded people in the cellars and on the barricades. The Germans systematically destroyed building after building and mowed down the civilian population wherever they encountered them. They forced women and children to precede their tanks and machine guns so that the Polish home army could not attack them. The end had to come. It came at eight o'clock in the evening of October 3, on the sixty-third day of the uprising, when the Polish High Command capitulated and General Bor and his staff, as well as the other Polish soldiers still alive, were taken away as prisoners.

Shortly before the end the women of Warsaw had sent a heartbreaking appeal to Pope Pius XII, which told of their heroic fight and suffering.

> Holy Father [they pleaded], we Polish women fighting in Warsaw are inspired by deep patriotism and devotion to our country. While we have defended our fortress for three weeks, we lack food and medical supplies. Warsaw is lying in ruins. The Germans are murdering the wounded in hospitals. They drive women and children before them, screening their tanks. There is no exaggeration in the reports of children fighting and destroying German tanks with bottles of gasoline. We mothers see our sons dying for liberty and their country. Our husbands, sons, and brothers are not regarded as combatants.
>
> Holy Father, no one helps us. The Russian armies, which have been standing for three weeks at the gates of Warsaw, don't move a step forward. The help which came from Britain is insufficient. The world ignores our fight. Only God is with us. Holy Father, Vicar of Christ, if you can hear us, bless us Polish women fighting for the Church and liberty.

No one helps us. . . . The world ignores our fight. This leitmotiv was taken up throughout the world. Even while the battle was going on, bitter controversies broke out everywhere. The Polish government-in-exile accused the Soviet Russian government of being responsible for the slaughter in Warsaw: it was said that the Russians had sent numerous appeals to the population of Warsaw to revolt and had promised them that the Russians would then come to Warsaw to help them. The Russians denied fiercely that they had done any such thing, explaining that they could not have possibly taken Warsaw at that time, in spite of the fact that they were only ten miles away, since Warsaw was one of the strongest of the Nazi points of defense. The Russians insisted that the uprising had been instigated by political schemers belonging to the Polish government-in-exile, who thus hoped to create a *fait accompli*—namely, to have the revolting people, under General Bor, take possession of the Polish capital for the government-in-exile before the Russians entered Warsaw. The commander in chief of the Polish Army, General Sosnkowski, who was relieved of his command soon afterward, also accused the English and the Americans of having "abandoned" the Poles, though the Allies had sent several hundred planes to Warsaw in spite of forbidding odds and in spite of the fact that the military value of such an exhibition was bound to be zero. Many bitter words were said on all sides.

"No one helps us. . . . The world ignores our fight." Have we not heard this refrain before? Is it not exactly the same thing the Jews in the Warsaw Ghetto said when they were waging their last all-out battle? At that time it was the Poles who did not want to help them, because "the time has not yet come." Now these very same Poles had to wage this very same battle, and now they too, in turn, felt that others were betraying them, because others were not coming to their aid, because "the time has not yet come."

There are, of course, some differences. The Jews fought to the last man. There was no giving up. Mordecai, Klepfisz, and the others had to see it through. They could not expect, as could General Bor, to be treated as honorable war prisoners. The English and the American governments, though unable to help the Poles militarily, at least helped them by threatening the Nazis with dire consequences if they did not treat the revolting civilian Poles as enemy soldiers. But they had not made any such statement in regard to the fighting Jews in the ghetto. When Warsaw revolted, it was all over the front pages, throughout the world; when the ghetto revolted, there were only scant items buried on back pages.

The Nazis had tried their best to keep secret from the world what they had been doing to the Jews of Poland and of other European countries. The world became the co-conspirator of the Nazis, by hushing up this news, by playing it down rather than up. Even while the battle of Warsaw was going on in the summer of 1944, the Russian Army had progressed to Lublin and was throwing open for inspection to the reporters of all free countries the annihilation camp of Majdanek. There were reports everywhere about this mammoth death factory. But there was little said about the victims, except that they were Poles, Russians, French, Germans, Hungarians, et cetera. In many reports the word "Jew" did not even figure. In others it was only mentioned that Jews, too, had been killed there.

But the truth is: while non-Jews were killed in the death camps of Poland in unheard-of numbers, the vast majority of the victims were Jews from all countries of Europe. Probably more than 90 per cent of the victims were Jews. A large percentage, particularly if one stops to think that except for Poland, where the Jews made up about 10 per cent of the population, the Jews represented hardly more than 1 to 2 per cent of the population of Europe. If no more than 3 or 4 per cent of the victims in the death camps had been Jews, they would have furnished their rightful quota, so to speak, for destruction. As it was, they furnished more than twenty times as much. As it was, more than four fifths of all the Polish Jews were killed and more than half of all other European Jews. But the reports did not say so. Even now that the Jews are dead, the world does not yet want to open its eyes to the fact that the Jews were considered by Hitler as his first and most important enemy.

Shortly after the battle of Warsaw was over, Dr. Shoskes received some new material on the uprising, which had been smuggled out of Poland. This material made it clear beyond any doubt that in this fight, too, Jews had taken part.

Five hundred Jews had been killed while fighting under the command of General Bor. The general himself estimated the total number of Jews in his army at several thousand. Most of them had previously been hiding out in Warsaw and neighboring villages, where they lived under assumed names, protected by Aryan documents. When General Bor called on the Poles to revolt, all the Jews came to volunteer. The general further stated that many of them were decorated for courage and that it was the Jewish units which succeeded in occupying the Napoleon Square in the center of the city—killing and taking prisoner many Germans.

The new information received by Dr. Shoskes also told how these Jews escaped from the ghetto. Since the story seems too utterly fantastic, let me quote an item from a German newspaper, the *Krakauer Zeitung* of October 5, 1944: "While cleaning up the city after the collapse of the uprising the German authorities in Warsaw discovered at last the tunnel which had served as a communication line for General Bor and his fighting army. It appeared that the tunnel was so well concealed in the district of the former ghetto that in 1943, after the destruction of the ghetto, it could not be found. It was through this tunnel, three kilometers long, that a part of the ghetto fighting men disappeared after the collapse of the ghetto uprising to join the Polish underground. The tunnel was searched for a long time. . . ." The Nazi paper concluded that here was another proof of Jewish shrewdness.

At the same time Dr. Shoskes received information about the end of Dr. Emanuel Ringelblum, pupil and friend of Professor Balaban and a well-known Jewish historian in his own right. Ringelblum and his family had taken part in the uprising and had been among those who were able to escape through the ghetto tunnel. For almost a year afterward he hid out in the cellar of a house in Warsaw. He used that time to continue working on a report dealing with the cultural life in the Jewish ghetto—a most amazing and inspiring account which is now in the possession of the Polish authorities in London. It tells the story of the Jewish schools, theaters, concerts, universities during the time of starvation and killing—not only in the Warsaw Ghetto but even in the death camps. "The pulse of the social and cultural work beat as long as the last trace of life remained in these places," Dr. Ringelblum wrote. He also mentioned the fact that he organized clandestine archives under the innocent name of *Society for the Pleasures of the Sabbath*, full of documents relating to the martyrdom of the Polish Jews: diaries, letters, memoirs, photos. The archives were buried in a safe place. Perhaps one day, when they are unearthed, the world will be able to read Professor Balaban's history of the ghetto. . . .

Dr. Ringelblum perished on March 7, 1944, when the Nazis detected his hiding place and entered it with machine guns and killed the historian, his family, and thirty-five other Jews. Those who forwarded his final report took part in the later uprising in Warsaw. Nobody knows yet how many of them are still alive.

"And they cried with a loud voice, saying, How long, O Lord, dost Thou not judge and avenge our blood?"

How long?

The story told in this volume has been called the story of Hitler's greatest crime. At first glance this seems to be a rather immodest title. Hitler and the Nazis have committed so many crimes, so many deeds which for many centuries human beings were thought incapable of, the atrocities and monstrosities committed by them are of such a gigantic scope, that it is difficult to classify them; indeed, such a classification seems almost unnecessary. But if we try to analyze what has been suffered, what has been done during the years of the Nazi reign in Germany and throughout Europe; if we try to find extenuating circumstances for some of the crimes and those who committed them; if we try to understand that some of the crimes were committed as follow-ups to open warfare and by people driven by shrewd means of propaganda into a paroxysm of super-nationalist feelings; if we attempt to understand—not forgive—the fact that many Germans acted atrociously because they believed that their enemies were acting equally atrociously; if we give them the benefit of one hundred million doubts—there still remains one crime that cannot be explained, cannot be understood, one crime that, no matter under what circumstances it was committed, can never be looked upon as anything but the act of ruthless wild animals who happened to look and move and speak like human beings.

Millions of people have been murdered, not in the heat of battle, not in the drunkenness after the battle. Millions of people have been murdered. Most of them had never tried to fight the Nazis; most of them could not even have fought them if they so wanted: old people, women, children. Millions of people were killed, slowly, scientifically, according to cold-blooded, well-thought-out plans. Millions of people have been assassinated, for no reason at all except one: that they were born, that they came from a long line of forefathers who happened to be Jews. Theirs was no guilt except the fact that they were Jews. They had no escape because their fate was sealed the date they were born.

A great deal has been said and written about revenge on the Germans, revenge for the treatment the Germans accorded to occupied countries where they starved the population, took the men away to forced labor, shot hostages without the slightest provocation. A great deal has been said and written by those who apologize for the Germans, pointing out that it is only a small clique of Germans that bears the responsibility for all these deeds; that the others, the great majority, just went along obeying orders, believing that they were fighting an enemy and that they had to do the things they did. And how about the millions of murdered Jews? How about their hundreds of thousands of assassins? Yes, they obeyed orders. No, they did not think twice about them. But is this an excuse? Even they, those unthinking, murdering robots, could not believe for one moment that here was a guilt to be avenged, a crime to be punished, an enemy to be fought.

Revenge, then—revenge on all the Germans? But why only on the Germans? Aren't there others just as guilty, those who were accessories before and during the deed? How about the governments of Allied countries which refused to do anything, anything at all, to stop the murder while the murdering was going on? How about the governments of the Allied and neutral countries which refused to let the Jews escape to safer places till the nightmare was over? How about the newspapers which buried the stories of what was going on in the Polish ghettos and camps on back pages? How about us who did not like to read these stories, who looked the other way, because it was all so dreadful and upsetting?

Yes, how about us? For all of us are guilty of this crime committed by the Nazis: because we knew and did nothing to stop it; because we knew and looked the other way; because we said this was none of our business, this was not our responsibility.

As if in this world, which is becoming smaller and smaller every day, there was anything which was not our responsibility! Yes, we are guilty, and we are becoming more guilty every day. Because we are still looking the other way. We are still trying not to know, still trying to forget the horrible things which have happened. Because it is all so dreadful and upsetting.

But we must not look the other way. We must learn what has gone on. And we must not forget. We must not stand before our children and future generations and say: "All these crimes were committed while we were alive, and we did nothing about them; we did not even know."

That is why we must know. That is why we must learn the facts, all the horrible and gruesome facts of this greatest crime in history. Only if we know, only if we never forget, will the fight of the Jews in the ghetto of Warsaw have the meaning they wanted it to have. If we forget, they will have died in vain. If we do not forget, if we keep their memory and the memory of their deeds alive for the generations to come, we will one day be recompensed for suffering with those who have suffered in the ghetto of Warsaw. We will take courage from their fight. We will know that a world in which there were such men and women cannot be without hope. We will understand that these Jews in the ghetto of Warsaw, too, were crucified for us, for all of us.

CURT RIESS